THE ESSENTIAL
COMTE

THE ESSENTIAL
COMTE

SELECTED FROM

Cours de Philosophie Positive

BY AUGUSTE COMTE

First published in Paris 1830–42

Edited and with an Introduction by

STANISLAV ANDRESKI

Translated and annotated by

MARGARET CLARKE

CROOM HELM LONDON

BARNES & NOBLE BOOKS NEW YORK
(a division of Harper & Row Publishers, Inc.)

FIRST PUBLISHED 1974
INTRODUCTION © 1974 BY STANISLAV ANDRESKI
TRANSLATION © 1974 BY CROOM HELM LTD

CROOM HELM LTD 2—10 ST. JOHN'S ROAD LONDON SW11

PUBLISHED IN THE USA 1974 BY
HARPER AND ROW, PUBLISHERS INC.
BARNES AND NOBLE IMPORT DIVISION

CROOM HELM ISBN 0—85664—049—2 CLOTH
0—85664—054—9 PAPER
BARNES AND NOBLE ISBN 06—490181—5 CLOTH
06—490182—3 PAPER

PHOTOSET, PRINTED AND BOUND
IN GREAT BRITAIN BY
REDWOOD BURN LIMITED
TROWBRIDGE & ESHER

CONTENTS

TRANSLATOR'S NOTE

Many of Comte's pleonasms and expletives—adjectives, adverbs, subordinate phrases, have been pruned away, as they are heavy in English and obscure rather than illuminate the thought.

Cross-references to parts of the six volume course not included in this selection are given in the Notes. Where Comte summarises the reference it is translated in the body of the test.

'Physics' is used in the nineteenth-century sense for 'natural science in general'. The fifth chapter treats of what Comte calls 'physics properly so called', the science of energy and matter to which the word is usually confined today. 'Art' is also used in a sense more of the nineteenth than of the twentieth century, which usually applies the word only to the fine arts. It has the meaning 'practical application of a science'.

INTRODUCTION

Comte's Place in the History of Sociology

The son of a humble and pious clerk in a small town, Isidore Auguste Comte would have kept no doubt to his station in life had he lived earlier; but he was born just in time (20 January 1798) to benefit from the widening of educational opportunities by the revolutionary and the napoleonic régimes. Early showing a great aptitude for learning, he was able to go through *lycée* despite the very modest income of his father, and got as far as the top educational institution of France–École Polytechnique. Despite a strong attachment to his mother, he kept a distance from her, did not get on well with his siblings and was on bad terms with his father. He travelled very little, never went outside France and spoke no foreign language. Once arrived in Paris, he never showed any desire to return to Montpellier.

Though theoretically in favour of strong authority even in his youth, the future author of an authoritarian utopia was a rebel in his behaviour, who continuously got into trouble with his teachers because of his obstinacy, bossiness and conceit; and, instead of making an academic career commensurate with his abilities and knowledge, he became an odd man out, able to get only occasional and ill-paid jobs as an examiner or tutor. For a couple of years he worked as Henri de Saint Simon's secretary, but their overweening ambitions could not be reconciled and they parted in bitter animosity which Comte harboured until the end of his life insistently denying his obvious intellectual debt to his former mentor. His occasional part-time employment at the École Polytechnique also came to an end after a row with the governors.

His longest lasting source of sustenance was the immoral earnings of his wife, who had been forced into this profession by poverty some years before she met Comte. He married her in full knowledge of the facts and with an ostensible intention of helping her; but his inability or unwillingness to earn a living repeatedly forced her to return to her trade. She was an intelligent woman who was interested in his work and used to turn up at his lectures even after they separated, and was willing to support him by the only method at her disposal. Although it was largely his own doing, Comte resented the situation and eventually turned against her. After the breach he lived in abject poverty, except for a short interlude after he received a donation which John Stuart Mill (who greatly appreciated the *Cours* though not the later writings) had raised in England. Until his death Comte continued to receive small sums as gifts from his friends and admirers, but they never sufficed to provide him with a decent living, largely because he quarrelled with his benefactors as soon as they disagreed with him on the smallest point.

Undeterred by poverty, Comte wrote an imposing array of volumes, the first of them published when he was only twenty-one. He produced the six volumes of *Cours de Philosophie Positive*—his most important work of which the present volume is a selective abridgement—when in his thirties, despite a two-year interruption due to mental illness which necessitated his confinement in an asylum.

He completed the *Cours* after his recovery and later wrote other books, including treatises on astronomy and geometry, but the quality of his work began to decline when he passed forty. The mental deterioration took a sudden dip when, at the age of forty-five, he fell madly in love with Clothilde de Vaux, an impoverished gentlewoman of thirty, whose husband had deserted her some years earlier and who at the time was enamoured of another man. Apart from being less attached to him than his prostitute wife, Clothilde seems to have been less intelligent and less appreciative of Comte's intellect and endeavours. After one apparently unsuccessful sexual encounter, Clothilde demanded that their relationship should remain strictly platonic. Comte submitted; and (as a psychoanalyst would nowadays say) sublimated his desire into a fervent quasi-religious worship of, first, Clothilde and then of women in general, placing them in his utopia on an absurdly elevated pedestal while nonetheless denying them freedom.

Clothilde's death (less than two years after they met) left Comte completely shattered. He eventually recovered the will to live and to continue his self-imposed task; but it seems that he achieved this by divesting himself of the remnants of rational thinking and plunging into mysticism. The hefty four volumes of his *Système de Politique Positive ou Traité de Sociologie* written during this period of his life—the first book to have the word 'sociology' in the title—are indelibly stamped with this spirit; and far from having the character of a scientific treatise, contain an incredibly verbose and repetitious sketch of a utopia. It was accompanied by a short book called *Le Catéchisme Positiviste*, written in the form of a dialogue between a woman who asks questions and a positivist priest whose answers leave no room for doubt.

Thus the young advocate of scientism (to use a recent term, unknown of course to Comte) ended as a mystic prophet and the self-proclaimed Grand Priest of the Religion of Humanity, who expected the Pope to resign in his favour, was sure that he could assure his longevity by will power, but died in utter destitution aged fifty-nine.

Auguste Comte proclaimed himself as the founder of sociology, and on the whole this title has been accepted, in consequence of which many (if not most) histories of this subject begin with him. And on one score at least there can be no doubt; this eminently successful terminological innovator (who also coined such indispensable words as biology and altruism) did indeed invent the name for it. On other scores his claim appears less justified.

Though now chiefly remembered for his invention of the word 'sociology', Comte also coined the term *positiviste* and *positivisme* which served as the principal appellation by which he set himself apart from other philosophers and politicians, and sought to characterise his works. Ever since, this term has continued to be bandied about and used in all kinds of possible and impossible senses; the latest fashion prevailing at the time of writing enjoins us to be anti-positivists, without worrying too much what a positivist is. In Comte's first formulation 'positivism' was (naturally and logically) used as the opposite of 'negativism', to distinguish between a positive and negative attitude to science as the ultimate source of knowledge. Positivists, according to early Comte, were people who believed in the supremacy of science as our guide, while the derogatory label of 'negativism' was affixed to those who negated this view and continued to uphold old pre-scientific dogmas. Unfortunately, no sooner had he made this distinction than Comte began to twist it, and apply it to everything he happened to assert or approve of. The pseudological premise for this semantic transition was his claim that all his beliefs and preferences were backed by science. The title of one of his latest books 'Positivist Catechism' well indicated the turn which his terminology had made: 'positivism' now came to mean the new religion which included such detailed prescriptions as the daily worship of a woman and a rather imaginative substitute for the sign of the cross, which the positivists were enjoined to make by touching certain parts of their heads, singled out in accordance with the findings of phrenology —the only kind of psychology which Comte regarded as scientifically acceptable and essential for sociology.

Comte was certainly neither the first to study society nor even the first to theorise about its nature. Attempts in this direction begin at the latest with Plato, while Aristotle (whom Comte regards as his principal fore-runner) explicitly formulated a number of general propositions about cause-and-effect or mutual dependence relationships between various aspects of social order. The same is true of Montesquieu and Condorcet —the other two of the three writers whom Comte acknowledged as predecessors of equal rank. He attributes to Montesquieu the discovery that social life is subject to natural law, and claims to have combined this idea with Condorcet's view of progress as the inevitable and universal intellectual advance of mankind. Though with less admiration, Comte also mentions Adam Smith in this context, but the list can be greatly enlarged to include at least Bodin, Turgot, Hume, Adam Ferguson, John Millar and Saint-Simon. Although they held a more static view of civili-sation—in the sense of not envisaging a continuous progress —Machiavelli, Hobbes and Bodin must also be included in the list of searchers for regularities in social behaviour.

To assess the contributions of an author who wrote on every major branch of learning then in existence (and in his later years spoke of him-self as having inherited the mantle of Aristotle as well as of St Paul) we must take care not to let our feelings about one aspect of his work affect our judgement on the other. I propose, therefore, to consider Comte's place as: (1) a scientist; (2) a philosopher in the present sense of the word; (3) sociological theorist; (4) a sociological historian and observer; (5) a reformer and prophet; (6) a methodologist. To assess his importance we must compare him with his predecessors and contemporaries, trace his influence upon the later thinkers, and try to find out what in his writings is both new and true, what is new but not true or true but not new, and what is neither. We must also bear in mind that an author of an influen-tial error is also a figure of importance.

To give an answer under the first heading is perhaps the easiest, because one does not need to be a specialist in the history of the natural sciences to see from a perusal of the *Cours* that Comte made no substan-tive contributions to any of the natural sciences. It seems that the electors who turned him down for a chair of mathematics at the École Polytech-nique (precisely on the ground that he had made no contributions to mathematics) were perfectly justified. What is worse, from about the age of thirty he failed to keep up with advances not only in the other sciences but even in his special field of mathematics, on the preposterous excuse that he did not want to clutter up his mind with inessential know-ledge. As on other occasions, his linguistic ingenuity did not fail him, and he baptised this policy by the high sounding name of 'mental hygiene'. Nonetheless, even his critics found his knowledge of the sciences truly impressive—which was all the more remarkable since it was acquired during the years of his youth. The fact that he was able to attract some uneducated workmen to follow his course on astronomy, and that many readers of the *Cours* owed to it their first acquaintance with the sciences, prove that he had a talent for explaining science to the uninitiated. Perhaps the secret of his success was that his expositions were more than simple popularised summaries of what the experts knew, and his characterisations of the essential features of each science exhibit a considerable dose of originality. In other words, his value derives from his quality as a commentator on the nature of the results and the methods of the sciences, rather than as a scientific discoverer.

Apart from their value as documents depicting a certain stage in intellectual history, his writings on the natural sciences are of importance to a historian of the social sciences because they have imprinted a certain idea of science on several generations of sociologists. Even by the standards of to-day Comte's comments on the sciences are not without merit, and can be especially recommended to a sociologist who has come exclusively from the arts side, and who can kill two birds with one stone by reading them; to learn something about the nature of the exact sciences, and at the same time to acquaint himself with the works of the writer regarded as the founder of his craft. This applies, however, only to Comte's general characterisations of the sciences; because his unfortunate habit of recognising no limits to his competence led him to pontificate on all kinds of specific issues on which he was hopelessly wrong. As these pronouncements are now of only antiquarian interest, they have not been included in the present selection.

When we look at him as a philosopher, we must remember that he used the term philosophy in the sense not far removed from that which it had in the days of Newton; that is, the sum of all knowledge. Actually, Comte would leave strictly technical details as falling outside philosophy, by which he meant the quintessence of all the fundamental tenets of the sciences rather than the minutiae. In any case his usage of the term was very much wider than the current one which omits the question of the empirical validity of the statements to the sciences, and addresses itself solely to the problem of the foundations of knowledge—or to put it in plain words, to the question of how we know that we know. To repeat: in contrast to modern philosophy of science from Mach and Peirce to Russell and Popper, which is *about* science, Comte's scientific philosophy consisted of the fundamental principles (as he conceived them) of all the sciences. It is not surprising therefore that as a philosopher in the narrower modern sense he does not loom large; and that analytic philosophers continue to refer to Descartes, Hume and Kant but leave Comte out.

Though of considerably more interest as a sociologist, his contribution to substantive theory (as distinguished from methodology, about which more anon) would not warrant putting him in the same rank as Montesquieu, Tocqueville or Marx. Comte's theoretical formulations, as well as the voluminous historical references adduced to illustrate them, focus on one theory to which he pinned the label 'The Law of Three Stages', and which asserts that civilisation as a whole, as well as the various provinces of knowledge and belief which make it up, regularly develop through three stages: the theological, the metaphysical and the positive—that is, scientific. Stripped of its tripartite character (prompted perhaps by the analogy with the Holy Trinity) and the misplaced emphasis on discontinuity, the Law of Three Stages boils down to the idea of progress from superstition to science, upheld by all the enlightened writers of the eighteenth century. (The late Pitirim Sorokin, incidentally, renamed Comte's stages as ideational, idealistic and sensate, and made claims to have created 'social and cultural dynamics' by asserting that instead of going in one direction mankind goes through them cyclically.) Nor were writers like Condorcet or Adam Ferguson or John Millar strangers to the notion that there is a connection between the stages of mental (or, better, cultural) development and the form of society—the credit for originating which is sometimes given to Comte. But when we look at the writings of Henri de Saint-Simon we find there all the sociological ideas which Comte claims to have invented; with this difference that Saint-Simon just talks and talks, without any attempt to systematise his assertions. In this field Comte's chief contribution was putting these ideas into pigeon-holes which (given the limitations of human minds) may not have been without utility.

Comte's shortcomings as an empirical sociological theorist seem to stem largely (and this brings us to the fourth aspect of his work) from the insufficient range of his information about social conditions—whether past or present. Montesquieu, Charles Comte* and Adam Smith tried to back their general propositions with masses of concrete details drawn from history, jurisprudence, accounts of travels and, last but not least, personal observations; since, like most great social, political and psycho-

* Author of *Traité de Législation* (1826), an exhaustive work on serfdom and slavery.

logical theorists, these men were outstandingly good (even if somewhat one-sided) observers, which Comte (like the most famous sociologist of today, Talcott Parsons) certainly was not. The two great figures who can be regarded as the most direct successors of Comte—Herbert Spencer and Karl Marx—also backed their theoretical assertions by a much vaster array of factual data than we find in Comte. Perhaps the most striking contrast in respect of the relationship between theory and data is offered by Comte's English contemporary Thomas Henry Buckle, who died in his early thirties on a fact-finding expedition in Asia, and who (in his unfinished book which bears a modest title—*An Introduction to a History of Civilisation in England*) tries to formulate an empirical theory of progress based on an astounding wealth of historical material. Whereas Buckle formulates his general propositions in an almost casual manner and then backs them with a massive display of historical illustrations, Comte's historical accounts consist of an endless churning around of the same, relatively restricted, assortment of data, wrapped up in pompous verbiage. In this respect he was a true begetter of the style dominant in the social sciences today.

Since there can be no factual data about the future, Comte's undistinguished command of this material constituted less of a handicap in his capacity as a planner of social reconstruction or (which in his case comes to the same thing) as an author of a utopia. His basic preoccupation was how to ensure stability of the social order, shaken by revolutions and undermined by the weakening of the influence of the Church. His prescription was to institute a new religion and a new Church which would provide the same services as the old in promoting social stability and consensus, but which, instead of preaching dogmas formed in the days of fetishistic thinking and therefore untenable in the light of knowledge supplied by science, would inculcate beliefs and attitudes proven by science and therefore, according to Comte, not open to doubt. Unlike Hume and the modern analytic philosophers, Comte never doubted that science can show which ultimate goals and values are good or bad; in other words he was not worried about the difficulties of jumping from 'is' to 'ought'.

The Religion of Humanity which he attempted to found turned out to be a dismal failure; and instead of becoming the first positivist pope, Comte died in abject poverty. Nevertheless, many of his visions have found an embodiment in a system which we might expect to be their opposite; namely, the social order erected by the disciples of Comte's contemptuous critic, Karl Marx, which in operation comes much closer to what Comte envisaged than to what Marx had in mind. It would not be very far from the truth to say that the communists have implemented Comte in the name of Marx. The inversion whereby the man who becomes the totem is not the one who preaches what the movement is doing, but the one who advocates the opposite is not surprising as it may seem at first glance.

The chief use of a political totem is in propaganda; and the aim of a propagandist is to make people believe that what his side is doing is something much nicer than in reality is the case; and to be of use for this purpose a totem must provide a smoke screen rather than guidance. Thus poor Comte's statement that 'dogmatism is the natural state of the human mind' is not a very good slogan for foisting a dogma on people, which can be done much better under the banner of freedom, equality and fraternity or in the name of God.

Though broached in his earlier works, his scheme for a new society was fully worked out only in one of his last publications: the massive four-volume *Système de Politique Positive ou Traité de Sociologie*, translated into English under the title of *System of Positive Polity*. As mentioned earlier, however, by the time he began to write this book Comte had already suffered a marked mental deterioration, with the consequence that his treatise is so verbose and repetitious that to read it is a test of endurance. Nevertheless, this indigestible treatise fixed the chief practical preoccupation of French sociology until the Second World War: which was to find a rationalistic substitute for religion. It must be said, however, that whereas Comte was sure that he had found all the answers, Durkheim realised that to achieve such a feat of social engineering, much more had to be discovered about how society works. Although Durkheim regarded Comte as obviously pre-scientific, on one important point he in fact transformed the latter's proposal into a descriptive proposition: namely, while Comte wanted to institute a religion of worship of Humanity, Durkheim maintained that all religion is in a sense worship of the group by its members. The latter view is debatable, to say the least; but, seeing unambiguous signs of social disintegration all around us, we cannot gainsay the topicality of the question whether a society can endure without a dogmatic creed.

Comte's beliefs that not only a dogma but also the ritual is essential for the maintenance of a social order has by no means lost its plausibility; and is fully shared by Chairman Mao who obliges his subjects to perform frequently elaborate faith-strengthening ceremonies while Comte's unlucky attempt to produce a catechism without supernatural beliefs has found a more successful embodiment in *The Little Red Book*. It could well be argued that the disuse of rituals constitutes an even more important source of the anomie which afflicts the western societies than the weakening of beliefs; although Comte would probably not agree with this view since he maintained that belief and ritual are equally essential as a social cement.

There can be no doubt that both as a theorist and a systematising historian Marx outclassed Comte and has made far more important contributions to our understanding of the causation of social processes. As even Lenin on several occasions complained, however, Marx said very little about how a socialist society ought to be organised, confining himself to a few exceedingly vague generalities, and devoting his energies not to the study of a system which he hoped for but to the one he hated and branded as doomed. In contrast, in his volume just mentioned, Comte specified even such details of the future society as the times and names of holidays . . . which no doubt disqualifies him as patron saint of a successful movement; because you stand a much better chance of becoming a revered prophet if you give your followers a *carte blanche* than if you leave specific instructions which they may want to disobey. Moreover, whereas Marx's prophecies about the coming of socialism and communism can never be proved wrong because he did not fix a time limit for these occurrences, Comte was so naive as to specify the dates on which the positivists would take over (or rather would be given) power . . . although it is only fair to remember that he indulged in these flights of fancy only towards the end of his life, after his mental illness; and there is nothing of this kind in his best work which is summarised in the present selection.

While the works of Marx enjoy the status of Holy Writ—which Comte prescribed for his own writings in the positivist social order —the place of the party in the Communist system corresponds to a considerable extent to that which Comte envisaged in his ideal society for the positivist lay priests alias sociologists. They too were supposed to be the guardians of the true doctrine and control the thinking of ordinary folk. Another point on which the Communists follow Comte is censorship—which Marx regarded with abomination while Comte approved . . . so long as it was in the hands of the right people. Likewise, the Communist habit of worshipping their stalwarts, building them monuments and mausolea, naming streets, towns, buildings and what not after them, is much more in line with Comte's project of replacing the Christian saints by positivist figures, than with Marx's insistence on the unimportance of individuals. Above all, the notion that their doctrine and programme were based on Science—as well as the name 'scientific socialism' for them—in all likelihood occurred to Marx and Engels in consequence of reading Comte. So, though in a rather perverse way, a number of Comte's crucial projects have been implemented by the worshippers of the man who had nothing but contempt for Comte's utopian schemes.

Though interesting, Comte's performance as a prophet would hardly warrant his inclusion among the founding fathers of sociology; and since we have seen that as an empirical theorist he was not outstanding either, the question arises why should we pay much attention to him at all. In other words, what is his place in the development of sociology apart from baptising it? The answer to this falls under the last of the headings into which I have divided various aspects of his work: namely, methodology. To be correct, the latter term is too restricted, because he certainly was not a methodologist in the present narrowly technical sense. We might better characterise Comte as a visionary or seer of scientific method who attempted to annex to its domain a new and vast field; the moulder of the ideas which presided over the rise of sociology and had considerable influence upon other branches of the study of society.

As an empirical theorist Comte was vastly inferior to his most outstanding immediate successors Karl Marx and Herbert Spencer, no match for his contemporary Alexis de Tocqueville, and not even as good as some much earlier writers. But, whereas his precursors and contemporaries went ahead trying to answer important questions about how society works, without much discussion about what they were doing and why they were doing it in this particular way, Comte was the crucial figure in establishing the idea that the methods of the natural sciences can and ought to be applied to the study of society. To repeat, he did not do it very well himself. When, after expostulating at great length about the need to study society in a positive (that is, scientific) manner, he comes to deal with a substantive problem, he forgets all his methodological arguments and rushes headlong into gratuitous pontification which contravenes every canon of methodology which he has persuasively advocated a few pages back. In this respect he is the true father of contemporary sociology with its bombastic proclamations of methodological purism, accompanied by pseudo-scientific practices which often descend to the level of folly or charlatanry.

Nowadays, when everybody (except a few backwoodsmen esconced in Oxford or Cambridge) takes for granted that thinking about human behaviour ought to follow the canons of scientific method, it is difficult to appreciate the merit of an author whose chief contribution was a ceaseless advocacy of this viewpoint. The very fact, however, that arguments to this point now seem so banal and superfluous, constitutes a justification for regarding Comte as great . . . just as our admiration for Eratosthenes or Copernicus is enhanced rather than diminished by the fact that today every dullard knows that the earth is round and goes round the sun. A person educated during the second half of the present century has to make an effort of historical imagination to realise how alien and abhorrent (not only to the uneducated masses but even to most academics) throughout the nineteenth century was the idea that the social order—that creation of God and the product of glorious deeds of semi-divine kings and heroes—was subject to natural causation; and that by studying it we could discover empirical laws in accordance with which it operates. Although he was much better as an empirical theorist and much more circumspect in his methodological pronouncements, Thomas Henry Buckle provoked a vituperative outcry among the academics (especially in England) by stating his conviction that general laws could be formulated about development of civilisation. Until the present century an advocacy of the application of the method of the sciences to the study of society was regarded even in the most enlightened parts of the world as a dangerous attack on the sacred foundations of the social order except when it concerned the restricted province of economics. To devote one's life to propagating such a blasphemy, one needed perhaps to be an obsessional visionary; and perhaps it was not a coincidence that the first standard bearer of the social sciences did not exactly enjoy robust mental health. Nor does it appear accidental that Marx and Engels—who, despite vituperating about most points of Comte's system, were his followers in this respect—combined an adamant insistence on the scientific character of their writings about society with visionary utopianism. No doubt the zeal of a prophet was needed to sustain a writer in such painful opposition to the established learned opinion.

Like most writers of his time, Comte got into a bit of a muddle in his usage of that baneful term 'law' which (by confusing description with prescription) continued to impede the progress of understanding until its various meanings were clarified by the analytic philosophers of the present century. Despite his weakness on this point, however, Comte bequeathed to sociology its most general concepts such as structure, function, equilibrium, system, self-regulation, mutual dependence of parts, social causation; even though he was less successful in analysing reality with their aid than his principal and most direct continuator Herbert Spencer. Another enduring bequest was his classification of the sciences in accordance with the increasing complexity of their subject matter, which corresponds inversely to the historical order of their rise and maturation. By crowning sociology as the last, the most difficult and the most embracing of them all, he provided its pioneers with confident hopes of great achievements, as well as with the weapon to defend the conspicuous imperfections of their craft.

As a moulder of scientific ideals and a marker of the field Auguste Comte has made a great contribution to intellectual progress, despite his sterility as an inductive theorist. His methodological ideals were better furthered by his successors who were inspired by them, but rejected his pseudo-empirical divagations and attempted to base their theorising on better factual foundations. Without the inspiration drawn from Comte's methodological vision neither Marx nor Spencer nor Durkheim nor Weber could have written their works as we know them.

I

Aim of the Course. General Considerations on the Nature and Importance of Positive Philosophy [1]

The object of this first lecture is to set forth clearly the aim of this course, that is, to determine in exactly what spirit the various branches of natural philosophy will be considered.

No doubt the nature of this course will only be completely understood, and a definite opinion formed about it, when the various parts have been developed in their order. Such is the usual drawback of definitions, when the system of ideas is extensive and the definitions precede the ideas. There are two aspects to generalities: either they are the conspectus of a doctrine still to be established, or the summary of one already established. But even if it is only as a summary that they acquire all their force, as a conspectus they are still extremely important, for they characterise from the start the subject under consideration.

As we understand it, an absolutely indispensable preliminary to a study as vast and hitherto as indeterminate as that which we are about to undertake, is the strict delimitation of the field of research. In obedience to this logical necessity, I must now indicate the considerations that have led me to give this new course, and that will each be developed in the detail demanded by its very great importance.

In order to explain adequately the true nature and proper character of positive philosophy, it is necessary to survey as a whole the progress of the human spirit, for a concept is understood only through its history.

Studying the total development of the human intelligence in its various spheres of activity, from its first trial flights up to our own day, I believe I have discovered a fundamental law to which it is subjected from an invariable necessity, and which seems to me to be solidly established, either by rational proof drawn from a knowledge of our nature, or by the historical test, an attentive examination of the past. This law is that each of our principal conceptions, each branch of our knowledge, passes successively through three different theoretical states: the theological or fictitious, the metaphysical or abstract, and the scientific or positive. In other words, the human mind, by its nature, employs in all its investigations three methods of philosophising, of an essentially different and even opposed nature: first the theological, then the metaphysical, and finally the positive. Hence there are three mutually exclusive kinds of philosophy, or conception systems regarding the totality of phenomena: the first is the necessary starting-point of human intelligence; the third its fixed and final state; the second is only a means of transition.

In the theological state, the human mind, directing its search to the very nature of being, to the first and final causes of all the effects that it beholds, in a word, to absolute knowledge, sees phenomena as products of the direct and continuous action of more or less numerous supernatural agents, whose arbitrary intervention explains all the apparent anomalies of the universe.

In the metaphysical state, which at bottom is a mere modification of the theological, the supernatural agents are replaced by abstract forces, veritable entities (personified abstractions) inherent in the various types of being, and conceived as capable in themselves of engendering all observed phenomena, the explanation of which consists in assigning to each its corresponding entity.

Finally, in the positive state, the human mind, recognising the impossibility of attaining to absolute concepts, gives up the search for the origin and destiny of the universe, and the inner causes of phenomena, and confines itself to the discovery, through reason and observation combined, of the actual laws that govern the succession and similarity of phenomena. The explanation of the facts, now reduced to its real terms, consists in the establishment of a link between various particular phenomena and a few general facts, which diminish in number with the progress of science.

The theological system arrived at the highest perfection of which it is capable when it substituted the providential action of a unique being for the interplay of the numerous independent divinities that had been imagined in the beginning. In the same way the metaphysical system reaches its consummation in the idea not of different particular entities, but of one great general entity, *nature*, as the unique source of all phenomena. The perfection of the positive system, towards which it toils unwearied, though destined probably never to attain it, would consist in seeing all observable phenomena as the particular cases of one single fact, as for instance the fact of gravitation.

This is not the place to demonstrate the fundamental law of development of the human mind, and to deduce its most important consequences. We will treat that law in proper detail in the part of the course devoted to the study of social phenomena. I am drawing attention to it now however in order to define the precise character of positive philosophy, in contrast with the two other philosophies which successively have dominated our entire intellectual system up to the last few centuries. For the present, in order not to leave unproved a law of this importance, whose application will frequently occur throughout the course, I will rapidly indicate the most telling evidence of its truth.

First of all it seems to me it should be enough to state this law for its truth to be immediately perceptible to all who have a knowledge of the general history of science. Indeed nearly every science today in the positive stage is known to have consisted in the past of metaphysical abstractions, and before that of theological conceptions. Unfortunately we shall more than once have occasion to note in the various parts of this course that in the most advanced sciences there are still considerable traces of the two primitive states.

This general evolution of human intelligence is easily confirmed, in a very notable though indirect manner, by that of individual intelligence. The starting point in the education of the individual is necessarily the same as that of the species, and the principal phases of the individual represent the epochs of the species. Now does not each one of us, when he looks at his own history, recall that he was successively a *theologian* in childhood, for his most important ideas, a *metaphysician* in his youth, and a *physicist* in his maturity? All men who are truly of this century provide us with this easy proof.

But in this brief explanation I must mention, besides the observations, general and particular, which prove the law, the theoretical considerations which demonstrate its necessity.

The most important of these considerations, and one rooted in the very nature of our subject, is the need, in every epoch, of some kind of a theory to link facts, together with the obvious impossibility in the primitive stages of mankind of forming theories from observation.

Since Bacon, intelligent people are agreed that there is no real knowledge save that which rests on observed facts. As applying to the full grown state of our intelligence, this principle is evidently incontestable. But if we look at its formative stage, it is no less certain that the human mind then could not, and should not, think in this way. For if on the one hand every positive theory is necessarily based on observation, on the other it is no less certain that in order to devote itself to observation the mind needs some kind of theory. If in contemplating phenomena we had no principles to which to attach them, not only would we find it impossible to combine isolated observations, and therefore to profit from them, but we would not be able to remember them, and most of the time the facts themselves would pass unperceived before our very eyes.

Thus between the necessity of observation for the formation of genuine theories, and the not less pressing necessity of constructing theories for the pursuit of observation, the human mind must have found itself trapped in a vicious circle, from which it could never have escaped, had not a natural way out been provided by the spontaneous development of theological conceptions, which offered a rallying point for its efforts and material for its activity. Such is the fundamental motive—apart from the weighty social ones which are not to be entered into at this stage—of the theological character of primitive philosophy, and the proof also of its logical necessity.

The necessity becomes still more apparent when we consider the perfect accord between theological philosophy and the nature of the investigations on which the human mind is engaged in its infancy. It is after all extremely remarkable that the questions which are most absolutely inaccessible to human powers: the inner nature of being, the origin and end of all phenomena, are precisely those that our intelligence undertakes in that primitive state, while all the truly soluble problems are looked upon as almost unworthy of serious consideration. The reason is obvious: only experience could teach us the limits of our strength, and if man had not begun by having an exaggerated opinion of it, he would never have attained the utmost of his capabilities. Such is human nature.

Let us try then to imagine, if we can, this universal, ingrained attitude of mind, and ask ourselves what would have been the reception given in such an epoch to positive philosophy, whose proper character is to regard as forbidden to human reason those sublime mysteries which theological philosophy explains with such admirable facility down to the last detail.

The same holds good of the practical inquiries that first occupy the human mind. They offer to man the goal of a limitless empire to be exercised over the external world, which is regarded as destined for his exclusive use, and presenting in its phenomena intimate and continuous relations with his existence. These fantastic hopes, these exaggerated ideas of the importance of man in the universe, which originate in theological philosophy and which wither away at the first breath of positive philosophy, are an initial stimulant without which it would be inconceivable that the human mind could address itself in the primitive state to painful toil.

Today we have put such a distance between us and these primitive attitudes, at least with regard to most phenomena, that we have difficulty in representing to ourselves their force and necessity. Human reason is now sufficiently mature for laborious scientific research to be undertaken without the imagination being activated by any of the ulterior motives that moved the astrologers and the alchemists. Intellectual activity is sufficiently stimulated by the hope of discovering the laws of phenomena, the desire of confirming or refuting a theory. But it could not be so in the infancy of the human mind. Without the attractive chimeras of astrology, without the energising illusions of alchemy, where was the constant ardour to come from that was necessary to collect these interminable series of observations and experiments which later served as a foundation for the first positive theories of one or other of these classes of phenomena?

This primary condition of our intellectual development was long ago perceived by Kepler, in astronomy, and justly appreciated in our own day by Berthollet,[2] in chemistry.

Thus we can see that if positive philosophy is the point of arrival of human intelligence, the state to which more or less it has tended, it has none the less had to use at the start, during many centuries, either as provisional method or as provisional doctrine, theological philosophy, a philosophy whose very character is to be spontaneous, and therefore the only possible one in the beginning, the only one that could offer sufficient interest to the awakening intelligence. We can now also see that in order to pass from this provisional philosophy to the ultimate philosophy, metaphysical doctrines and methods had to be adopted as a transitional philosophy. In order to complete the outline of the great law I have indicated, we must consider this last point.

Evidently our understanding, advancing only by scarcely perceptible degrees, could not pass abruptly, without intermediaries, from theological to positive philosophy. Theology and physics are so profoundly incompatible, their conceptions are so radically opposed, that before renouncing the one, in order to employ the other exclusively, human intelligence had to use intermediary conceptions, of a bastard nature, and suited for that very reason to the gradual transition. Such is the natural destiny of metaphysical conceptions: they have no other real use. By substituting in his study of phenomena for the supernatural directive action a corresponding inherent entity, although conceived at first as an emanation of the supernatural directive, man habituated himself little by little to considering only the facts, for the notions of these metaphysical agents were gradually refined to the point of being, for any sound mind, merely the abstract names of phenomena. It is impossible to imagine by what other procedure our understanding could have passed from considerations that were frankly supernatural to the purely natural, from the theological to the positive regime.

Now that we have established, as far as is possible without a detailed discussion—which would at present be out of place—the general law of development of the human mind, we can easily determine the exact nature of positive philosophy. Which is the essential aim of these lectures.

We see that it is the nature of positive philosophy to regard all phenomena as subject to invariable natural *laws*, the discovery of which, and their reduction to the least possible number, is the aim and end of all our efforts, while causes, either first or final, are considered to be absolutely inaccessible, and the search for them meaningless. There is no need to insist on a principle so familiar to all who have made any serious study of the observational sciences. Everyone knows that in positive explanation, even when it is most perfect, we do not pretend to expound the generative *causes* of phenomena, as that would be merely to put the difficulty one stage farther back, but rather to analyse the circumstances in which the phenomena are produced, and to link them one to another by the relations of succession and similarity.

To cite a most striking example, we say that the general phenomena of the universe are *explained* by the Newtonian law of gravitation, because this theory shows, on the one hand, the immense variety of astronomical facts as being one and the same fact seen from different points of view: the mutual attraction of molecules proportional to the product of their masses and inversely proportional to the square of their distances; and on the other, this fact as an extension of a phenomenon which is very familiar, and for that reason regarded as perfectly well known: the weight of bodies on the surface of the earth. As for determining what that attraction and that weight are in themselves, and what their causes, these are questions that we regard as insoluble, as outside the domain of positive philosophy, questions that we rightly resign to the imagination of the theologians and the subtleties of the metaphysicians. The clear proof of the impossibility of obtaining answers to such questions is that every time people have tried to say something rational on the subject, even the greatest minds have only been able to define these two principles by one another, declaring that attraction is nothing but weight, and that weight is simply the attraction of the earth. When one aspires to know the inner essence of things and the mode of their generation, such 'explanations' will raise a smile: actually they are the most satisfactory obtainable, for they show two orders of phenomena which had long been regarded as having no connection with one another, as identical. No intelligent person today would seek to go any further.

It would be easy to multiply examples: there will be hosts of them in the course of these lectures, for such is the spirit that today governs the great intellectual enterprises. To cite one only of these contemporary projects, we have M. Fourier's[3] fine series of researches on the theory of heat. It furnishes quite decisive proof of our remarks. In this work, whose philosophic character is eminently positive, the most important and most precise laws of thermological phenomena are revealed without the author having once inquired into the essential nature of heat, or mentioned, otherwise than to indicate its inanity, the agitated controversy between the partisans of calorific matter, and of heat as the vibration of a universal ether. Nevertheless the greatest questions, of which several had never before been raised, are treated in this work, thus providing palpable proof that the human mind may find inexhaustible material for its most profound speculations, without concerning itself with insoluble problems, and keeping strictly to researches of a positive order.

Now that the spirit of positive philosophy has been defined as exactly as is possible in a general summary, we have to examine its present stage of development, and what remains to be done to complete its formation.

The first thing to consider is that the different branches of our knowledge have not gone through the three phases of development indicated above at an equal speed, and consequently have not arrived simultaneously at the positive stage. There is an invariable and necessary order according to which our conceptions progress, each after its kind, and which must be carefully studied as a necessary consequence of the aforesaid law. This order will be the special theme of the next lecture. For the present it is enough to say that it finds itself in conformity with the diverse nature of phenomena, that it is determined by the degree of their generality, simplicity, and mutual independence, three considerations which though distinct contribute to the same end. Thus astronomical phenomena to begin with, as the most general, simplest, and most independent of all the others, after these the phenomena of terrestrial physics, those of chemistry, and finally those of physiology, have proved amenable to positivist theory.

It is impossible to assign a precise origin to the positivist revolution. It can be said with truth that as with all great human events, it was accomplished both unremittingly and gradually, particularly since the work of Aristotle and of the Alexandrian school, and subsequently the introduction of natural science into western Europe by the Arabs. However, since it is advisable to choose a period, if we are to avoid too great a dispersal of ideas, I will choose that great movement of the human mind which took place two centuries ago, through the combined action of the precepts of Bacon, the concepts of Descartes, and the discoveries of Galileo, as the moment in time when the spirit of positive philosophy began to assert itself in the world, as against the theological and the metaphysical spirit. It is then that positive conceptions cast off the superstitious alloy of scholasticism which more or less disguised the real nature of all previous work.

Since that memorable epoch the rise of positive, and the decline of theological and metaphysical philosophy have been very marked. So marked, that today it has become impossible for any observer, conscious of the times, not to recognise that positive studies represent the final destiny of human intelligence, and that human intelligence will separate itself definitely from the vain doctrines and provisional methods which were only suited to its infancy. Thus this fundamental revolution will necessarily be fully accomplished. If therefore there still remains a conquest to be made, a branch of the intellectual domain to be taken over, one can be sure that the transference will take place, as it has taken place in all the others. It is extremely improbable that the human mind, disposed as it is to unity of method, should retain indefinitely its primitive manner of philosophising for any one class of phenomena, once it has come to adopt a new philosophic procedure of an exactly opposite character for all the rest.

Thus everything comes down to a simple question of fact: does positive philosophy, which in the last two centuries has experienced so great an extension, embrace today all orders of phenomena? Obviously it does not, and consequently a great scientific operation still remains to be carried out if it is to acquire the character of universality indispensable to its final form.

For the four principal categories of natural phenomena which we have just enumerated: astronomical, physical, chemical and physiological, leave a gap where the social phenomena ought to be. Though implicitly included with the physiological, they deserve to form a separate category, by reason both of their importance and of the difficulties attending their study. This last order of conceptions, which relates to the most peculiar, complicated and dependent of phenomena, was bound for that reason to progress more slowly than all the preceding ones, quite apart from other obstacles which we shall consider later. At any rate it is evident that it has not yet entered the domain of positive philosophy. The theological and metaphysical methods, which are no longer employed in any other order of phenomena, either as a means of investigation or even of argumentation, are still exclusively used for both these purposes in all that concerns social phenomena, although their inadequacy is already fully recognised by all intelligent persons, for whom the vain and interminable contestation between divine right and the sovereignty of the people has become a source of inexpressible boredom.

Here then is the great, the only lacuna that must be filled if we are to complete the formation of positive philosophy. The human mind has created celestial and terrestrial physics, mechanics and chemistry, vegetable and animal physics, we might say, but we have still to complete the system of the observational sciences with *social physics*. Such today is the greatest, and in several most important respects, the most pressing need of our intelligence, and such the aim of this course.

The concepts which I shall endeavour to present in relation to the study of social phenomena, and of which the rudiments are already perceptible, I hope, in this lecture, cannot pretend to confer straightway on social physics the same degree of perfection as on the previous branches of natural philosophy: such an ambition would be entirely unrealistic, since even these branches are very unequal in their relation to these concepts. But they are meant to bring about in this class of sciences that positive character which has already been assumed by all the other sciences. If this condition is once really fulfilled, the philosophic system of the moderns will at last be whole and complete, for obviously no observable phenomenon could fail to be included in one or other of the five great established categories of astronomical, physical, chemical, physiological and social phenomena. All our fundamental conceptions will have become homogeneous, and philosophy will definitely have arrived at a positive state. No longer subject to any change of character, it will only need to develop indefinitely through the constant acquisitions that will result from new observations or more profound reflection. Having thus

27

acquired what it lacked, the character of universality, positive philosophy will be able to substitute itself entirely for theological and metaphysical philosophy of which the one quality at the present moment is that universality. Ceasing to be objects of preference on this ground, these philosophies will only exist historically for our descendants.

Our special aim in this course being now explained, its second general aim, which makes it a course of positive, and not merely of social philosophy, is easily understood.

For the foundation of a social physics, completing the system of the natural sciences, makes possible and even necessary a summation of the various departments of knowledge which have arrived at a fixed homogeneous state, so as to co-ordinate them and present them as branches of a single tree rather than isolated entities. Before proceeding to the examination of social phenomena, therefore, I shall consider in turn the different positive sciences already in existence, in the encyclopaedic order indicated above.

There is no need to point out that there can be no question of a series of special courses on the various branches of natural philosophy. Quite apart from the time this would take up, clearly such a project would be beyond me and, I may add, beyond anybody, in the present stage of our knowledge. Even a course of the nature of the present one, if it is to be properly understood, demands a series of preparatory studies of the different sciences under consideration. Unless this condition is fulfilled, the philosophical reflections of which these sciences are the subject are difficult to understand and impossible to judge. To cut matters short, it is a *Course in Positive Philosophy* that I propose to give, not in positive sciences. What we have to do is to consider each fundamental science in its relation to the entire positive system, as also the spirit that characterises that science both in its method and in its results. Most of the time I shall have to confine myself to quoting the results from the specialists, merely endeavouring to appreciate their importance.

As regards our aim, which is both special and general, I must observe that these two objects, although distinct, are inseparable. On the one hand it would be impossible to conceive a course in positive philosophy which did not include the foundation of social physics, since an essential element would be lacking; the conceptions therefore would not have the character of generality which should be their principal attribute, marking off the present study from series of special studies. On the other, how can we proceed with any certainty to a positive study of social phenomena unless our minds are first prepared by a consideration of the positive methods which have already been tested in connection with less complex phenomena, and unless they are furnished with a knowledge of the principal laws of these phenomena, laws which all have a more or less direct bearing on the social facts?

Although all the fundamental sciences do not inspire equal interest in the vulgar mind, there is not one we can afford to neglect in a study like the present. As far as importance for the happiness of the human race is concerned, all of these sciences are of equal value, on any close examination. Those whose results seem at first sight to be of less practical interest command our notice either for the perfection of their methods, or as the foundation of all the other sciences. This latter aspect will be recommended to your particular attention in the next lecture.

A course as novel as the present one is bound to lend itself to misinterpretations and misunderstandings. Let me just say a few brief words on that 'universal knowledge' which the unreflecting might regard as the tendency of this course, but which we regard as totally contrary to the spirit of positive philosophy. These remarks will have the additional advantage of showing the positive spirit in a new light and from a new angle.

In the primitive state of our knowledge there is no division between intellectual subjects; all the sciences are simultaneously cultivated by all the minds. This mode of study, at first inevitable and even indispensable, changes little by little, as the various orders of concept develop. By the law of necessity each branch of the scientific system detaches itself gradually from the parent trunk, when it has developed sufficiently to be cultivated independently, that is, when it has reached the point of permanently and fully occupying a number of minds. It is to this distribution of the various kinds of research among different orders of scientists that we owe the so remarkable development in our day of each distinct class of human knowledge, rendering manifestly impossible in our time that universality in research which was so easy and so common in antiquity. In a word, the division of intellectual labour, constantly raised to an ever higher degree of perfection, is one of the most important and characteristic attributes of positive philosophy.

But while saluting the prodigious results, and recognising the division as basic to the organisation of the scientific world, one is struck by the very considerable disadvantages associated with its present state, through the excessive particularity of the ideas by which the individual intelligence is occupied. This unfortunate effect is no doubt inevitable up to a point, and inherent in the principle of division; by no possible means can we ever aspire to emulate the ancients in their command of the whole field of knowledge, for this command derived from the undeveloped state of knowledge. We can, however, it seems to me, by the proper methods, avoid the more pernicious effects of specialisation, without diminishing in any way the stimulus given by distinct orders of research. On everyone's admission, the dividing line between the various branches of natural philosophy is in the last resort artificial. Let us not forget that despite this admission few indeed are the scientific minds which embrace the whole of even one science, that science being in its turn only a part of the great whole. Already the majority confine themselves to a more or less extensive section of a particular science, not concerning themselves overmuch with the relation of their particular research to the general system of positive knowledge represented by their science. Let us hasten to remedy this evil, before worse things come upon us, for there is indeed grave danger that the human mind will lose itself in minute investigation. Let us not be blind to the fact that it is precisely on this point that the partisans of theological and metaphysical philosophy can attack positive philosophy with some hope of success.

The true means of arresting the deleterious effect on the future of the intellect of over-specialised research cannot obviously be a return to the ancient confusion, which would be a retrograde step for the human mind, and happily today has become impossible. The remedy consists on the contrary in perfecting the division of labour. All that is required is that the study of scientific generalisation should become still another speciality. That a new class of scientists, prepared by a suitable education, and not devoted to any particular branch of natural philosophy, should occupy itself simply and solely with the present state of the various positive sciences, determine the spirit of each one of them, discover their relations and inter-connections, and reduce their particular principles to a lesser number of common principles, all this in conformity with the fundamental maxims of the positive method. That at the same time the other scientists, before devoting themselves to their respective specialities, should be rendered capable, by an education in the totality of positive knowledge, of profiting immediately from the light shed on their studies by the scientists specialising in generalities, and in their turn of rectifying the latter's results—a condition of things to which contemporary scientists are getting closer every day. Once these two conditions are fulfilled, and it is evident that they can be fulfilled, the division of labour in the sciences will be extended with impunity as far as is necessary for the development of the various orders of knowledge.

When a distinct class, constantly checked by all the other classes of scientist, has as its proper and permanent function the linking of each particular discovery as it appears to the general system, there will no longer be any fear that too much attention to detail is preventing the grasp of the whole. In a word, the modern organisation of the world of science will have taken shape, and will only have to develop indefinitely while retaining that shape.

By making the study of scientific generalities a distinct section of intellectual work, we shall simply be extending the principle of division which has detached the various specialities one after the other. As long as the different positive sciences were little developed, their mutual relationships had not sufficient importance to produce, at least permanently, a particular class of work. By the same token the necessity of this new type of work was much less pressing. But today the sciences have each acquired separately sufficient scope for the examination of their mutual relationships to constitute a special study, and at the same time this special study becomes indispensable if the dispersal of ideas is to be avoided.

This is how I see the part to be played by positive philosophy in the general system of the positive sciences. And the aim of this course is to play this part.

Now that I have defined as exactly as is possible in a first sketch the general spirit of positive philosophy, I think I should rapidly indicate the principal advantages to be derived from these studies, as long as the essential conditions relating to the progress of the human mind are properly fulfilled. I shall confine myself to four fundamental features.

First, the study of positive philosophy, by considering our intellectual faculties only in their results, furnishes the true means of determining the logical laws of the human mind, hitherto sought in ways little suited to their discovery.

To explain what I think on this subject, I must remind you of a philosophical concept of the highest importance, developed by M. de Blainville[4] in the fine introduction to his *General Principles of Comparative Anatomy*. Every active entity, according to this concept, and especially every living entity, with all its phenomena, can be studied under two aspects, the static and the dynamic, i.e. as capable of action, and as acting. All possible considerations necessarily belong to one or the other of these modes. Let us apply this maxim to the study of intellectual functions.

If these functions are viewed under their static aspect, the study of them will consist in the determination of the organic conditions on which the functions depend. It will be a branch of anatomy and physiology. If they are considered under their dynamic aspect, it will simply amount to tracing the course actually followed by the human mind in action, through the examination of the methods really employed to obtain the exact knowledge that it has already acquired: and this constitutes the essential aim of positive philosophy, as I have defined it in this lecture. In a word, if we regard all scientific theories as so many great logical facts, it is simply and solely by the study of these facts that we can rise to the knowledge of the laws of logic.

Such are the only two methods, complementary to one another, by which one can arrive at a few truly rational notions of intellectual phenomena. Under no consideration will there be any room for that illusory psychology, final avatar of theology, which today is in process of resuscitation, and which aims at discovering the fundamental laws of the human mind by contemplating it in itself, that is, by abstracting it from causes and effects—disdaining either to study the physiology of our intellectual organs, or to observe the rational methods by which scientific researches are actually carried out.

The preponderance of positive philosophy has come about gradually since the days of Bacon; today it has acquired so great an ascendancy even over minds ignorant of its immense development, that metaphysicians busy with the study of our intelligence could not hope to arrest the decay of their so-called science except by a change of attitude, with the result that they now present their doctrines as likewise founded on the observation of facts. With great subtlety they now distinguish between two kinds of observation of equal importance, the one external, the other internal, the latter being directed to the examination of intellectual phenomena. This is not the place to enter into a detailed discussion of this sophistry. I will merely point out the reason why the so-called contemplation of the mind by the mind is a pure illusion.

Only recently it was believed that vision was explained by the luminous action of bodies on the retina, producing images representative of forms and colours. Physiologists pointed out that if the impressions of light acted as *images*, another eye would be needed to look at them. Have we not in the present instance a case of the same kind?

We see that from an ineluctable necessity the human mind observes all phenomena directly, except its own. For who could conduct such a type of observation? One can understand that a man might be able to observe moral phenomena in the passions that inflame him, for the anatomical reason that the organs that are the seat of these passions are different from the organs of observation. But even although every man may have had occasion to make such observations on himself they could never have great scientific importance, and the best way to know the passions will always be to observe them as a spectator: for every pronounced state of passion, that is every state essential to this very study, is necessarily incompatible with the state of observation. But as for examining in the same manner intellectual phenomena as they appear, this is manifestly impossible. A thinking individual cannot divide himself into two, one half reasoning, and the other watching it reason. The observed and the observing organ become identical in this case. How could observation take place?

The so-called psychological method therefore is in principle invalid. And consider to what absolutely contradictory antics it leads! On the one hand you are told to insulate yourself, as much as possible, from every external sensation, above all you must refrain from intellectual work; for if you were to do the simplest sum, what would become of *internal* observation? On the other hand, after having by dint of precautions attained to the state of intellectual sleep, you must busy yourself contemplating the operations taking place in your mind, when nothing at all is taking place in it! Our posterity will doubtless one day see these pretensions transferred to the comic stage.

The results of so strange a method are in perfect conformity with its principle. In the space of two thousand years that metaphysicians have been cultivating psychology, they have not been able to agree on a single intelligible and solidly established proposition. Even today they are split into a multitude of schools in constant debate over the first elements of their doctrine. *Internal observation* engenders almost as many divergent opinions as there are individuals to pursue it.

The men of science, that is, dedicated to positive studies, are still asking the psychologists to cite one single real discovery, great or small, due to their vaunted method—in vain. This is not to say that all their work has been absolutely without result for the general progress of our knowledge, quite apart from the great service they rendered by keeping our intelligence active at a time when it had no substantial pabulum. But it can be affirmed that everything in their writings that is not, in the words of an illustrious positive philosopher, (M. Cuvier)[5] metaphor mistaken for reasoning, and that does present some real idea, has been attained not by their so-called method, but by genuine observation, called forth from time to time by the progress of the sciences, of the human mind's actual procedures. And even then the sparse notions announced with drum and trumpet and due to the psychologists' infidelity to their own method, are either very inflated or very incomplete, and quite inferior to the unostentatious remarks made by scientists on the procedures they employ. It would be easy to cite striking examples, but we will not labour the point at this juncture: among other things you might consider what has happened to the theory of signs.

The considerations I have submitted on the science of logic become still more cogent in the art of logic.

When it is a matter not only of knowing what the positive method is, but of knowing it well enough to be able to use it effectively, it must be seen in action. What we must study are the important applications of it that have already been made and tested. In other words it is by the philosophic examination of the sciences that we shall grasp it. It cannot be studied apart from the research in which it is employed; or at any rate such a study would be lifeless, barren of results for the mind engaged in it. Anything that one could say about it in the abstract would be so vague and so general as to have no influence on intellectual procedures. When we establish as a logical thesis that all our knowledge must be based on observation, that we must sometimes go from facts to principles, and sometimes from principles to facts, and a few other aphorisms of that ilk, we know the method much less clearly than anyone who has studied a single positive science, even without any philosophic intention. It is because they have overlooked this fact that our psychologists imagine that their lucubrations are science, and that they understand the positive method from having read the precepts of Bacon or the discourses of Descartes.

I am not sure whether, later on, it will be possible to conduct a course on method quite independently of the philosophic study of the sciences, but I am convinced that it is not possible at present, as the great logical procedures cannot yet be explained with sufficient exactitude apart from their application. I will venture to add that even if this were eventually possible, it is only through the study of the regular application of scientific methods that a system of good intellectual habits can be acquired, and this after all is the aim of the method.

Such then must be the first great result of positive philosophy: the experiential manifestation of the laws obeyed by our intellectual faculties when fully developed, and consequently a precise knowledge of the general rules to be observed in any fruitful search for truth.

A second consequence, of no less importance and greater urgency, is to bring about the remodelling of our system of education.

All intelligent persons are already agreed that our European education, which is still essentially theological, metaphysical and literary, must be replaced by a *positive* education, in tune with the spirit of our time, and adapted to the needs of modern civilisation. The various and repeated attempts during the last hundred years, above all recently, to spread and to augment positive instruction, attempts in which the various European governments have eagerly participated even when they did not initiate them, are sufficient evidence that on all sides this necessity has come to be felt. But while seconding these useful projects as much as possible, we must not shut our eyes to the fact that in the present state of our ideas these projects cannot realise the true aim, which is the fundamental reform of general education. The exclusive specialism, the exaggerated remoteness which still characterise our understanding and cultivation of the sciences influence also the teaching of them. Let any intelligent person decide to study the principal branches of natural philosophy, with a view to making out a system of positive ideas, he will find himself obliged to study each branch separately, with the same method and in the same detail as if he wished to become a specialist in astronomy, chemistry, etc., so that such a study becomes almost impossible and at any rate highly incomplete even for the loftiest intelligence in the most favourable circumstances. In general education it would be out of the question. And yet a *sine qua non* of general education is certainly a schema of positive conceptions covering all the great orders of natural phenomena. Such a schema, on a scale either small or large, must become, even for the masses, the permanent basis of all planning; it will form the mentality of our descendants. The regeneration of our intelligence is already far advanced. If natural philosophy is to complete it, it is essential that the various sciences of which it is composed be presented to every mind as the branches of a single trunk, and reduced to what constitutes their spirit, that is, their principal methods and most important results. Only thus can the teaching of science become the basis of a new and rational general education. Naturally this basic instruction should be followed by specialised scientific studies. But it is essential to grasp that all specialities, even though absorbed with a great deal of trouble, would not produce any real renewal of our system of education if they did not have as a preliminary basis that general instruction which is the result of positive philosophy as defined in this course.

Not only must the special study of scientific generalities reorganise education, it will also contribute to the advancement of particular sciences; and this is the third virtue of positive philosophy to which I will draw your attention.

35

The divisions which we establish between our sciences, though not arbitrary, as some believe, are certainly artificial. In reality the subject of all our research is one; we only split it up in order to insulate difficulties with a view to solving them. More than once it happens that, contrary to our classical divisions, important questions demand a combination of specialities, such as can scarcely be effected in the scientific world as at present constituted; and thus these problems run the risk of remaining unsolved much longer than is necessary. Such is the case and such the difficulty with regard to the basic doctrines of each positive science. Striking examples of this might be quoted; I will give a few.

In the past we have Descartes's admirable conception of analytical geometry. This basic discovery, which changed the face of mathmatical science, and which must be regarded as the veritable germ of all its subsequent developments—what is it but the link between two sciences which up to that time had been isolated from one another? But it is questions still hanging in the balance that give even more decisive proof of a necessary pluridisciplinarity. I will confine my remarks to the important chemical doctrine of definition proportion. All appearances to the contrary the recent discussion on the basic principle of that theory cannot be regarded as closed. For, as it seems to me, here we have no mere question of chemistry.[6] I think I may say that to arrive at a final decision on the point, that is, to decide whether we should regard fixed numbers for the combination of molecules as a law of nature, it is necessary to combine chemistry with physiology. What makes this clear is that on the admission of the illustrious chemists who have contributed most to the establishment of this doctrine, all that can be said is that it is constantly confirmed by the composition of inorganic bodies. But it is found just as constantly at fault in organic compounds, to which hitherto it has been impossible to extend it. Before raising it to the status of an essential principle, should not account be taken of this immense exception? Might it not be connected with the general character of organic bodies, none of whose phenomena admit of invariable numbers? However that may be, it is obvious that a totally new order of considerations, belonging both to physiology and to chemistry, is here called for if any final conclusion is to be reached on this great question of natural philosophy.

I think I should bring forward here a second example of the same kind, one which, as it relates to a research subject of a much more detailed character, is still more conclusive as to the importance of positive philosophy in the solution of questions requiring the combination of several sciences. Again I take it from chemistry. I refer to the still undecided question whether nitrogen must be regarded, in the present state of our knowledge, as a simple or a compound body. You know by what purely chemical arguments the illustrious Berzélius[7] was enabled to sway the opinion of almost all contemporary chemists in favour of the simplicity of this gas. But what I must draw attention to is the influence exercised on the mind of M. Berzélius, as he himself has declared in an important statement, by the physiological observation that animals that feed on non-nitrogenous matter store just as much nitrogen in their tissues as carnivorous animals. This shows that in order to decide if nitrogen is or is not a simple body, it will be necessary to bring in physiology and to combine with the chemical considerations properly so called a new series of researches on the relation between the composition of living bodies and their diet.

It would be useless to multiply examples of these pluridisciplinary problems, insoluble except by a combination of several sciences which at the present moment are cultivated independently of one another. The cases I have cited sufficiently demonstrate the importance of positive philosophy in the advancement of every natural science, for its role is to organise such combinations on a permanent footing; nor could they properly be formed without this philosophy.

Finally I must here and now draw attention to a fourth and last quality of positive philosophy, the one that deserves our closest scrutiny, for it has most practical importance at the present moment, that of offering the one solid basis for the social reorganisation that will alone bring to an end the state of crisis in which the most civilised nations have been plunged for so long. The latter part of these lectures will be specially devoted to establishing this proposition and there it will be fully developed. But the outline of the great scheme which I have wished to convey in this lecture would lack one of its main elements if I neglected so important an aspect.

A few simple reflections will serve to justify what might appear an over-ambitious claim.

There is no need to prove to this audience that ideas govern and revolutionise the world, in other words that the entire social machinery rests in the last resort on opinion. You are aware that the great political and moral crisis of our present society is the result, in the final analysis, of intellectual anarchy. Our most deadly disease is the profound divergence of minds with regard to all the fundamental maxims whose fixity is the prime condition of a true social order. So long as individual minds do not assent to a certain number of general ideas forming a common social doc-

37

trine, there is no hiding the fact that the state of nations will remain revolutionary, in spite of all political palliatives, and that institutions will be only provisional. It is equally certain that if the union of minds in a communion of principles can once be established, suitable institutions will necessarily spring from it, without serious disturbance, for the greatest disorder of all will have been dissipated. Here then is the point on which should be concentrated the efforts of all those who see how important is a truly normal social condition.

From the lofty standpoint of these considerations the nature of present society is easily perceived, as also the means by which it may be reformed. In the light of the law stated at the beginning of this lecture, all the observations that can be made on the present state of society amount to this: that the present mental disorder is, in the last analysis, due to the simultaneous use of three incompatible philosophies, the theological, the metaphysical and the positive. Clearly if any of these three philosophies achieved universal and complete surpremacy, there would be a definite social order; clearly what we suffer from is disorganisation. The coexistence of these three opposed philosophies prevents agreement on any essential point. If this is true, all we have to do is to find out which of these three philosophies can and must prevail in the nature of things. Then every sensible man, whatever may have been his private opinion before the question was settled, must endeavour to contribute to the triumph of that one philosophy. Once research has been reduced to these simple terms, it does not appear that its results can long be in doubt; it is obvious for all kinds of reasons, of which I have explained some of the most important, that positive philosophy alone is destined to prevail in the ordinary course of events. Its advance has been constant for many hundreds of years, while its antagonists have been constantly in retreat. Rightly or wrongly, it is no matter: the fact is indisputable, and it suffices. It may be deplored, but it cannot be either removed or neglected, if we are not to indulge in vain dreams. This general revolution of the human mind is today almost accomplished; all that we have to do is to complete positive philosophy by including in it the study of social phenomena, and then reduce it to a single body of doctrine. When this work is sufficiently advanced, the definite triumph of positive philosophy will come about spontaneously, and will re-establish order in society. The marked preference shown today for positive knowledge, as distinct from vague and mystical conceptions, by the most eminent as well as by the most vulgar minds, augurs well for the reception of this philosophy, when it has acquired the one quality that it still lacks: universality.

To sum up: theological and political philosophy today dispute the task —beyond the strength of either—of reorganising society. The contest is between them and them alone. Up till now positive philosophy has only intervened to criticise them both, in which duty she has acquitted herself well enough to discredit them completely. Let us put her in the position of playing an active part, and give over worrying about useless debates. Let us complete the vast intellectual operation that was begun by Bacon, Descartes and Galileo; let us construct without more ado the system of general ideas destined to prevail in human society, and the revolutionary fever which torments civilised peoples will be at an end.

From these four points of view the salutary influence of positive influence had to be indicated, as it seemed to me, in order to complement the general definition which I have endeavoured to give.

Before closing, one last observation: one that will, I hope, prevent an erroneous opinion being formed in advance on the nature of this course.

In assigning to positive philosophy the aim of reducing the totality of acquired knowledge to one single body of homogeneous doctrine, relatively to the different orders of natural phenomena, I have no intention of making a general study of these phenomena as the diverse effects of one single principle, as subject to one and the same law. Although this question will receive separate treatment in the next lecture, I believe I must make this declaration at once, in order to meet half-way the criticism, entirely without foundation, that might be directed against me by those who, on a false assumption, would class this course among the universal explanations daily spawned by minds totally unacquainted with the methods and results of science. Nothing of the kind is here; and those who from the introduction might still conceive some doubts will receive ample proof as the course proceeds.

I am profoundly convinced that these universal explanations of all phenomena by a single law are fanciful in the extreme, even when attempted by the most competent minds. I think that the means at the disposal of the human mind are too inadequate, and the universe too complicated for such scientific perfection ever to be within our grasp; besides I believe that a very exaggerated idea has been formed of the resultant advantages, even if such perfection were possible. In any case it seems quite obvious that we are too far from it in the present state of our knowledge to attempt those universal explanations until a considerable time has elapsed. If there were any hope of attaining it, this could only be by attaching all natural phenomena to the most general positive law known to us, the law of gravitation, which already links all astronomical phenomena to some phenomena of terrestrial physics. Laplace[8] developed the idea that chemical phenomena might be viewed as the molecular effects of Newtonian gravitation, modified by the shape and relative position of the atoms. But besides the inconclusiveness which would probably always be a feature of such a conception, through the absence of the data on the inner constitution of the bodies, it is almost certain that the difficulty of applying it would make it necessary to retain the division between astronomy and chemistry, which today is accepted as natural. Therefore Laplace presented this idea as a mere philosophic toy, incapable of exercising any real and useful influence on the progress of chemical science. Furthermore, even if this difficulty were overcome, we should not even then have attained to scientific unity, since it would be necessary to attach physiological phenomena also to the same law; which would certainly have its difficulties. And yet the hypothesis just mentioned is, all things considered, the most favourable to the desired unity.

No further details seem necessary to convince my hearers that the aim of this course is not at all to present natural phenomena as at bottom identical, save for the variety of circumstances. Positive philosophy no doubt would be more perfect if this were so. But such a condition is in no wise necessary to its systematic formation, nor to the realisation of the great and happy consequences it is destined to produce. For that, the only indispensable unity is unity of method, which can and does exist and is already in great part established. As for doctrine, it is not necessary for it to be one; all that is necessary is that it be homogeneous. Thus it is from the viewpoint of unity of method and homogeneity of doctrine that we are to consider in this course the various classes of positive theory. While we do work to cut down as much as possible the number of general laws necessary for the explanation of natural phenomena, and this is indeed the philosophic aim of science, we should think ourselves rash if we aspired even in the most distant future to reduce them to one only.

I have endeavoured, in this exposition, to determine as exactly as I could the aim, spirit and influence of positive philosophy. I have therefore marked out the goal towards which my research has always tended, and will continue to tend, in this course and by any other means. No one is more firmly convinced than myself of the inadequacy of my intellectual resources, even if they were much greater than they are, for so vast and sublime a task. But what cannot be accomplished either by a single mind or in a single lifetime, may be clearly proposed by one person. Such is my ambition.

I will complete the prolegomena in the next lecture, by an exposition of the plan, that is, by determining the encyclopaedic order that must be established between the different classes of natural phenomena, and consequently between the corresponding positive sciences.

II

Plan of this Course, or General Considerations on the Hierarchy of the Positive Sciences[9]

Now that you are in possession of the leading ideas that will be presented on the principal branches of natural philosophy, we must draw up the plan to be followed, that is, the most suitable classification of the various basic positive sciences, so that we may study them one by one from our chosen point of view. This second discussion is indispensable, if the spirit of the course is to be understood from the start.

You will of course understand that we have no intention of criticising, which would be easy enough, the numerous classifications that have emerged, one after another, during the last two centuries, for the system of human knowledge viewed in its entirety. It is now accepted that all encyclopaedic 'ladders of knowledge', constructed, like those of Bacon and D'Alembert,[10] according to some kind of distinction between the various faculties of the human mind, are for that very reason radically defective, even when the distinction is not, as often happens, more subtle than real; for in each of its spheres of activity our understanding employs simultaneously all its chief faculties. As for the other classifications proposed, suffice it to say that every discussion excited by them has resulted in some basic defect being discovered, so that none of them has obtained unanimous assent and there exist almost as many opinions as individuals. These various attempts have been generally so ill-conceived that they have created a prejudice in intelligent minds against every enterprise of this nature.

But why linger over these well known facts? More important is to find the cause. The defects of these encyclopaedic attempts so frequently repeated, can easily be explained. I need not point out that since projects of this nature fell into disrepute through their lack of solid basis, these classifications have been the business of people almost totally ignorant of the subjects classified. But apart from this question of personnel, there is a much more important element, part and parcel of the subject itself, by reason of which it has not been possible to attain to a satisfactory encyclopaedic system. It is the absence of homogeneity in the different parts of the intellectual system, some having become positive, while others have remained theological or metaphysical. In this jumble it was impossible to establish a rational classification. How dispose profoundly contradictory conceptions within a single system? This has been the stumbling block of all classifiers, although none of them was quite aware of it. It was very apparent, nevertheless, to anyone well acquainted with the real situation of the human mind, that such an enterprise was premature, and that it could be undertaken with success only if our principal conceptions had become positive.

Since this fundamental condition may now be regarded as fulfilled, it is possible to proceed to the truly rational and lasting systematisation of parts which have at last become homogeneous.

Furthermore, the general theory of classification has recently been established by the philosophic research of botanists and zoologists, and allows us to hope for real success in our task by offering us a sure guide in the true principle of classification, which had never been clearly grasped until now. This principle emerges as soon as the positive method is applied to the problem of classification, for, like any other problem, it must be treated by observation and not by *a priori* considerations. By the positive method classification results from the study of the objects to be classified, and is determined by the affinities indicated by their affiliation, so as to be itself the expression of the most general fact relating to these objects, and elucidated by the comparison in depth of the objects.

Applying this rule to the present case, we shall classify the various positive sciences according to their mutual interdependence; such interdependence, to be real, can only be deduced from the phenomena appertaining to the sciences.

But before carrying out so important an encyclopaedic operation in this observational spirit, we must clearly outline its limits, so as not to wander too far afield.

All human labour is either speculative or active. Thus our knowledge is divided first of all into theoretical and practical. It is evident that a course like the present is concerned solely with theoretical knowledge; it is not a question of observing the entire system of human ideas, but only the fundamental conceptions behind the different orders of phenomena, conceptions basic to all our thinking, and themselves without anterior basis. It is speculation that concerns us in this work, and not application, except in so far as application can throw some light on speculation. This is perhaps what Bacon meant, though dimly, by his *prima philosophia*, which he says must be extracted from the totality of the sciences, and which has been interpreted in such various and strange ways by the metaphysicians who undertook to comment on his thinking.

There is no doubt that when we view the labour of humanity in its totality, the study of nature seems destined to furnish the rational basis of man's action upon nature, since knowledge of the laws governing phenomena means that we can anticipate these phenomena, and play off one against another in active life. Our natural means of acting on the bodies surrounding us are extremely feeble, and quite disproportionate to our needs. Every time we produce a big effect upon nature, it is because the knowledge of natural laws has enabled us to introduce modifying elements, however feeble in themselves, among the circumstances surrounding phenomena, so as in certain cases to modify in our interest the final result of a complex of causes. In short: *science = foresight, foresight = action*: such is the simple formula expressing the general relation of science and art, taking these words in their full sense.

But in spite of the great importance of this relationship, which should never be forgotten, to conceive science merely as the basis of art would be to have a very imperfect idea of it, and one which unfortunately is all too prevalent today. Whatever be the services rendered to *industry* by scientific theory, and although, to quote Bacon's incisive phrase, power is necessarily proportionate to knowledge, we must not forget that the sciences have a more immediate and more elevated destiny: that of satisfying the fundamental need of our intelligence to know the causes of phenomena. To realise how deeply implanted in us is this need we have only to consider the physiological effects of *astonishment*, and the terrible sensations we experience when anything seems to happen contrary to the laws of nature with which we are familiar. The need to arrange facts in an order we can grasp (the very object of all scientific theories) is so native to our being that if we were not able to satisfy it by positive conceptions we should inevitably return to the theological and metaphysical explanations which were its first fruits.

I thought it advisable to make this point, as it is necessary to guard against the too great influence of present habits, thanks to which a just and noble idea of the importance of the sciences has no chance of forming. If the very nature of our being did not correct, in the minds of scientists, the narrow and defective outlook of the age, human intelligence, confined to researches of immediate practical utility would for that same reason, as Condorcet[11] very truly remarked, be arrested in its progress, even as regards those applications to which speculative research had been imprudently sacrificed: for the most important applications invariably derive from theories created in the pursuit of pure science, and often cultivated for centuries without any practical result. We have a remarkable example of this in the Greek geometrists' speculations on conic sections which, after many generations, by leading to the renewal of astronomy, brought the art of navigation to the degree of perfection it has attained in these latter days, and which it never would have attained without the purely theoretical research of Archimedes and Apollonius;[12] in the words of Condorcet: 'The sailor who escapes being wrecked through an exact observation of latitude owes his life to a theory conceived two thousand years ago by men of genius who were concerned solely with geometric speculations.'

Evidently therefore after having conceived the study of nature as a rational basis for acting on nature, the human mind must proceed to theoretical research, totally removed from any practical consideration, as the means at our disposal for discovering the truth are so feeble that if we do not concentrate them exclusively on that one aim, if we impose on the search for truth the condition of satisfying some immediate practical requirement, we shall nearly always fail to arrive at truth.

What is certain is that the knowledge of nature, and the knowledge of the procedures for turning nature to our advantage, form two essentially different systems, which it is proper to consider and to cultivate separately. And as the first system is the basis of the second, this is the one that should be first considered in a methodical study, even if one's aim is to embrace the totality of human knowledge both speculative and applied. The theoretical system seems to me to constitute the sole subject of a rational course in positive philosophy: at least that is how I understand it. Certainly it would be possible to conceive a more extensive course, one bearing on practical as well as on theoretical generalities, but I do not think that such an enterprise, quite apart from its extent, can be properly attempted in the present state of the human mind. It seems to me to require considerable preliminary work of a peculiar nature: that of deriving from scientific theories the particular conceptions that serve as a basis to practice.

At the present stage of development of the human intellect, sciences are not immediately applied to arts, at least where the application is most perfect and most accomplished. Between the two orders of ideas there exists an intermediate order whose philosophic character is not as yet completely determined, but which is quite perceptible as a social class. Between the scientists properly so called and the managers of production, an intermediate class has grown up in our day, that of the *engineers*, whose special function is to organise the relation between theory and practice. Not at all concerned with the progress of scientific knowledge, they use this knowledge in its actual state, and derive from it the industrial applications of which it is capable. Such is at least the general tendency, although there is still a great deal of confusion. The body of doctrine belonging to this new class, and which will serve to constitute the genuine theories of the different arts, may well yield philosophic insights of great insight and some importance. But any study which included these theories conjointly with those founded on the sciences would be premature: doctrines half-way between pure theory and direct practice have not yet been formed. Up till now we have only had fragments of such doctrines relating to the most advanced sciences and arts, and giving us a glimpse of the nature and the possibilities of similar studies for human labour. Monge's fine conception of descriptive geometry must be regarded as the most important example of this. 'Descriptive geometry' is really a theory of the art of building. But clearly such incomplete concepts should not form an essential part of a course in positive philosophy, which should include only doctrines of a fixed and clearly determined character.

The difficulty of constructing such intermediate theories will be better understood if we realise that every art depends not on one corresponding science but on several, so much so that the most important arts borrow directly from almost all the principal sciences. Thus the true theory of agriculture—to mention only the most essential of all arts—demands a combination of physiological, chemical, physical, and even astronomical and mathematical knowledge. It is the same with the fine arts. By this we can see why it has not been possible to form these theories as yet, since they presuppose the development of all the different fundamental sciences. Whence still another motive for not including this type of idea in a course on positive philosophy: far from contributing to the formation of this philosophy, general theories proper to the arts are likely to be one of the most useful results of its construction.

To sum up, we must consider only scientific theories, not their application. But before proceeding to the methical classification, I must make another important distinction, this time between the pure sciences.

With reference to the orders of their phenomena, there are two kinds of natural sciences: the abstract and general have as their object the discovery of the laws governing the different classes of phenomena, in every conceivable case; the concrete, particular descriptive, sometimes

46

called 'natural' sciences, apply the said laws to the natural history of existing beings. The first are fundamental, and our studies will be exclusively concerned with them; the second, whatever be their intrinsic importance, are truly secondary, and must therefore not form part of a study in itself extensive enough to render any possible limitation advisable.

A distinction such as this between the two kinds of pure science will offer no difficulty to those who have any special knowledge of the different positive sciences. It is pretty well the same as that made in scientific treatises between dogmatic physics and natural history. A few examples will serve to bring out this distinction, whose importance has not yet been sufficiently appreciated.

It emerges when we compare general physiology on the one hand with zoology and with botany on the other. To study in general the laws of life, and to determine the mode of existence of each living body, are obviously two undertakings of a very different character. And the second is necessarily founded on the first.

It is the same with chemistry relatively to mineralogy. The first is obviously the rational basis of the second. In chemistry we consider all possible combinations of molecules, in all imaginable circumstances; in mineralogy we consider those combinations which actually take place in the constitution of the terrestrial globe, and under the influence of the circumstances peculiar to that globe. What clearly shows the difference between the chemical and the mineralogical point of view, although the two sciences are concerned with the same objects, is that most of the facts envisaged by chemistry have only an artificial existence, so that a body such as chlorine or potassium will be extremely important through the extent and the force of its affinities, while it will have no importance in mineralogy; conversely a compound such as granite or quartz, the object of many mineralogical considerations, will evoke but a slight interest in the chemist.

And what renders the logical necessity of the distinction between the two great sections of natural philosophy still more apparent is that each section of concrete physics supposes the previous study of the corresponding section of abstract physics, and also requires knowledge of the general laws relating to all orders of phenomena. Not only, for example, does the study of the earth, considered from all points of view, require a previous knowledge of physics and chemistry, but it cannot be carried out properly without, on the one hand, astronomical knowledge, and on the other, physiological knowledge; so that it depends on the entire system of fundamental science. It is the same with all the 'natural' sciences. For this reason *concrete physics* has so far made little progress, for it is as a sequel to *abstract physics* that it has been possible to begin a rational study of it, when all the principal branches of the latter had acquired their definite character, and this has not happened till our time. Up till now it has been possible to collect merely disparate material on the subject, and that very incomplete. Known facts cannot be co-ordinated to form special theories of the different entities of the universe, until the fundamental distinction to which we have drawn attention is more clearly perceived and more overtly developed and until, as a result, the specialists in the natural sciences have recognised the necessity of founding their research on a knowledge of all the fundamental sciences—a condition which today is very far from being fulfilled.

All of which confirms our reasons for limiting ourselves, in a course on positive philosophy, to the study of general science, not including the particular descriptive sciences. Indeed we see a fresh advantage to be gained from the study of the generalities of abstract physics: that of furnishing the rational basis of a truly systematic concrete physics. In the present state of the human mind there would be a kind of contradiction in wishing to combine in the same course the two orders of science. It could also be said that even if concrete physics had already attained the degree of perfection of abstract physics, and it were possible to embrace both in a course of positive philosophy, it would still be necessary to begin with the abstract section, as invariably furnishing the basis of the other. Besides, it is clear that the study of the generalities of the fundamental sciences is sufficiently vast in itself to make it necessary to exclude everything that is not absolutely indispensable: and what relates to the secondary sciences must always be, whatever happens, different in kind. The philosophy of the fundamental sciences, presenting as it does a system of positive conceptions with respect to every order of real knowledge constitutes that *prima philosophia* sought by Bacon which must be carefully reduced to its simplest expression, as it is destined to serve from now on as the permanent basis of all human speculation.

There is no need to labour this point any further. I have said enough to justify the limits I have set myself in the study of our subject.

We see then, as a result of what has been said in this lecture: 1. that human science is composed of speculative and applied sciences and that it is solely with the first that we are concerned; 2. that theoretical sciences, that is, sciences properly so called, are divided into the general and the particular, and that we are to consider only the first, to limit ourselves to abstract physics, whatever be the interest of concrete physics.

Our proper subject being now exactly circumscribed, we can proceed to the encyclopaedic problem, a truly satisfactory classification of the fundamental sciences, which is the real subject of this lecture.

But first we must realise that however natural the classification is, it will always necessarily contain something artificial, if not arbitrary, and will therefore be imperfect.

The end to be kept in view is the arrangement of the sciences in their natural sequence, i.e. according to their dependence on one another, so that they can be successively expounded without turning in a vicious circle. Now this is a condition which it seems to me cannot be quite fully met. Bear with me while I develop this point which is important if we are to understand the real difficulty of this type of research. And this will also be an opportunity to establish a general principle as regards the exposition of our knowledge.

Every science may be expounded in two essentially different ways, the historical and the dogmatic, any other being merely a combination of these two.

In the first knowledge is expounded in the order in which it has been acquired by humanity, following as much as possible the way in which it has been acquired.

In the second the system of ideas is presented as it could be conceived today by a single mind which sought, from a suitable point of view and with sufficient knowledge, to recreate the science as a whole.

The first mode is obviously the one in which we begin the study of any incipient science; it is the mark of such a science that it requires, for the exposition of its matter, no new study save that of its formation, and that its didactics consist in the chronological study of the various original works that have contributed to its progress.

The dogmatic mode presupposes that all these particular labours have been recast in a general system and present themselves in a natural logical order, and is therefore only applicable to a science which has already reached an advanced stage of development. As the science progresses, the *historic* order becomes less and less practicable, because of the long series of points that it is necessary to cover; while the *dogmatic* order becomes ever more possible, as well as necessary, because new conceptions enable one to present previous discoveries from a more direct point of view.

For example, the education of a geometrist in antiquity consisted simply in the study of the very small number of original treatises produced up to that time on the various parts of geometry, which really

49

meant the writings of Archimedes and Apollonius; while on the contrary a modern geometrist has generally finished his education without reading a single original work, except on the most recent discoveries, which can only be known by this means.

The tendency of the human mind, therefore, as far as the exposition of knowledge is concerned, is to substitute the dogmatic order for the historic order, as being alone suitable to the perfected state of our intelligence.

The general problem with which intellectual education is confronted is that of bringing one single intelligence, generally of mediocre calibre, to the point of development attained, through a long sequence of centuries, by a great number of superior geniuses applying all their strength during the whole of their lives to the study of one subject. Clearly then, even although it is easier and quicker to learn than to invent, it would be impossible for education to attain its end if every individual mind were to be forced to cover all the stages through which the collective genius of the human race has passed. Hence the ineluctable necessity of the dogmatic order, especially evident today for the most advanced sciences, the exposition of which no longer shows the actual filiation of particulars.

But to prevent exaggeration it should be added that any mode of exposition involves a certain combination of the dogmatic with the historical order, the first alone being destined to become more and more preponderant. Indeed the dogmatic order cannot be strictly followed; implying as it does a redigestion of acquired knowledge it is not applicable at every epoch of science to recently constituted parts, the study of which can only be pursued in the historical order. In such cases it is not subject to the drawbacks that cause it to be rejected most of the time.

The only fundamental defect that might be imputed to the dogmatic method is that it leaves one in ignorance of the way in which the various departments of human knowledge have emerged, and although this has little to do with the acquisition of knowledge, it is in itself a source of profound interest to every philosophic mind. If this were a real motive for preferring the historic order, it would have considerable weight with me. But it is easy to see that there is only an apparent connection between studying a science in the mode termed historical, and knowing the real history of that science.

For not only have the various parts of each science been simultaneously developed under the influence of one another, while they must be separated in the dogmatic order—a fact which would tend to make us prefer the historic order, but the different sciences, as becomes more and more apparent, have mutually and simultaneously perfected one another, even the progress of the sciences and the arts has been interdependent, through innumerable mutual influences, and finally all have been linked to the general development of human society. This vast interdependence is so real that often in order to understand how a scientific theory came to be generated, one is led to consider the improvement of some art which has no rational link whatsoever with it; or even some social advance, without which the discovery would not have taken place. Thus the true history of any science, that is, the emergence of the discoveries of which it is composed, cannot be known except by the study of the history of humanity. That is why all the facts and proofs collected up till now on the history of mathematics, astronomy, medicine, etc., however valuable, can only be regarded as raw material.

The so-called *historical* mode of exposition, even if it could be rigorously followed for the details of every science in particular, would remain purely hypothetical and abstract in the most important respect, for it would consider the development of that science in isolation. Far from exhibiting the true history of the science, it would tend to convey an entirely false impression of that history.

Certainly I am convinced that the history of science is of the greatest importance. I even think that one does not know a science completely as long as one does not know its history. But such a study must be considered as entirely separate from the dogmatic study of science, without which the history would be unintelligible.

We have now determined the conditions that must be accepted, and that can be fulfilled, if we are to construct the encyclopaedic ladder of the fundamental sciences.

We realise that however perfect it may be supposed to be, the classification cannot be in strict conformity with the historical filiation of the sciences. Whether we like it or not, we shall have to present as anterior to another science one that will need to borrow from it in more or less important respects. All that we can do is to see that this does not happen with the concepts peculiar to the individual science, for then our classification would be entirely vitiated.

Thus to me it appears undeniable that in the general system of the sciences astronomy must be placed before physics, yet several branches of physics, especially optics, are necessary to complete the account of astronomy.

Such minor defects are inevitable, and cannot invalidate a classification that in other respects fulfils the main conditions. They arise from what is necessarily artificial in the compartmentalising of intellectual labour.

And although as we have seen we cannot take historic order as the basis of our classification, I must point out that an essential property of the encyclopaedic ladder I am about to propose is its general conformity with scientific history, in the sense that in spite of the real and continuous simultaneity of development of the different sciences, those that are classed as earlier are in very truth older and more advanced than those presented as later. This must be so if we take, as we should, as principle of our classification, the natural and logical sequence of the sciences, the starting-point for the species being necessarily the same as that for the individual.

With a view to specifying with all possible exactness the difficulty of the encyclopaedic problem which we have to solve, it will be useful to introduce a very simple mathematical proposition that will sum up the arguments of this lecture. Here it is:

We propose to classify the fundamental sciences. It will soon become apparent that, all things considered, it is not possible to reduce them to less than six. Most scientists would indeed admit a greater number. Now we know that six objects can have 720 different arrangements. So the fundamental sciences might have 720 different classifications, among which it is our business to choose the one that best satisfies the principal conditions of the problem. We see that in spite of the great number of encyclopaedic ladders proposed up to the present, only a relatively small number of the possible arrangements have come under discussion; nevertheless I think I can say without exaggeration that if we examined all the 720, there is perhaps not one in favour of which one could not argue very plausibly. Observing the arrangements that have been proposed, we see that the most extreme differences exist between them: the sciences placed by some at the head of their encyclopaedic system are sent to the other end by others, and vice versa. Thus it is in the choice of one single rational order from the very considerable number of possible systems that the precise difficulty of the problem consists.

Faced with this question, let us remember that the principle of a natural and positive classification of the fundamental sciences should be sought in the comparison of the orders of phenomena whose laws these sciences exist to discover. What we wish to find out is the real relationship of the various scientific studies. And that relationship can only be derived from the phenomena.

Considering from this point of view all observable phenomena, we find we can divide them into a small number of categories, arranged so that the study of each category is founded on a knowledge of the principal laws of the preceding one, and is the foundation for the study of the following one. The order is determined by the degree of simplicity, or what amounts to the same thing, of generality in the phenomena, resulting in successive dependencies, and consequently greater or less difficulty in study.

A priori we can decide that the most simple phenomena, those least complicated by others, are necessarily the most general. Clearly what is observed in the greatest number of cases is for that very reason most independent of the circumstances proper to individual cases. Hence it is by the study of the most general or most simple phenomena that we must begin, proceeding by successive degrees to the most particular and the most complex, if we would understand natural philosophy in a truly methodical manner. For the order of generality or of simplicity, as it determines the sequence of the various fundamental sciences according to the successive dependence of their phenomena, determines also their degree of difficulty.

At the same time—and here we have a subsidiary cause which converges with the preceding ones—the most general and simple phenomena being necessarily the most remote from man, will be studied in a calmer and more rational spirit, which is another reason for the corresponding sciences developing more rapidly.

This being the basic rule which must guide us in the classification of the sciences, I now proceed to the construction of the encyclopaedic ladder which will decide the plan of the course.

When we first consider natural phenomena in their totality, we find ourselves dividing them, in conformity with the principle we have just established, into two great classes, the first comprising all the phenomena of inorganic, the second of organic bodies.

The second class are obviously more complicated and highly individualised than the first; they depend on the first, while the first are not at all dependent on the second. Hence the necessity of studying physiological phenomena only after those of inorganic bodies. In whatever way we explain the differences of these two kinds of bodies, what is certain is that all the phenomena, mechanical or chemical, of inorganic bodies are to be observed in organic bodies, with in addition a quite special order of phenomena, the vital phenomena properly so called, those that belong to *organism*. This is not the place to examine if these two classes of bodies are or are not of the same *nature*, an insoluble question far too much debated in our day, from some kind of a theological and metaphysical atavism;

53

the question does not fall within the domain of positive philosophy, which professes total ignorance of the intimate *nature* of any entity. It is not at all necessary to consider inorganic and organic bodies as different in *nature* to recognise the necessity of separating the study of them.

Doubtless we have rather confused ideas as to how we should look on the phenomena of living bodies; but whatever decision may be arrived at on this subject, the classification we are establishing will in no wise be affected. Even if it were proved—as seems barely possible from the present state of physiology—that physiological phenomena are merely mechanical, electrical, and chemical phenomena, modified by the structure and composition proper to organic bodies, our fundamental division would subsist none the less. For even with such a hypothesis, it still remains true that general phenomena must be studied before we proceed to the special modifications they undergo in certain entities as a result of a particular disposition of the molecules. Thus our division, which at present is based for most intelligent people on a divergence of laws, can maintain itself indefinitely through the subordination of phenomena and the rules of study, whatever link be established with certainty between the two classes of bodies.

We cannot here develop a general comparison between organic and inorganic bodies; it will be the subject of a special study in the physiological section. For the present it is enough to recognise in principle the logical necessity of separating science that treats of the inorganic from that which treats of the organic, and to proceed to the study of *organic physics* only after establishing the general laws of *inorganic* physics.

We will now determine the subdivisions of each of these two great halves of natural philosophy.

As regards *inorganic physics*, in conformity with the order established by the relative generality and dependence of phenomena, we see it must be divided into two sections, one treating the general phenomena of the universe, and the other the particular phenomena of terrestrial bodies. Whence celestial physics or astronomy, geometrical or mechanical; and terrestrial physics. The necessity of this division is exactly similar to that of the division that preceded it.

As astronomical phenomena are the most general, the most simple and the most abstract of all, obviously natural philosophy must begin with them, since the laws to which they are subject influence those of the other phenomena, while they on the contrary are independent of these phenomena.

In all phenomena of terrestrial physics we observe first and foremost the effects of universal gravitation, plus some other effects proper to these phenomena and modifying those of gravitation. It follows that when we analyse the most simple terrestrial phenomenon, not only a chemical phenomenon, but even a purely mechanical one, we invariably find it to be more composite than the most complex celestial phenomenon. Thus the mere movement of a heavy body, even if only a solid, is a more complex subject of research, if we take all the determining circumstances into account, than the most difficult astronomical question. The necessity is thus demonstrated of separating quite definitely celestial from terrestrial physics, and of studying the second of these two only after the first, which is its rational basis.

Following the same principle terrestrial physics is subdivided into two distinct parts, according as to whether it regards bodies from the mechanical or the chemical point of view. Whence physics, properly so called, and chemistry. The latter, if understood with any pretence to method, presupposes a knowledge of physics. All chemical phenomena are necessarily more complicated than physical phenomena; they depend on them without influencing them. Everyone knows that chemical action is subject first of all to the influence of weight, heat, electricity etc., and has also something of its own that has modified the influence of these agents. This fact shows that chemistry can only follow in the wake of physics, and is at the same time a distinct science. For whatever opinion one may adopt about chemical affinities, and even if one only sees them as the modifications of gravitation produced by the shape and mutual disposition of the atoms—as is possible—it cannot be doubted that the necessity of continually taking these special conditions into consideration excludes the possibility of treating chemistry simply as an appendix of physics. We are therefore obliged in all cases, if only to facilitate study, to maintain the division and order of precedence which today is regarded as deriving from the heterogeneity of the phenomena.

Such then is the rational classification of the principal branches issuing from the general science of inorganic bodies. An analogous division is called for in the general science of organic bodies.

All living beings present two distinct orders of phenomena, those of the individual and those of the species, especially when the species is sociable. In relation to man especially this distinction is fundamental. The second kind of phenomenon is obviously more complex and more peculiar than the first; it depends on it without influencing it. Hence the two great sections of *organic physics*: physiology, and social physics, founded on physiology.

In all social phenomena we observe first of all the physiological laws of the individual, and then something peculiar that modifies the effects of these laws, stemming from the action of individuals on one another, which is of great complexity in the human species, through the action of each generation on the following one. Obviously therefore, in order to study social phenomena properly, you must start with a profound knowledge of the laws of individual life. On the other hand this necessary subordination of one study to the other does not imply, as some eminent physiologists are inclined to believe, that social physics is a mere appendix of physiology. Although the two types of phenomena are certainly homogeneous, they are not identical, and the separation of the two sciences is of fundamental importance. It would certainly be impossible to treat the collective study of the species as a deduction from the study of the individual, since the social conditions which modify the action of physiological laws become in social physics the primary consideration. Thus social physics must be founded on a body of direct observation proper to it alone, always having regard to its intimate and necessary relation to physiology.

Perfect symmetry could be established between the division of organic physics and that of inorganic physics, as treated above, on the model of the popular distinction between vegetable and animal physiology. Such a subdivision could easily be related to the principle of classification which we have constantly followed, since the phenomena of animal life are, in general at least, more complex and more special than those of vegetable life. But the search for such symmetry would be puerile if it led us either to underestimate or to exaggerate the genuine analogies or the real differences of the phenomena. And it is certain that the distinction between animal and vegetable physiology, if it has great importance in what I have called *concrete physics*, has none at all in *abstract physics*, the only subject that concerns us here. Knowledge of the general laws of life, in our view the true object of physiology, demands the simultaneous consideration of the whole series of organisms, without any distinction between the vegetable and the animal, a distinction which, by the way, is becoming more and more blurred from day to day, as the phenomena are studied more in depth.

As a result of this discussion positive philosophy splits up into five fundamental sciences, the sequence of which is determined by a necessary subordination, independent of any hypothesis, and based on the comparison of the corresponding phenomena. These sciences are: astronomy, physics, chemistry, physiology, and social physics. The first of these sciences considers the most general phenomena, the most simple, the most abstract, the most removed from humanity; these phenomena influence all the others, without being influenced by them. The phenomena considered by the last are, on the contrary, the most peculiar, the most complex, the most concrete, the most directly interesting to man; they depend, more or less, on all the preceding ones, without exercising any influence on them. Between these two extremes the degree of specificity, of complexity and of personality in the phenomena gradually increases, as does also their sequential dependence. Such is the real interrelation of the various fundamental sciences, as established by true philosophic observation, not vain and arbitrary logic-chopping. Such is to be the plan of this course.

I have been able here to expound only very briefly the principal ideas on which the classification rests. In order to understand it completely, we should now have to examine it in relation to each fundamental science. This we shall proceed to do by special studies of each rung of the 'ladder'. The construction of the encyclopaedic ladder, which we resume with each of the five great sciences in succession, will lend more exactitude to the classification, and above all will give proof of its solidity. Its advantages will become all the more apparent when we see each science classifying itself also internally in accordance with the same principle, and thus the entire system of human knowledge will appear resolved into its component parts down to the secondary detail, thanks to one single concept consistently followed through: that of the degree of abstraction of the conceptions. But work of this kind, besides taking us too far afield, would be out of place in this lecture, in which I must keep to the general point of view of positive philosophy.

Nevertheless, if the importance of the fundamental hierarchy, of which I shall make constant use during these lectures, is to be fully understood, I must point out its essential properties.

First we must note, as decisive proof of the exactness of the classification, its agreement with the kind of co-ordination implicitly admitted by scientists in their study of the various branches of natural philosophy.

It is a condition of encyclopaedic ladders of science, much neglected by their builders, that those sciences which the human mind in its forward course has been led, without premeditation, to cultivate separately, should be presented as distinct, and that a subordination should be established between them in conformity with their actual relationships as manifested in their daily development. Such an agreement is obviously the surest sign of a good classification, for the divisions spontaneously introduced into the scientific system have been determined by long felt needs of the human mind, which ill-considered generalisations have not been able to mislead.

But although our classification entirely fulfils this condition—a fact which stands in no need of proof—this does not mean that the habits now established through experience among scientists render superfluous the encyclopaedic work that we have carried out. They have merely rendered possible the operation, in which there is all the difference of a rational conception from a purely empirical one. And this classification is far from being ordinarily understood, much less followed with all the necessary precision, nor is its importance properly appreciated: one need only consider the grave offences daily committed against the encyclopaedic law, much to the detriment of the human mind.

Conformity with the real order of development of natural philosophy is a second characteristic of the classification. It is verified by all that we know of the history of the sciences, particularly during the last two centuries, in which it is possible to observe their progress with more exactitude.

It will readily be understood that the rational study of certain fundamental sciences, since it requires the previous cultivation of all the sciences that precede it in the encyclopaedic hierarchy, has been able to make real progress and assume its true character only after a considerable development of the anterior sciences concerning phenomena more general, more abstract, less complex, independent of other phenomena. It is therefore in that order that progress, although apparently simultaneous, must have taken place.

This fact seems to me so important that I do not think it possible really to understand the history of the human mind without reference to it. The general law which dominates the whole of history, and which I have propounded in the first lecture, cannot be properly understood if it is not combined with the encyclopaedic formula that we have just established. For it is according to the order enunciated in that formula that the different human theories have attained successively first the theological, then the metaphysical, and finally the positive stage. If in practice one does not take into consideration this law of necessary progression, one will often meet with difficulties that seem insurmountable; for clearly the theological or metaphysical state of certain fundamental theories must have temporarily coincided, and did indeed so coincide, with the positive state of those anterior to them in the encyclopaedic system. Which tends to render less perspicuous the working of the general law, and the obscurity can only be dissipated by the classification.

In the third place the classification has the very remarkable property of marking the relative perfection of the different sciences, which consists in the degree of exactness of knowledge, and in its greater or less co-ordination.

It can easily be seen that the more phenomena are general, simple and abstract, the less they depend on other phenomena, the more exact will be the knowledge relating to them, and the more complete will be the co-ordination of that knowledge. Thus the study of the phenomena of organic bodies must be at once less exact and less systematic than that of the phenomena of inorganic bodies. And so, in inorganic physics, the celestial phenomena, by reason of their greater generality and independence of other phenomena, have given rise to a science much more precise and interconnected than that of terrestrial phenomena.

This situation which is so striking in the practical study of science and which has often given rise to illusory hopes and unjust comparisons, is completely explained by the encyclopaedic order which I have established. I shall have occasion to develop these observations fully in the next chapter, when I shall show that the possibility of applying mathematical analysis to the study of phenomena, which is the means of producing the highest degree possible of co-ordination in that study, is exactly determined by the rank occupied by the phenomena in my encyclopaedic ladder.

Before I pass on to the next point I must put my hearers on their guard against an error sufficiently glaring, but still very common. It consists in confusing the degree of exactness of our knowledge with the degree of its certitude, whence the very dangerous prejudice that as the first is obviously very unequal so also is the second. Thus people often speak, though perhaps less than formerly, of the unequal certainty of the sciences, and this tends to discourage the cultivation of the more difficult sciences. It is clear however that exactness and certitude are two very different qualities. A quite absurd proposition can be extremely exact, as for instance that the sum of the angles of a triangle is equal to three right angles; and a very certain proposition may have very little exactness, as for instance that every man will die. If then the various sciences are very unequal in exactness, they are not at all unequal in certitude. Each science can offer results as certain as those of any other, as long as its conclusions are contained within the degree of exactness of its phenomena, a condition not always easy to fulfil. In any science, everything that is simply conjectural is only more or less probable, and this is not the domain of the science; everything that is positive, that is, founded on well attested facts, is certain: here there is no distinction.

Finally, the most interesting property of our encyclopaedic formula, from the number and importance of its applications, is that it delivers the general plan of an entirely rational scientific education. The plan is the formula.

It is indeed evident that before undertaking the methodical study of some one of the fundamental sciences, one must necessarily have prepared oneself by the examination of the sciences on our encyclopaedic ladder which treat of anterior phenomena, since such phenomena always influence considerably the phenomena whose laws one is seeking to know. This consideration is so very obvious that, in spite of its great practical importance, I see no reason why I should insist further on it at the present moment; it will reappear later in connection with each fundamental science. I will merely point out that if it is eminently applicable to general education, it is particularly applicable to the special education of scientists.

Thus the physicists who have not made a preliminary study of astronomy, at least in a general way, the chemists who, before concerning themselves with their own science, have not previously studied astronomy and then physics; the physicists who have not prepared themselves for their specialised work by a preliminary study of astronomy, physics and chemistry, have failed to fulfil one of the fundamental conditions of their own intellectual development. And this is obviously still more the case of those undertaking the positive study of social phenomena without having acquired a general knowledge of astronomy, physics, chemistry and physiology.

As these necessary conditions are rarely fulfilled in our time, and as none of our institutions is so organised as to secure their fulfilment, we can say that no rational education as yet exists for scientists. This fact is, in my view, of such importance, that it is responsible for the backward state of the more difficult sciences, a state so little suited to what the more complex nature of their phenomena would demand.

As for general education, it is still more necessary to fulfil the condition in that sphere. Scientific instruction, it seems to me, is incapable of producing the general results that should be contributing to the renovation of our entire intellectual system, if the principal branches of natural philosophy are not studied in their proper order. Remember that in almost every intelligence, even the highest, ideas are connected in the order in which they were first acquired; and that not to begin at the beginning does irretrievable harm. Only a very small number of thinkers in each century can, in full maturity, like Bacon, Descartes and Leibnitz,[13] make a clean sweep, in order to reconstruct from top to bottom the system of their intellectual acquisitions.

The encyclopaedic law as a basis of scientific education must also be considered in relation to method, as well as doctrine, if its importance is to be properly appreciated.

From this point of view, if the general plan of study we have outlined is carried out, it will result in a perfect knowledge of the positive method, such as could not be obtained in any other way.

Indeed, since natural phenomena have been classed so as to leave the truly homogeneous within the bounds of one study, while heterogeneous ones have been relegated to different studies, it follows that the positive method will be constantly modified in a uniform manner throughout one science, and will constantly undergo different modifications of increasing complexity as it passes to the other sciences. We shall thus be certain of knowing it in all the varieties of which it is capable, which would not have been the case if we had adopted an encyclopaedic formula that did not fulfil the conditions stated above.

This new consideration is of fundamental importance; for if we saw in the first lecture that it is impossible to know the positive method apart from its use, we must now add that no clear and exact idea can be formed unless we study its successive application to the various principal classes of phenomena in their proper order. One single science, however judiciously chosen, would not attain this end. For while the method is essentially identical in all the sciences, one or other of its characteristic procedures is developed in each science as a speciality, and would pass unperceived in the other sciences as being too little in evidence. In certain branches of natural philosophy it is observation, in others experiment, and a certain nature of experiment, that constitutes the principal means of exploration. In the same way some general precept, now constituting an integral part of the method, was first furnished by a certain science; and although it has since been transferred to others, it is best studied at its source if one wishes to know it properly. Such for instance is the theory of classifications.

If we confined ourselves to the study of only one science, we would of course have to choose the most perfect one in order to have a deeper understanding of the positive method. But the most perfect science being also the most simple, one would have only a very incomplete knowledge of the method; one would not get to know the modifications it must undergo in order to adapt itself to more complex phenomena. For this purpose each fundamental science has advantages peculiar to itself; which proves clearly the necessity of considering them all, under pain of forming narrow conceptions and inadequate habits.

Let me insist once more, with regard to method, on the necessity, if we would know it well, not only of studying the various fundamental sciences philosophically, but also in the encyclopaedic order established in this lecture. What rational conclusions can any mind, not superlatively endowed, arrive at, if it busies itself straight away with the most complex sciences, before it has learned from the examination of the most simple phenomena, what a *law* is, what it is to *observe*, what a positive conception is, and what a logical sequence? Yet such is the ordinary procedure of our young physiologists, who tackle at once the study of living bodies, without as a rule having been prepared otherwise than by a preliminary education in one or two dead languages, and having at the most a superficial knowledge of physics and chemistry, practically worthless as regards method, since as a rule it has not been obtained in a rational manner by starting from the point of departure of natural philosophy. How important it is to reform so defective a plan of study you may well imagine. Similarly, with respect to social phenomena, would it not be a mighty step towards normality for modern societies to recognise the logical necessity of proceeding to the study of these phenomena only after training the intellect by the examination in depth of all anterior phenomena in their order? It could even be said that this is the heart of the matter. Indeed few sound minds today are not convinced that social phenomena must be studied by the positive method. But alas! this maxim remains sterile, as far as renewing social theory is concerned, for those who busy themselves with this study have no means of knowing in what the positive method exactly consists, and have never examined it in its anterior applications. The theory therefore remains in the theological and metaphysical state, in spite of the efforts of would-be positive reformers.

From these four principal points of view we can measure the importance of the positive classification established for the fundamental sciences.

But in order to complete the general plan of this course, there now remains to consider an immense and all-important lacuna, which I left purposely in my encyclopaedic formula, and which my hearers have doubtless already noticed. In our scientific system we have not noted the position of mathematical science.

This intentional omission was motivated by the very importance of this science, so vast and so fundamental. Our next lecture will be entirely devoted to determining its general character, whereby its encyclopaedic rank will also be determined. But not to leave incomplete in so important a respect the great synoptic table that I have endeavoured to sketch in this lecture, let me here indicate in brief, and in anticipation, the general results of the examination to be undertaken in the next lecture.

In the present state of development of our positive knowledge we should, I think, regard mathematical science less as a constituent part of natural philosophy than as the true and fundamental basis of all such philosophy since Descartes and Newton, although in actual fact it is both one and the other. Today however mathematical science is far less important for the real and very precious knowledge it contains, than as constituting the most powerful instrument that the human mind can employ in its search for the laws of natural phenomena.

In order to convey a clear and exact conception of this position, we shall have to divide mathematical science into two sciences, of quite distinct character: abstract mathematics or *computation*, taking the word in its widest meaning, and concrete mathematics, consisting on the one hand of geometry, and on the other of mechanics. The concrete part is necessarily founded on the abstract part; in its turn it becomes the basis of all natural philosophy, since we can regard all the phenomena of the universe as roughly either geometrical or mechanical.

The abstract part alone is purely instrumental, being nothing but a huge and admirable extension of natural logic to a certain order of deductions. Geometry and mechanics must on the contrary be looked upon as true natural sciences, founded, like all sciences, on observation, although by reason of the extreme simplicity of their phenomena they are capable of an infinitely greater degree of systematisation; and this has sometimes caused the experimental nature of their first principles to be overlooked. But these two physical sciences have this peculiarity that, in the present state of the human mind, they are already, and in future will be, employed more as method than as information.

It is obvious that by placing mathematical science at the head of positive philosophy we are but extending the application of that principle of classification founded on the successive dependence of the sciences according to the degree of abstraction of their phenomena, which furnished us with the encyclopaedic series set forth in this lecture. We are merely restoring to this series its true first term, whose very importance required that it be treated apart. Clearly the geometrical and the mechanical are of all phenomena the most general, the most simple, the most abstract, the most irreducible, the most absolutely independent of other phenomena, of which they are indeed the basis. The study of these two sciences is obviously an indispensable preliminary to that of all other orders of phenomena. Thus it is mathematical science that must constitute the point of departure of any rational scientific education, whether general or specialised, and this explains the universal usage which has long been empirically established on this subject, though it had in the beginning no other cause than the greater age of mathematical science.

We have therefore fixed the plan that should guide us in the study of positive philosophy, not by vain and arbitrary speculation, but as the solution of a philosophic problem. The final result: mathematics, astronomy, physics, chemistry, physiology and sociology, such is the encyclopaedic formula which, alone among the numerous classifications applied to the six fundamental sciences, conforms to the natural and invariable hierarchy of phenomena. Surely I do not need to insist on the importance of this result, with which the reader must so familiarise himself that he is ready to apply it continually throughout the course.

We may then summarise this lecture as the explanation and justification of the great synoptic table which heads this work, and in constructing which I have tried to follow as closely as possible, in respect to the internal subdivisions of each science, the same principle of classification as furnished us with the general series of the sciences.

III

Philosophical Considerations on all Mathematical Science [14]

Mathematical science is the oldest and most perfect of the sciences, yet its general idea has not yet been clearly outlined. Its definition and its subdivisions have remained up till now vague and uncertain. The plural by which it is usually designated would in itself be enough to indicate the absence of philosophic unity, as commonly understood.

The truth is that it is only at the beginning of the last century that the various fundamental conceptions constituting this great science had attained a development that allowed the spirit of the whole to emerge. Since that time geometricians have been, quite properly, too absorbed in perfecting its different branches and in applying them to the most important laws of the universe, to attend to the general system of their science.

But today the progress of specialised parts is no longer so rapid as to prevent the view of the whole. The science of mathematics is now sufficiently advanced, both in itself and in its most important applications, to be in that firm and consistent state that lends itself to the co-ordination of parts in a single system, as a preparation for future progress. Indeed this important philosophical operation is indicated by the latest improvements in the science, for these improvements confer on its principal parts a character of unity which did not exist before. Such is the spirit that shines pre-eminently in an immortal author's *Theory of Functions* and *Analytical Mechanics*.[15]

In order to form a correct idea of the object of mathematical science as a whole, we may begin with the usual vague definition: that it is the *science of magnitudes*, or, to speak more positively, *the science whose aim is to measure magnitudes*. This scholastic view no doubt needs a great deal more precision and depth. But the idea is at bottom correct; it is even sufficiently general, when properly understood. And it is important, in such matters, to make use of generally admitted ideas, wherever possible. Now let us see how, starting from this rough notion, we ran rise to a true definition of mathematics, to a definition worthy of the importance, the extent, and the difficulty of this science.

Measuring a magnitude conveys to the mind no other idea than that of comparing the magnitude to another similar and supposedly known one which one takes as the *unit* of all magnitudes of the same kind. Thus when one defines mathematics as having for its object the measurement of magnitudes, one is giving a very imperfect idea of it. How could there be any ground here for a science, and especially a science as vast and profound as mathematical science is rightly reputed to be? Instead of an immense sequence of rational investigations offering inexhaustible material to the intellect, we should have a series of mechanical procedures in order to obtain, by means of operations analogous to the superimposition of one line over another, the relations of the quantities measured to those by which one measures them. Yet the definition has no other defect than that of not being sufficiently analytic. It does not lead to any error touching the final aim of mathematics; but it presents as a direct object one that almost always is indirect, thereby obscuring the true nature of this science.

To get a true idea, let us first of all consider a commonly attested fact. The fact is that the *direct* measurement of a magnitude, by superimposing a unit of measurement or some similar procedure, is generally an absolutely impossible operation: so that if we had no other means of determining magnitudes than such immediate comparisons, we should have to give up trying to know most of the magnitudes that interest us.

The truth of this observation will at once become apparent if we consider the easiest of the possible cases: that of measuring a straight line by another straight line. No one can deny that this is the simplest of comparisons, yet it can scarcely ever be effected. The necessary conditions of measuring a straight line directly cannot, on reflection, be met, as far as the lines we wish to know about are concerned. The first and most obvious of these conditions, that of being able to go from one end of the line to the other in order to apply the unit of measurement throughout its length, evidently excludes the greater number of the most interesting distances: first the distances between the different celestial bodies, or between the earth and another celestial body and then most of the terrestrial distances, which so frequently are inaccessible. And even if this first condition is met, the length must be neither too small nor too great, for there again direct measurement would be impossible; and it must be conveniently situated, etc. The slightest circumstance which in the abstract appears to introduce no fresh difficulty, will in the concrete often be enough to preclude direct measurement. Many a line for instance that could be exactly measured with the greatest of ease when horizontal, need only be vertical to prove immeasurable. In a word direct measurement of a straight line presents such a complex of difficulties, especially when it is to be carried out with any degree of precision, that we scarcely ever meet with any that can be measured exactly, if of any length at all, except the purely artifical ones, created expressly for the purposes of direct measurement, and serving as a standard for all the others.

And what I have just said with regard to lines, holds good still more for surfaces, volumes, speeds, times, forces, etc. and in general all other magnitudes that can be exactly measured, and that by their nature present many more obstacles to direct measurement. We need not labour the point: the impossibility of directly measuring most of the magnitudes that interest us is sufficiently demonstrated. This is what necessitates the creation of mathematical science. Forced to give up direct measurement in almost every case, the human mind was bound to resort to indirect measurement, and that is how mathematics came into being.

The method constantly employed, the only method for the discovery of magnitudes that cannot be directly measured, is to link these magnitudes to others that can be directly measured, in accordance with which the former can be known, by means of the relations that exists between the two. This is the object of mathematical science in general. But to get a proper idea of it we must realise that there are many degrees of indirectness of measurement. In a great number of cases, and these often the most important, the magnitudes that are going to determine those that concern us cannot themselves be directly measured, and become the subject of the same problem, and so on; so that in numerous instances a long series of intermediaries has to be established between the unknown magnitudes, the real object of the research, and the magnitudes capable of direct measurement which will finally serve to determine them, yet appear to have no link with them.

A few examples will serve as illustrations.

Consider in the first place a very simple natural phenomenon, but one that raises a real question in mathematics, of some practical consequence: the phenomenon of the vertical fall of heavy bodies.

Observing this phenomenon even a complete stranger to mathematical conceptions will at once recognise that the two quantities it presents: the height from which the body falls and the time during which it falls, are interconnected, since they vary together, and remain fixed simultaneously: to use the language of geometers, they are *functions* of one another. This phenomenon becomes a mathematical problem when it is a question of supplying the measurement of one of the two magnitudes, if it cannot be direct, by the direct measurement of the other. Thus the height of a precipice can be indirectly calculated by merely measuring the time a body takes to fall to the bottom of it; and if the procedure is properly followed, this inaccessible height can be known with as much precision as if it were a horizontal line placed in the circumstances most conducive to easy and exact measurement. On other occasions it is the height itself from which a body falls that is easily known, while the time taken in the fall cannot be directly observed: then the same phenomenon will give rise to the opposite problem, that of determining the time by the height. As when one wants to know for example the length of time taken by the vertical fall of a body from the moon to the earth.

In this example the mathematical problem is very simple, at least if one does not take into consideration variations in intensity of weight, or resistance of the fluid traversed by the body in its fall. But to make the question a much bigger one, all one needs to do is to consider the phenomenon in its most general form, the fall as oblique, all the main circumstances being taken into consideration. So that now instead of two variable qualities linked by a relationship which is easy to follow, the phenomenon will have a great number of them: the space traversed, both vertically and horizontally, the time taken up in transit, the speed at each point in the course, and even the intensity and direction of the initial impetus, which may also be regarded as variable; finally, in certain cases, the resistance of the medium and the gravitational force. All these quantities will be so interlinked that each in its turn can be determined by the others, which will involve as many distinct mathematical operations as there are coexistent magnitudes in the phenomenon considered. A quite simple change in the physical conditions of a problem may, as in this example, promote an elementary mathematical calculation to the rank of those difficult problems whose complete solution still challenges the greatest forces of the human mind.

Take a second example, this time from geometrical phenomena. The problem is to determine a distance that cannot be measured directly. It is generally taken as part of a *figure*, or system of lines in which the other elements are immediately observable. In the simplest case, to which all the others may be reduced, the distance in question will belong to a triangle, in which either another side and two angles, or two other sides and one angle, can be directly determined. Then knowledge of the distance required, instead of being directly obtained, will result from a mathematical calculation involving deduction from the observed elements, in accordance with the relation of this distance to them. These calculations will assume greater complexity if what we have supposed to be known elements cannot be determined except indirectly, with the aid of new auxiliary systems, whose number can become quite considerable. Once the distance is determined, this knowledge will frequently furnish new quantities, the subjects of further mathematical problems. Thus when we know at what distance an object is situated, however inaccessible it be, the mere observation of its apparent diameter—and this is always possible—will make it possible to determine indirectly its real dimensions, and by an analogous series of calculations, also its area, volume, even its weight, and a host of other properties which it would seem impossible for us to know.

It is by investigations such as these that man has attained to the knowledge, not only of the distance of the stars from the earth, but from one another; their true size, shape, even the unevenness of their surface; and what seems still more to elude our means of investigation, of their mass, average density, and the conditions of the fall of heavy bodies on their surface. Through the power of mathematical theory these results and many others relating to the different classes of natural phenomena have needed no measurements but those of a very small number of straight lines, rightly chosen, and of a greater number of angles.

We have now succeeded in defining mathematical science exactly, by assigning to it the aim of measuring magnitudes *indirectly*, and by affirming that in it and through it *magnitudes are determined by one another according to their mutual relation*. Such statements no longer convey the idea of an *art*, as do the definitions of the past, but of a science, now revealed as an immense sequence of intellectual operations, capable of assuming greater and greater complexity by reason of the chain of intermediaries that have to be established between unknown quantities and those that can be measured directly, by reason also of the number of variables coexisting in a problem, and the nature of the relations between these magnitudes furnished by the phenomena under consideration. According to this definition, it is of the essence of mathematics to regard all the quantities associated with a given phenomenon as interconnected, with a view to deducing them from one another. Now obviously there is no phenomenon that will lend itself to such considerations; whence the indefinite extent and even logical universality of mathematical science: we shall endeavour later on to delimit its domain as exactly as possible.

Our analysis clearly justifies the name given to this science. This name which has now so definite a meaning, really signifies *science* in general. Such a name was absolutely exact for the Greeks, who had no other real science. If it was retained by the moderns it was to show that mathematics is the *science* par excellence. For the definition to which we have been led, if we exclude from it numerical precision, is the definition of any real science. Is not the aim the mutual determination of phenomena according to their interrelations? Every *science* consists in the coordination of facts; if we had only detached observations, there would be no science. Indeed it could be said that *science* is destined to exempt from direct observation, as far as the phenomena will permit, by making it possible to deduce from the smallest number possible of data the greatest possible number of results. Is not this the real use, both speculative and practical, of the *laws* that we manage to extract from natural phenomena? On this principle mathematics is only extending to the utmost, both as to quantity and quality, the kind of research in the subjects of its competence which is pursued to a greater or less degree by every real science in its particular sphere.

Hence it is by the study of mathematics, and mathematics alone, that one can acquire a true idea of what a *science* is. Here alone is to be discovered the exact method employed by the human mind in all positive research, for nowhere else are questions solved in a manner so complete and rigorous dedutions pushed so far. Here likewise our intelligence has given the greatest proof of its strength, for the ideas have the highest degree of abstraction possible in the positive order. Any scientific education which does not begin with this study is basically defective.

So far we have looked at mathematical science as a whole, and made no account of its subdivisions. Now, in order to complete this general view, and to get a right idea of the philosophic character of this science, we must consider its fundamental subdivisions. Secondary subdivisions will be examined later.

The principal subdivisions are not to be derived rationally from the nature of the subject except as they present themselves spontaneously in the course of the analysis of a mathematical problem. So, now that we have defined the object of mathematical work, let us examine the various orders of research of which it is composed.

The complete solution of any mathematical problem falls naturally into two parts, essentially distinct, and always in the same relation to one another. We have seen that the aim of all mathematical research is to determine unknown magnitudes according to the relation existing between them and known magnitudes. Obviously this relation must be exactly known. The first kind of research gives us what I call the *concrete* part of the solution. This finished, the nature of the problem changes; it becomes a pure question of numbers, of determining unknown numbers by their relation to known numbers. This second kind of research gives us the *abstract* part of the solution. Hence the division of mathematical science into two great sciences abstract and concrete.

The above analysis applies to every complete mathematical problem, however simple or complex. A single example will serve as illustration.

Returning to the phenomenon of the vertical fall of a heavy body, and taking the simplest case, we see that in order to determine the height from which the body has fallen by the duration of its fall, and vice-versa, we must first discover the exact relation of these two quantities, or, to employ the term of the geometers, the *equation* that exists between them. Until this first inquiry is terminated, every endeavour to determine numerically the value of one of these two magnitudes by that of the other would be premature, for it would have no basis. It is not enough to know vaguely that one depends on the other, everyone sees this at once; we must determine in what this dependence consists, which may be difficult. Here it is the main part of the problem. The scientific spirit is so modern and still so rare, that no one perhaps except Galileo had even noticed the acceleration of velocity of a falling body, excluding the hypothesis to which our intelligence would naturally resort, inclined as it is to suppose the simplest *functions* for every phenomenon, simply because it finds them easier to deal with, the hypothesis that the height is proportionate to the time. In a word this first inquiry leads to the discovery of the law of Galileo. When this concrete part is finished, the research becomes of an entirely different nature. As we know that the spaces traversed in each second by the body increase as the sequence of odd numbers, the deduction of the height from the time or of the time from the height becomes a question of numbers and abstraction, which means finding that, according to the given law, the first of these two quantities is a known multiple of the second power of the other, whence we can conclude the value of the one, given that of the other.

In this case the concrete question is more difficult than the abstract one. It would be the other way round if we considered the same phenomenon in its most general form, as I did above for another purpose. Sometimes it will be the first, and sometimes it will be the second of the two parts that will be the principal difficulty, as the mathematical law of the problem may be simple, but difficult to obtain, and in other instances easy to obtain, but exceedingly complex. So that the two great sections of mathematical science, regarded as a whole, are exactly equivalent in range and difficulty, as also in importance.

These two parts, distinct in their objects, are not less so from the nature of their research.

The first we call *concrete*, because it obviously depends on the kind of phenomena considered, and must necessarily vary with these phenomena; while the second is completely independent of the nature of the objects examined and is only concerned with their numerical relations, we therefore call it *abstract*. The same relations may exist in a great number of different phenomena of extreme diversity, if they are looked on by the geometer as propounding an analytical problem capable of being solved once for all. For example the law which furnished the space-time ratio for the vertical fall of a body in the void applies also to other phenomena having no analogy with these or with one another, for it is the law that expresses the relation between the area of a spherical body and the length of its diameter; it likewise determines the decrease in intensity of light or heat in proportion to the distances of objects illumined or heated, etc. The abstract part common to these various mathematical problems having been treated for one of them is *ipso facto* treated for all of them; while the concrete part will have to be repeated for each one separately, without any one solution offering assistance for the others. There can be no establishing of general methods which will infallibly discover the relations between quantities in the case of various phenomena; such a task necessarily involves special methods for the different classes of phenomena, geometrical, mechanical, thermological etc. But on the other hand, whatever be the source of the quantities considered, uniform methods can be established for deducing them from one another, if we know their relations. The abstract part of mathematics therefore belongs to its general domain, the concrete to its specialised sections.

We may say that concrete mathematics has an essentially experimental, physical, phenomenological character; while abstract mathematics is purely logical and rational. This is not the place to discuss in detail how the human mind has gone about discovering the mathematical laws of phenomena. But whether precise observation has suggested a law, or, as happens so often, has merely confirmed the law extracted by reason from the most common facts, what is certain is that the law is looked upon as real only in so far as it shows itself in agreement with the results of experience. Thus the concrete part of every mathematical problem is necessarily based on the consideration of the external world, and however great the part reason play in it, can never resolve itself into a mere series of intellectual operations. The abstract part on the contrary, when it has been properly detached from the other, cannot but consist in a more or less prolonged series of rational deductions. Once one has discovered the equations of a phenomenon, the mutual determination of its quantities, however difficult, depends entirely on reason. It is for the intelligence to deduce from the equations the results that they imply, and there can be no further resort to the external world, the consideration of which must be rigorously excluded, so that effort may be concentrated on the real difficulties of the work.

IV

Philosophical Considerations on Astronomical Science [16]

Up till now astronomy has been the only branch of natural philosophy in which the human mind has been liberated from every theological and metaphysical influence, direct or indirect; thus it is particularly easy to bring out its real philosophic character. But if we are to have a true idea of its nature and composition, it is absolutely necessary to set aside the vague definitions of it that are still being given, and to mark the boundaries of the positive knowledge that we can acquire of the stars.

Of the three senses that reveal the existence of distant bodies, that of sight is obviously the only one employed for the discovery of heavenly bodies. There could be no astronomy for any species that was blind, however intelligent it might be; and for ourselves, the unseen stars, perhaps more numerous than the seen ones, are excluded from study, and their existence can only be suspected by induction. Any research which cannot be reduced to actual visual observation is excluded where the stars are concerned, which are thus of all natural entities those that we know under the most unvarying aspects. We can see the possibility of determining their forms, their distances, their magnitudes and their movements, but it is inconceivable that we should ever be able to study by any means whatsoever their chemical composition or mineralogical structure, still less the nature of the organic bodies living on their surface, etc. To express the matter in scientific terms, the positive knowledge we can have of the stars is limited to their geometrical and mechanical phenomena, and can never be extended by physical, chemical, physiological and social research, such as can be expended on entities accessible to all our means of observation.

Certainly it would be rash to fix the boundaries of our knowledge for every part of natural philosophy; becoming immersed in detail, we should make them either too wide or too narrow. And judgement on this matter is much influenced by the state of intellectual development. The man who is a stranger to mathematical science cannot understand that the distances and dimensions of the heavenly bodies can be calculated, since these bodies are not physically accessible, while the semi-initiated will admit this possibility quite readily, but will deny that of weighing (indirectly) the sun and the planets. Nevertheless it seems to me that it is necessary to set certain limits to the different sciences, so that the human mind does not lose itself in vague and vain inquiry, and at the same time does undertake what is really viable by more or less indirect procedures, however difficult it may be to reconcile these two stipulations. Astronomical research does seem to me to reconcile them in the maxim stated above, that it is confined solely to the categories of geometrical and mechanical phenomena. Such a rule is not at all arbitrary. It results from a comparison of the objects to be studied with the means of studying them. Only its application may present certain difficulties, which under examination will disappear in each particular case, if we continue to follow the same fundamental principle. To clinch the matter, let us take the celebrated problem of the atmospheres of the celestial bodies. Even before ingenious means were discovered of exploring them, research on them might well be thought to be possible by reason of the luminous phenomena that they must necessarily produce: but it is evident from that very fact that our knowledge of these gaseous envelopes is necessarily limited to that of their existence, to a lesser or greater extent, and refractive force; in no way can we determine their chemical composition or even their density; we should err gravely, for instance, if we supposed, as some have done, that the atmosphere of Venus is as dense as that of the earth because of the horizontal refraction of about half a degree that they have in common, for the chemical nature of the gases influences their refractive power, quite as much as their density.

As to problems in general relating to the stars, if we clearly perceive that the problem depends on more or less direct visual observations, we do not hesitate to declare it to be accessible; if on the other hand we recognise unmistakably that it would by its nature demand some other kind of exploration, we should not hesitate to reject it as radically insoluble; lastly, we may perceive neither one thing nor the other very clearly, in which case we should suspend our judgement, until the progress of knowledge provides us with some definite indications—a very rare attitude unfortunately, and yet a very necessary one. This rule is easily applicable. Scientific observation after all never employs and could not employ any other means than vulgar observation would employ in analogous circumstances; all that it does is to perfect them and extend their use.

The determination of temperatures is probably the only subject which might make the limit we have set up appear too narrow. But whatever hopes may have been aroused by our immortal Fourier's[17] epoch-making creation of mathematical thermology, and especially by his calculation of the space temperatures in which we circulate, I still believe that the average temperature of the stars must for ever elude us. Even if all the thermological influences affecting the exchange of heat between the various celestial bodies were mathematically analysed, which scarcely appears possible, there would still be one eternal unknown, and that perhaps the chief factor for certain stars: I refer to the internal state of each star, and the, in many cases, not less unknown mode of absorption of its heat by its atmosphere. Thus Newton's calculation of the temperature of the comet of 1680 at its perihelion was certainly fallacious, for such a calculation, even if repeated with all the means now at our disposal, could only give us the temperature that our earth would have if, with no change in its present constitution, it were transported into the position of the comet, and in view of the physical and chemical differences, this may have been very far indeed from the temperature of the comet. Such being the case, I do not think I am limiting astronomy too much by assigning to it the discovery of the laws governing the geometrical and mechanical phenomena presented by the celestial bodies, that, and that only.

To the limitation of the nature of the phenomena to be observed must be added another limitation, that of the bodies with which we shall be concerned. This second restriction, as we must be careful to note, is not absolute, like the first, but in the present state of our knowledge it is almost as necessary.

Those philosophical spirits who have little familiarity with astronomy, and even astronomers themselves have not up till now sufficiently distinguished between what might be called the *solar*, and the *universal* point of view. Yet such a distinction seems imperative if we are clearly to separate what may become perfect science from what seems destined to a perpetual nonage, at least in comparison. No doubt the solar system of which we form a part is a very restricted subject of study, capable of being completely explored, and leading to a most satisfactory state of knowledge. While on the contrary the very idea of *universe* is necessarily undefined: however extensive our real knowledge of it may become in the future, we can never attain to a true conception of the stars as a whole. The difference is extremely striking today, since side by side with the high perfection reached by solar astronomy during the last two centuries, is the absence in sidereal astronomy of the first and simplest element of any positive research: the determination of the interstellar intervals. No doubt we have every reason to suppose that these distances will soon be calculated, at least within certain limits, for certain stars, and that in consequence we shall possess with regard to these stars, other important information which theory is poised to deduce from this fundamental datum, such as their mass, etc. But the important distinction made above is not at all affected. Even if the day came when we were able to study in detail the relative movements of some multiple stars, the knowledge, however valuable, especially if it involved the group to which our sun probably belongs, would obviously leave us no whit nearer a true knowledge of the universe.

There exists in all important respects and in all classes of research, a constant and necessary harmony between the extent of our real intellectual needs and the scope of our knowledge present and future. This harmony is not, as popular philosophers incline to believe, the result or the indication of a final cause. It derives from an obvious necessity: the need to know only what affects us more or less directly. And on the other hand, for the very reason that this need exerts its pressure, sooner or later it becomes a sure stepping-stone to knowledge. This relationship is confirmed in the present case. The study of the laws of the solar system to which we belong is of overwhelming interest to us, so we have brought it to a high degree of exactitude. And even as an exact conception of the universe is beyond us, so also it has no real importance for us, except as a subject of curiosity. A day-to-day application of astronomy to the phenomena shows us that the interior phenomena of the solar systems, the only ones that can affect their inhabitants, are essentially independent of the general phenomena connected with the mutual interaction of the suns, just as our meteorological phenomena are independent of planetary phenomena. Our tables of celestial events drawn up a long time in advance, and exclusively concerned with our own world, have been up till now in complete agreement with direct observation, however exact. This manifest independence of our solar system is fully explained by the vast disproportion which we know exists between the immense distances of the suns from one another and the small intervals between the planets. If, which is highly probable, planets with an atmosphere, Mercury, Venus, Jupiter, etc. are really inhabited, we can regard the inhabitants as in some sort our fellow-citizens, since, from what is so to speak our common fatherland, there must necessarily result a kind of community of thoughts and even of interests, while the inhabitants of other solar systems will be perfect strangers. We must therefore separate more completely than is usually done the solar from the universal point of view, the idea of the world from that of the universe: the first represents the highest attainment possible to us, and also the only one possible to us.

Without therefore entirely renouncing any hope of sidereal knowledge, we must look on positive astronomy as consisting essentially in the geometrical and mechanical study of a small number of celestial bodies composing the *world* of which we are part. It is only within these limits that astronomy merits by its perfection the supreme rank that it occupies today among the natural sciences. As for those innumerable stars scattered in the sky, they have no interest for astronomy other than as signposts for our observations, their position being regarded as fixed in relation to the internal movements of our system, which alone concern us.

As we consider in succession the different orders of natural phenomena, it will be incumbent on me to stress a very important philosophic law which has passed unnoticed up to the present, and of which we have here the first instance. It is that as phenomena become more complex they are open to increasingly numerous and varied modes of exploration, although the increase in difficulty is not entirely compensated by the augmentation of resources; despite this proportion of difficulty and resource, the sciences concerned with the most complex phenomena are the most imperfect, as is shown by the encyclopaedic ladder at the beginning of this work. Astronomical phenomena being the most simple are also those whose means of exploration, are the most limited.

The art of observation has three procedures: 1. Observation properly so called, that is, the direct examination of the phenomenon as it naturally presents itself; 2. experiment, i.e. the consideration of the phenomenon modified by artificial circumstances which are introduced expressly with a view to exploration; 3. comparisons, that is, consideration of a graded series of analogous cases, in which the phenomenon is more and more simplified. The science of organic bodies, which studies the phenomena most difficult to access, is also the science where the three procedures are combined. Astronomy, on the contrary, is necessarily confined to the first. Experiment is obviously impossible, and as for comparison, it would only exist if we could directly observe several solar systems, and this can never happen. There remains observation, reduced, as we have noticed, to the smallest possible range, since it involves only one of our senses. Measuring angles and counting intervals of time: such are the only means by which our intelligence can proceed to the discovery of the laws that govern celestial phenomena. But these means are none the less perfectly adapted to the nature of astronomical phenomena, nothing else being required for the observation of geometrical or mechanical phenomena, magnitudes or movement. The only conclusion one can draw is that of all the branches of natural philosophy astronomy is the one where direct observation plays the least significant part, and reasoning incomparably the greatest: this is the source of its intellectual dignity. Nothing truly interesting is ever decided in astronomy by mere inspection, contrary to what takes place in physics, chemistry, physiology, etc. It can be said without exaggeration that the phenomena, however real, are the constructs of intelligence, for one cannot actually *see* the shape of the earth, or the curve described by a planet, or even the daily movement of the sky; our mind alone furnishes these various notions, combining, by a prolonged and complex process of reasoning, impressions which in their isolation would be almost totally insignificant. These fundamental difficulties, which generally inspire an almost insurmountable repugnance in the vulgar, are an additional attraction for minds of a certain order.

The combination of these two essential features, extreme simplicity in the phenomena to be studied, and great difficulty in observing them, is what makes astronomy a peculiarly mathematical science. The necessity, on the one hand, of constantly deducing from a small number of direct measurements, either angular or horary, quantities which are not in themselves immediately observable, renders the continual use of abstract mathematics absolutely indispensable. On the other, as astronomical problems are in themselves either geometrical or mechanical problems, they naturally fall within the domain of concrete mathematics. Finally, the perfect regularity of the astronomical forms, as geometry, and the admirable simplicity of the movements taking place in a medium whose resistance has so far proved negligible, under the influence of a small number of forces working according to a very simple law, as mechanics, allow of the application of the methods and theories of mathematics to a far greater extent than in any other science. There is perhaps not a single analytical procedure, nor a single geometrical or mechanical doctrine, that does not find employment today in astronomical research; most of them indeed until now have had no other purpose. It is in the thorough study of these applications that one acquires a proper sense of the importance and reality of mathematical speculation.

It is when we consider the eminently simple nature of astronomical research, and the consequent facility with which the resources of mathematics can be applied to it, that we understand why astronomy has been placed by common consent at the head of the natural sciences. It merits this supremacy 1. by the perfection of its scientific character, and 2. by the supreme importance of the laws which it reveals.

I have not to consider here its extreme practical utility in the measurement of time, in the exact description of the globe, and above all in the improvement of navigation: such considerations could not become a means of classing the different sciences, which in reality are essentially of equal value in that regard. But it behoves us to remark at this point that in astronomy is exemplified absolutely irrefutably the necessity of the loftiest scientific speculations for the satisfaction of the most vulgar practical needs. Take for instance the problem of determining longitude at sea. Its intimate connection with the body of astronomical theory was indicated in the very infancy of this science by its most eminent pioneer, the great Hipparchos. Since that epoch nothing essential has been added to the fundamental idea of this connection, but it needed all the immense improvements effected up till now in astronomical science for such an application of it to become at last feasible. Without the speculations of the geometers on celestial mechanics, by which the precision of astronomical tables has been improved out of all knowledge, it would be impossible to determine the longitude of a vessel with the degree of exactitude now obtainable; and far from science being more demanding in this respect than practice requires, if we cannot as yet know our position in equatorial waters within a dozen miles, it is certainly because our tables are not yet sufficiently exact. The narrow minds that would blindly arrest the development of the sciences, restricting them to researches of immediate practical utility will no doubt be astonished by these remarks.

Examining the present philosophical state of the fundamental sciences, we are bound to recognise that astronomy is still the only science truly purged of every metaphysical or theological consideration. Its method is its first title to supremacy. In astronomy may be seen what truly constitutes a science, and it is on this model that we must endeavour to constitute all the other fundamental sciences, always having regard to the more or less profound differences that arise from the growing complexity of the phenomena.

No doubt abstract geometry and rational mechanics are in reality natural sciences, the first of the natural sciences, as I have endeavoured to show; they are superior to astronomy because of the perfection of their methods, and the general nature of their theories. We have proved them to be the true foundation of all natural philosophy, and this particularly notable as touching astronomy. But however real their physical character, their phenomena are of too abstract a nature to be habitually appreciated as such, especially by reason of the spirit that continues to vitiate their teaching methods. We need to see those combinations of figures and movements made specific through actual bodies —which is what astronomy does so effectively—for their reality to be brought home to us. Although the knowledge of geometrical and mechanical laws is in itself extremely valuable, in the present state of the human mind such knowledge is employed as a means of investigation in the study of other natural phenomena, rather than as a science in its own right. Thus the first rank in natural philosophy remains with astronomy.

Those who see in science a mere accumulation of observed facts, need only consider astronomy with some attention to realise the narrowness and superficiality of their view. Here the facts are so simple, and moreover so uninteresting, that it is impossible not to perceive that their interconnection alone and their laws constitute the science. What in reality is an astronomical fact? As a rule, nothing but: Such and such a star has been seen at such and such a precise moment at such and such a precise angle—in itself, not at all important. It is the continual combination and mathematisation of these observations that alone create the science, even in its most imperfect state. It is not when the priests of Egypt or Chaldaea made a series of more or less exact empirical observations on the heavens, that astronomy was born, but when the first Greek philosophers began to reduce the general phenomena of the diurnal movement to a few geometrical laws. The aim of astronomical research is to predict with certainty what will be the actual state of the sky in a more or less distant future, and the establishment of the laws of the phenomena offers the only means of attaining that aim, without the accumulation of observations being of any use except to furnish a solid foundation for speculation. In a word, there was no real astronomy as long as it was not possible to foresee with some certainty, at least by graphs, and above all by trigonometrical calculation, the moment of the rising of the sun or of some stars on a given day and at a given place. This has been the essential mark of science ever since its beginning. Further progress has consisted in bringing to these predictions ever greater certitude and precision, in borrowing from direct observation as few data as possible, in order to predict the most distant eventualities possible. No section of natural philosophy therefore can lend greater weight to the axiom: the aim of every science is foresight; an axiom that distinguishes science from erudition, that mere recording of happenings without any view to the future.

Not only is the nature of science more marked in astronomy than in any other branch of knowledge; it may even be said that with the development of the theory of gravitation, astronomy attained the highest philosophic perfection possible to any science, namely the reduction of all phenomena both as to their nature and their degree to one single general law, providing that only solar astronomy is taken into consideration. The increasing complexity of their phenomena puts the realisation of such perfection in any other of the fundamental sciences beyond the range of possibility. Yet such must be the model that all classes of scientists must have constantly before their eyes, and which they must continually strive to approach, as far as the corresponding phenomena permit. To this model we must constantly return if we would renew our contact with positive *explanation* in all its purity, without any question of first or final cause; here also we must learn the true nature and conditions of scientific *hypotheses*, no other science having made so extensive and so proper a use of this powerful instrument.

Such being the great principles of astronomical philosophy, it will be my business to apply them more systematically than has already been done to improving the philosophic character of the other principal sciences.

In general every science, in accordance with the nature of its phenomena, must have perfected the basic positive method in some area of its activity. What we are bent on doing is to pick out these ameliorations one by one, then arrange them in the hierarchic order established in the second lecture, and so produce in the final result a perfect exposition of the positive method. A method which, I hope, will leave no further doubt as to the utility of similar comparative procedures for our future intellectual progress.

V

Philosophic Considerations on Physics [18]

This second branch of natural philosophy has only begun to detach itself from metaphysics and to assume a truly positive character since Galileo's discoveries on the fall of bodies; while the science considered in our fourth lecture has been positive, in its geometric aspect, since the foundation of the school of Alexandria. We can therefore expect to find physics in a far less satisfactory scientific state than astronomy (quite apart from the greater complexity of the phenomena): whether from the speculative point of view, as regards the purity and the co-ordination of its theories, or from the practical point of view, with respect to the scope and precision of its predictions.

This science has gradually taken shape during the last two centuries, under the stimulus of Baconian precept and Cartesian concept. Descartes considerably rationalised its procedures by establishing the universal conditions of the positive method. But however important such lofty authority might be, the dominion of primitive metaphysical methods was so established, and the positive spirit, which could only develop by exercise, was so imperfectly understood, that physics has not been able to acquire complete positivity in so short a time; for after all did not astronomy itself lack it on the mechanical side up to the middle of the modern period? Indeed we shall find that from this point on the traces of the metaphysical spirit will become ever more marked as the successive fundamental sciences come under consideration. Astronomy alone is completely liberated. The antiscientific influence is not confined to a few unimportant details affecting only the mode of exposition: it considerably falsifies the very conceptions of each science. By comparing, after the manner of our study, more directly, more rationally, and more profoundly than has hitherto been done, the philosophy of physics with the perfect model offered us in astronomical philosophy, and by gradually improving the method of the more complex sciences through application of the general precepts furnished by the analysis of the less complex sciences, I trust I shall be able to convey the possibility of impressing positivity on all the sciences, although by the nature of their phenomena they are far from offering the same possibility of perfection.

First we must delimit to the best of our ability the field of research that belongs to physics proper.

Not separating physics from chemistry, we could say that together they have as their object the knowledge of the laws of inorganic nature. Consequently their study is easily and markedly distinguished both from the science of life, which follows it on our encyclopaedic ladder, and from the astronomical science that precedes it, whose object is the consideration of the great natural bodies in their forms and movement. By contrast, the distinction between physics and chemistry is very hard to determine, and becomes more difficult every day with the ever more intimate relations that modern discovery is continually developing between the two sciences. Nevertheless the division between them is real and necessary, although less marked than any other in our encyclopaedic series. I think I can prove this on three general grounds, distinct though equivalent, each one of which in isolation might perhaps in some cases be insufficient, but which in combination do not seem to me to leave any room for doubt.

First there is the contrast, already vaguely apparent to the philosophers of the seventeenth century, between the necessarily general nature of physical research and the specialism inherent in chemical research. Every particular in physics is more or less applicable to any body; while on the contrary every chemical notion concerns a particular action on certain substances. This fundamental opposition is quite pronounced. Thus not only is gravity, the prime object of physics, manifested in the same way in all bodies, not only do all bodies exhibit thermological effects, but all are more or less resonant, and subject to optical and electrical phenomena; in all these properties they show only differences of degree. But in the composition and decomposition which is the subject of chemistry, we are concerned, in the last analysis, with specific properties, even in the most analogous combinations. Magnetic phenomena, it is true, appear to present a notable exception to the generality characteristic of physics, for they belong to certain not very numerous substances. This would appear to relegate them to the domain of chemistry, where they obviously do not belong. But the objection must disappear now that it is recognised, through M. Oersted's fine series of discoveries, that these phenomena are simply a modification of electrical phenomena, whose generality is indisputable. Under the influence of M. Oersted's[19] conception it becomes plainer and plainer every day, as science progresses, that the magnetic modification is not, as was believed, proper to one or two substances only, that all substances are more or less subject to it, though with more differences of degree than with any other physical property. This apparent exception, evidently the sole exception, cannot really alter the generality of all the phenomena in the domain of physics, in contrast with chemistry.

Thus there is no point whatsoever in the distinction habitually made today between the properties of physics, as being of a universality either necessary or contingent, a distinction which tends to throw doubt on the whole definition of the science. Such scholastic subtleties can only be the aftermath of the metaphysical spirit, for which bodies were knowable in themselves, quite apart from the phenomena associated with them, which were regarded as essentially fortuitous, whereas for the positive philosopher they are the primary basis of our conceptions. Now indeed that gravity has been recognised as universal, can we continue to look on it as a contingent quality, that is, can we imagine bodies without it? In the same way is it really in our power to conceive a substance without some kind of temperature, or sound effect, or luminosity, or even electric action? In a word, for positive philosophy generality and contingency are mutually exclusive, contingency appertaining only to those properties whose absence really occurs in certain cases.

The second consideration that serves to distinguish physics from chemistry is less important and less substantial than the preceding, although it is quite cogent. It is that in physics the phenomena are always related to mass, in chemistry to molecules. Whence the name *molecular physics* by which chemistry used to be known. Although this distinction is not without reality, it should be realised that physical actions are generally as molecular as chemical influences, if they are studied sufficiently in depth. Gravity itself provides us with an example of this. Physical phenomena pertaining to mass are usually nothing but the apparent results of those that operate in the smallest particles: this holds good for all phenomena except those of sound and perhaps of electricity. And as for the necessity of a certain mass for action to be manifest, this is just as necessary in chemistry; so that, in this respect also, there does not appear to be any real difference. Yet this ancient perception, communicated by a nascent science to philosophic minds, must have some sort of a basis which should be investigated, for the further development of the science cannot do away with such a comparison if it has been properly established. It seems to me that the incontrovertible fact of which this distinction is but the abstract, but no longer strictly scientific enunciation, is that one at least of the bodies in which chemical phenomena operate, must be in a state of extreme fragmentation, and even, in the majority of cases, of fluidity, if the action is to take place, while this condition is never indispensable to the production of a physical phenomenom, and is even unfavourable to such production, though it does not always suffice to prevent it. Thus there is a real distinction, however ill defined, between the two orders of research.

A third and last generalisation is perhaps the best calculated to separate physical from chemical phenomena. In the former, the constitution of bodies, that is the arrangement of their particles, may change, although generally it remains intact; but the nature of these bodies, that is, the constitution of their molecules, remains unalterable. In the latter, on the contrary, not only is there always a change of state in one or other of the bodies under consideration, but the mutual action of these bodies alters their nature, and it is this modification that actually constitutes the phenomenon. Most of the agents considered in physics are no doubt capable, when their influence is energetic or prolonged, of bringing about composition or decomposition absolutely identical with that determined by chemical action; hence the natural link between physics and chemistry. But with this degree of action they would quit the domain of physics and enter that of chemistry.

Our scientific classifications, if they are to be truly positive, cannot rest on the vague and uncertain estimate of the agents responsible for the phenomena we study. If such a method were strictly applied, the result would be total confusion and the disappearance of the most real and useful distinctions. We all know, for instance, that several modern philosophers, among them the great Euler,[20] have attributed to the same universal ether not only the phenomena of heat and light, as well as of electricity and magnetism, but also those of gravity, terrestrial and celestial, and it would be impossible to demonstrate conclusively that they are in error. Later, others have entrusted to this imaginary fluid the production of the phenomena of sound, for which the air did not seem to them an adequate medium. Finally we see today certain distinguished physiologists, adherents of German 'naturism', attributing the phenomenon of life itself to universal gravitation, to which chemical action has often been attributed. By combining these various hypotheses, which are as plausible united as separate, one would arrive at the vague idea of a single agent of all observable phenomena, and no one could disprove it. Thus all classification founded on the consideration of agents must be fallacious. The only means of dispelling these uncertainties, without entering into endless debate, is to recall the object of positive study, which is the knowledge of the laws of phenomena themselves that must provide the basis of our scientific classifications, if these are to have any rational consistency. Following this directive, we no longer walk in darkness or uncertainty; we can go forward with philosophic assurance.

Not to look beyond the present question, even if one day all chemical phenomena were to be positively analysed as due to the action of physics, which perhaps will be the general result of this generation's scientific research, the fundamental distinction between physics and chemistry would be affected. For it would still be true that in any fact described as *chemical* there is something more than in a fact of physics, namely the altered molecular composition of the bodies, and in consequence the alteration of their properties. Such a distinction cannot be affected by any scientific revolution.

We can now define the object of physics, confined to its proper limits: It is a science which consists in the *study of the laws governing the properties of bodies viewed as mass, and always so circumstanced as to maintain intact the composition of their molecules, and even as a rule their agglomerative state.* In addition philosophy demands, as I have already pointed out, that any science worthy of the name establish a system of prediction. We must therefore add to our definition that the aim of physical theory is to *foresee as exactly as possible all the phenomena that a body will present in any conceivable combination of circumstances,* exclusive of those that would transform that body. That this aim is seldom completely attained, still less exactly, there is no doubt; which only means that the science is imperfect. Even if its imperfection were much greater, its function would still be the same. I have noted elsewhere that, to grasp the character of any science, it is necessary to assume that it is perfect; after that one can take into consideration the fundamental difficulties that are always bound up with ideal perfection, as we have done for astronomy.

This exposition of the aim of physics enables us to see how much more complex is research in that subject than in astronomy. In astronomy research is limited to the consideration of bodies under the two most elementary aspects conceivable: form and movement, every other point of view being rigorously excluded. The bodies of physics, on the contrary, being accessible to all our senses, are necessarily seen in the conditions of their real existence, and consequently are to be studied in a great many different, and complementary connections. If we duly appreciate the difficulty that this involves, we can see that *a priori* such a science will be much less perfect than astronomy, that it would indeed be an impossible science if the extension of the means of exploration did not compensate, up to a point, for the increase in basic obstacles. Here we see in operation the laws of compensation I have established,[21] according to which phenomena, as they become more complex, become for that very reason more explorable in a greater number of directions.

Of the three procedures that make up our art of observation, as we remarked in the fourth chapter, the last, comparison, is scarcely more applicable to physical than to astronomical phenomena. Although it can sometimes be used to some effect, by its nature it is meant for the study of the phenomena proper to organic bodies. But in physics the two other modes of observation are developed to the full. Observation, properly so called, limited in astronomy to the use of only one sense, now attains its full scope. The multiplicity of the points of view relating to properties in physics is rooted in the use we make of all our senses with regard to them. Nevertheless if reduced to pure observation, however varied its use, physics would doubtless be extremely imperfect. But here enters the second exploratory procedure, which if properly directed constitutes the main strength of physicists in questions of any complexity. This happy expedient consists in observing bodies under artificial conditions expressly created to enable one to watch the course of the phenomena which are to be analysed from a specific point of view. Such an art is eminently adapted to physical research, concerned as it is with the general and permanent properties of bodies, which properties are subject only to varying degrees of intensity, and therefore admit of a practically limitless choice of circumstances to be introduced at will. It is really in physics that experiment triumphs, because our ability to modify bodies, the better to observe the phenomena, is subject to almost no restriction, or at least develops much more freely than in any other part of natural philosophy.

When we come to examine later the science of life, we shall see that it presents fundamental difficulties where experiments are concerned, because of the necessity of so devising the experiment as to maintain the state of life, that is, of normal life. This demands a very complex set of conditions both external and internal, which can only vary within very narrow limits, and of which the modifications are mutually evocative: so that one can never establish in physiology what is so easy in physics: two cases exactly similar in every respect, except that which one wishes to analyse; and this is the only basis of a decisive experiment. The use of experiments must therefore be extremely restricted in physiology, although no doubt they can be very useful, if undertaken with all necessary care; we shall see later that the place of this tool is supplied, to a certain extent, by pathological observation. In chemistry the domain of experimentation generally seems even wider than in physics, since up till now only those facts have been considered that proceed from artificial circumstances established by human intervention. But the willed character of the circumstances does not constitute in my view the principal philosophic characteristic of experimentation, which rather consists in the freest possible choice of the case best calculated to reveal the behaviour of the phenomenon, whether this case be natural or artificial. Such a choice is in reality far more open in physics than in chemistry, of which the phenomena result from the combination of a greater number of influences than in physics, so that the circumstances producing the phenomena cannot be varied as much, nor the different determinant conditions isolated as completely. For that reason not only do we owe the creation of the art of experimentation to the development of physics, but it is peculiarly suited to that science, however valuable the resources it offers to the more complex branches of natural philosophy.

After the experimental method, mathematical analysis is the principal basis of advancement in physics. Here indeed is where mathematical analysis stops, as far as natural philosophy is concerned. We cannot hope to extend it beyond this point with any hope of success, even to include chemical phenomena. The relative fixity and simplicity of physical phenomena naturally lend themselves to the instrumental use of mathematics, although this again is less adapted to physics than to astronomy. Such use may appear in two forms, the one direct, the other indirect. The first occurs when it is possible to observe a fundamental law in the phenomena, which becomes the basis of a series of analytical deductions. This was the case of the great Fourier who created his beautiful mathematical theory of the distribution of heat, a theory entirely founded on the principle that the thermological action between two bodies is proportional to the difference in their temperature. Most of the time, however, mathematical analysis only intervenes indirectly, that is, after the phenomena have been reduced by dint of a more or less difficult experimental procedure to a few geometrical or mechanical laws; and then it is not properly to physics that the analysis applies, but to geometry and mechanics. Examples of this are, as to geometry, the theories of reflection or refraction, and for mechanics, those of weight and of a part of acoustics.

Whether the introduction of analytical theories in physical research be mediate or immediate, it is important not to employ them without extreme caution, and close scrutiny of the point of departure, which alone can establish certainty of deduction. Such deduction is then prolonged and varied by the method with admirable results, the genius of physics always remaining the guide in the use of this powerful instrument. It must be admitted that these conditions have rarely been met by the geometrists, who for the most part, taking the means for the end, have confused physics with a host of studies founded on hazardous hypotheses, or even on fanciful conceptions, which can only be regarded by good scientists as so many mathematical exercises, of which the abstract value is sometimes quite outstanding, but which can never influence the progress of physics. The unjust contempt for purely experimental study which the preponderance of analysis creates, even tends to vitiate the direction of research, and if it were not kept within bounds would deprive physics of its necessary foundations, causing it to retrograde to a state of uncertainty and obscurity, little different in spite of an impressive façade from its ancient metaphysical condition. Physicists have no means of avoiding these fatal encroachments, except to become good enough geometrists themselves to direct the use of the analytical instrument, as of the other apparatus they employ, instead of abandoning the application of that instrument to minds that have no clear or profound idea of the phenomena which they are using it to explore. This condition, that physicists should also be geometrists, is already indicated by the position of physics on our encyclopaedic ladder, and could certainly be met if the preliminary education of physicists were more efficiently organised. They would then have no need to have recourse to geometers, except in the very rare cases requiring the full development of analytic procedures. Not only would they thus put a stop to the false scientific position which so irks them today, they would notably advance the scientific system as a whole, by hastening the development of sound mathematical philosophy. The philosophy of analysis is no doubt beginning to be quite well known, although it still awaits improvements. But as for true mathematical philosophy, which organises the relation of the abstract to the concrete, it is still in its infancy, as its formation was bound to be late. It could only emerge from the extensive comparison of studies in the various orders of mathematical phenomena, and it can only develop by an increasing number of such studies, pursued in a truly positive spirit, and of necessity far more advanced among physicists than among geometrists. The attention of geometrists should be directed to the instrument, apart from its use; physicists alone, as a rule, can sense the need to modify the means according to the end in view. Such would be their respective functions under a rational distribution of scientific work.

Although the application of analysis to the study of physics has not yet been philosophically organised, with the result that it has frequently been delusive, it has already done yeoman service to the progress of knowledge. Where it has been possible to comply with all the requisite conditions, analysis has brought that admirable exactitude to the different branches of physics, and above all that perfect co-ordination which invariably distinguish its proper use. What would the study of weight, of heat, of light, be without it? Nothing but series of disconnected facts that would permit of no prediction, except by introducing experiment at every step, while today these studies are rational to a degree that enables them largely to fulfil the purpose of all scientific work. Nevertheless we must not hide from ourselves the fact that physical phenomena, in proportion to their greater complexity, are less accessible to mathematical methods than astronomical phenomena, both as regards extent of application and certainty of result. Especially on the mechanics side, there is not a problem in physics that is not far more complex than any problem in astronomy, if one takes into consideration all the circumstances liable to exercise a real influence on the phenomenon. The case of weight, however simple it appears, and actually is, relatively to all the others, offers striking proof of this, even if we confine ourselves to solids, through the impossibility of taking the resistance of the air sufficiently into account in our calculations, yet this resistance modifies the actual movement quite definitely. And so, *a fortiori*, is it with other physical researches liable to become mathematical researches, which would, as a rule undergo this transformation only by dint of getting rid of more or less essential conditions of the problem; from which we may conclude that deductions from such incomplete analysis must be regarded with the greatest reserve. The utility of analysis in questions of physics would be greatly augmented, if it were not so exclusively used, and if resort were had more frequently to experiment which, ceasing to be a mere determinant of coefficients, as happens too often today, would furnish points less wide apart for the incidence of the mathematical method. This procedure has already succeeded in a few cases, too few unfortunately. No doubt the co-ordination becomes less perfect; but should one regret this illusory perfection, if it can only be obtained by modifying more or less fundamentally the reality of the phenomena? The combining of analysis and experiment, without subordinating one to the other, is still an almost unknown art; it is the final step in the creation of a method suited to the proper study of physics. This art will be practised only when physicists and not geometers undertake the guidance of the analytical instrument.

Now that we have considered the proper object of physics and the basic tools appertaining to that object, I must determine its encyclopaedic position. Naturally after the discussion at the beginning of this lecture, little more remains to be said. Yet I must justify here and now the rank I have assigned to this branch of natural philosophy in the scientific hierarchy.

If we look at physics in relation to the sciences I placed as its antecedents, it is easy to recognise not only that its phenomena are more complicated than those of astronomy—that is obvious—but also that the study of these phenomena cannot attain a truly rational character except through a profound, though general knowledge of astronomy, either as a model or as a basis. We have seen that the science of the heavenly bodies, as much from the mechanical as from the geometrical point of view, by reason of the simplicity of its phenomena, offers the most perfect type of the universal method to be applied, as much as possible, to the discovery of natural laws. What more suitable preparation could there be for the intellect, before it undertakes the more difficult investigations of physics, than the philosophical study of such a model? How are we to proceed rationally to the analysis of more complex phenomena if we have not made ourselves sufficiently acquainted beforehand with the way in which simpler phenomena are to be studied? Here the progress of the individual must follow the same lines as that of the species. It is through astronomy that the positive spirit was first introduced into natural philosophy, after it had been developed by mathematical studies. Can individual education really be excused from the same progression? If the science of the celestial bodies was the first to teach us what the positive *explanation* of a phenomenon is without any inquiry into its *cause*, either first or final, or the way in which it is produced, from what purer source could we draw today so fundamental an instruction? Physics, more than any other natural science, must imitate this model, since its phenomena are of all the least complex, after those of astronomy, and such imitation will therefore be more complete than elsewhere.

Apart from this fundamental relationship with respect to method, astronomical theory in general is a preliminary datum for the study of terrestrial physics. The position and the movements of our planet in the cosmos of which we form a part, its shape, its size, its general equilibrium, must necessarily be known before we can really understand any one of the physical phenomena occurring on its surface. The most ele- ·

mentary of these, and the one present in almost all the others, weight, cannot be truly studied apart from the universal celestial phenomenon of which it is only a particular case. Indeed I have noted elsewhere, that important phenomena, above all that of the tides, naturally effect a real, though almost imperceptible, transition from astronomy to physics. The subordination of physics to astronomy is therefore indisputable, in whatever way we look at it.

Physics must therefore be intimately, though indirectly dependent on mathematics, since mathematics is the basis of astronomy. But besides this mediate connection, we have noted above the immediate link between physics and the primary basis of natural philosophy. In most of the branches of physics we have to do, as in astronomy, with essentially geometrical or mechanical phenomena, although the circumstances are generally, in the case of physics, much more complex. This complexity no doubt prevents, as we have seen, the geometrical and mechanical theories from being applied in a manner nearly as perfect in scope or in precision as for the heavenly bodies. But the abstract laws of space and movement must be observed none the less; and the application of these laws cannot fail to furnish important and extremely valuable information. Yet however obvious this dependence is from the doctrinal point of view, it is in connection with method that the mathematical affiliation of physics is particularly important. Recollect that the general spirit of positive philosophy was first formed by the cultivation of mathematics, and that to know this spirit in all its purity we must go back to its original source. Mathematical theorems and formulae are rarely applicable to the study of natural phenomena, once extreme simplicity is not retained for the actual conditions of the problem. But the true spirit of mathematics, so distinct from that of algebra, with which it is too often confused, is always to be applied, and a thorough acquaintance with it is for me the most notable gain to be achieved by physicists from the study of mathematics. It is only through being habituated to the eminently simple and lucid truths of geometry and mechanics that the mind can develop its natural positivity, and prepare itself for genuine demonstrations in the most complex studies. Nothing can take the place of this subject as a means of training the intellect. It should be noted that geometrical notions being still clearer and more fundamental than mechanical ones, the study of geometry is of still greater importance to physicists as a means of education than that of mechanics although mechanics is of more immediate and extensive use in the various branches of science. Yet, whatever be the importance of this preparatory study, we must not ima-

93

gine that it can fully suffice, even as intellectual training, if it is not completed by the study of astronomy which will show, by simple but crucial examples, how the mathematical spirit must be modified to adapt itself to the exploration of natural phenomena. We see therefore that the preliminary scientific education of a physicist is necessarily more complex than that of an astronomer, since apart from their common mathematical basis, which is a sufficient preliminary for the astronomer, the physicist must add at least the general study of the heavenly bodies. The encyclopaedic position therefore that I assigned to physics is certainly correct.

Its rank is no less evident from the opposite relationship, that with the sciences coming after it.

It cannot be an accident that not only in our language, but in that of all thinking peoples, the generic term assigned from the first to the study of nature has during the last hundred years become the name of the science we are considering. So universal a usage must arise from a deep, though vague feeling of the necessary preponderance of physics in the system of natural philosophy, which it dominates entirely, except for astronomy, and astronomy is only an emanation of mathematics. Indeed it will be conceded that the study of the common properties of bodies manifested in all their states with only differences of degree, and revealing therefore the constitution of matter, must invariably precede that of the modifications proper to various substances and to their various arrangements. The necessity of following this order is apparent quite independently of the logical requirement of studying the more complex phenomena after the less complex. If we take the science of biology, for instance, whatever opinion one may adopt on the nature of the phenomena of organic bodies, it is obvious that these bodies are subject to the universal laws of matter, modified as to their manifestations by the circumstances peculiar to the living state. When we come to examine, in the seventh lecture, the philosophy of this science, we shall see how vain are the notions by which people seek to establish an opposition between vital phenomena and the general laws of physics. Besides, as life never occurs except under the continual and necessary influence of a given set of external circumstances, how could it be the subject of positive study if abstraction had to be made of the laws relating to these external modifiers? Thus any physiology that is not based on a previous knowledge of physics cannot have real scientific consistency. The subordination to physics is still more striking in chemistry, as we shall see. Without admitting the premature and perhaps hazardous hypothesis of certain eminent physicists, who want to attribute all chemical phenomena to purely physical action, it is obvious that every chemical action takes place invariably under physical influences, as necessary as they are inevitable. What phenomenon either of composition or of decomposition would be intelligible if one took no account of weight, heat, electricity, etc.? And could one appreciate the chemical force of those various agents if one did not know the laws governing the influence proper to each one of them? It is enough to mention these agents to remove any doubt as to the strict dependence of chemistry on physics, while physics is, on the other hand, by its very nature, independent of chemistry.

These considerations, while they clearly demonstrate the rank of physics in the hierarchy of the basic sciences, demonstrate at the same time its enormous philosophic importance, since they show it to be the basis of all the sciences that my encyclopaedic formula has placed after it. As for the action that physics exercises on the general intellectual system of man, such action is necessarily less profound than that of the two extremes of natural philosophy: astronomy and physiology. These two sciences, by determining our ideas on the two universal subjects which are correlated to all our concepts, man and the universe, must certainly act upon human thought in a more radical manner than the intermediate sciences, such as physics and chemistry, however indispensable their contribution. Nevertheless the influence of the intermediate sciences on the general development and ultimate emancipation of human intelligence is extremely marked. To take physics alone, it is obvious that the fundamental nature of the opposition between positive and theological or metaphysical philosophy is very much felt in this science, although less than in astronomy, by reason of its lesser scientific perfection. The relative inferiority, however, is compensated by the much greater variety of phenomena embraced by physics, whence arises a far more pluralistic, and therefore more apparent antagonism to theology and metaphysics. The intellectual history of the last centuries shows that it is chiefly in the domain of physics that the decisive struggle of the positive against the metaphysical spirit has formally taken place: in astronomy the discussion has not been very noticeable, positivism having triumphed almost without effort, except on the subject of the movement of the earth.

It is important to note also that it is with physics that natural phenomena begin to be really modifiable by human intervention, which could not take place in astronomy, but will be more and more in evidence throughout the entire remainder of the encyclopaedic series. If the extreme simplicity of astronomical phenomena had not given scientific prediction with regard to them tremendous range and extreme exactitude, the impossibility of intervening in them in any way would have rendered their complete emancipation from theological and metaphysical supremacy extremely difficult; perfect prediction here has been more useful to man than his petty action on all the other natural phenomena. As for the latter, human intervention, however restricted, acquires great compensatory importance, in view of the low degree of prediction possible in these sciences. It is fundamental to the nature of theological philosophy to conceive phenomena as subject to supernatural wills, and consequently as eminently variable and irregular. Now for the public, which cannot really enter into any speculative discussion on the best way to philosophise, this type of explanation can be refuted by two means, the eventual success of which with the public is certain: the exact prediction of phenomena, which causes the immediate disappearance of any idea of a directing will; and their modification according to our convenience, leading to the same result from another point of view, by presenting such a will as subordinate to our own. The first procedure is the more philosophic; it is what, when it is possible, best convinces the vulgar —which has not been the case up to the present to any considerable degree, except with regard to celestial phenomena; but the second, when very evident, is not less sure of universal assent. It is thus, for example, that Franklin destroyed once for all in even the rudest intelligence, the religious theory of thunder, by proving the guidance that man can impose within certain limits on this meteor, while the ingenious experiments to establish the identity of the phenomenon with an ordinary electric discharge, although of much greater scientific value, could be decisive only in the eyes of physicists. The discovery of this power of guiding the thunderbolt thus really contributed as much to the downfall of theological prejudice, as, in the other case, the exact prediction of the return of comets. By a philosophic law now disclosed for the first time, the more defective our scientific prediction becomes as the complexity of phenomena increases, the more our action on these phenomena acquires scope and variety. Thus in proportion as the antagonism between positive and theological philosophy is less pronounced from the point of view of prediction, so it is more pronounced from that of intervention, and as far as the general influence of this debate on the vulgar mind is concerned, the final result is just about the same, although the compensation is not absolutely exact.

If we now consider physics from the point of view of method and scientific perfection, apart from the importance of its laws, we can see that its comparative value exactly corresponds to the rank it occupies in the encyclopaedic hierarchy that I have established. The degree of speculative efficiency of any science is judged by two criteria, which are always correlative, although quite distinct from one another: coordination and prediction. The latter aspect is the surest and most decisive criterion, as it relates to the final aim of all science. Now in each of these two respects, physics, whatever be its future progress, by reason of the variety and complexity of its phenomena, must be inferior to astronomy. Instead of that perfect mathematical harmony we admire in the celestial science, which has now been reduced to a strict unity, physics presents us with numerous branches, nearly always isolated from one another, and each separately establishing only feeble and equivocal connections between its own principal phenomena; in the same way the rational and precise prediction of the entire course of celestial events for any moment in time, from a very small number of direct observations, is here replaced by a very limited foresight, which in order not to be uncertain, can scarcely lose sight of immediate experiment. But on the other hand, the speculative superiority of physics on both counts to all the rest of natural phenomena, is equally indubitable, even relatively to chemistry, *a fortiori* to physiology, as I shall show in my philosophical examination of these two sciences, of which the phenomena are by their very nature much more disconnected, and therefore permit of still less foresight. It is important to note here also that the philosophical study of physics has a quite special usefulness, as a general means of intellectual education, that it would be impossible to find elsewhere to the same degree: namely that of inculcating a profound knowledge of the art of experiment, which we have recognised as peculiarly adapted to physics. It is to this that true philsophers, whatever be the object of their customary researches, must always come back, to learn in what the true experimental spirit consists, to learn also the conditions demanded by experiments that will reveal unequivocally the course of phenomena, and finally to get an idea of the ingenious precautions by which, in this difficult exercise, the falsification of results may be prevented. Every fundamental science not only exemplifies the characteristics of the positive method, which are bound to show themselves in a greater or less degree, but also yields insights proper to the science, as we have seen in the case of astronomy, and it is always at their source that these particular notions of the universal logic should be studied, if they are to be properly appreciated. Mathematical science alone teaches the necessary conditions of positivity; astronomy illustrates the true study of nature; physics acquaints us with the theory of experimentation; from chemistry we must borrow the art of nomenclature, and finally the science of organic bodies alone can reveal the true theory of classification.

VI

Philosophic Considerations on Chemistry [22]

The final aspect under which the existence of any body must be studied by natural philosophy is that of the modifications experienced by substances as a result of their molecular reactions. This new order of phenomena, without which the great operations of terrestrial nature would be simply incomprehensible, is the most complex and important of all those manifested by inorganic nature. In no act of their existence do inert bodies seem so near to being alive as when, through their interaction, they bring about the perturbations characteristic of chemical transformation. As it is the fundamental trait of theological and metaphysical philosophy to conceive every phenomenon as analogous to life, [23] which is the only phenomenon known to us by immediate feeling, one can understand why that primitive manner of philosophising was bound to exercise on the study of chemical phenomena a more intense and persistent dominion than on any other class of inorganic phenomena.

We must note in addition that for the above-mentioned natural effects only extremely complex phenomena offer themselves to our direct observation: vegetable combustion, fermentation, etc., the exact analysis of which is almost the final stage of science; for the most important chemical phenomena, or those at least to which our means of exploration are best adapted, are only produced in exceedingly artificial circumstances, and the idea of these must have come very late and been implemented with much difficulty. It is easy today, even for the most mediocre intelligence, to induce new phenomena of some scientific interest, as it were by chance, through establishing neglected relations between the numerous substances already known; but in the infancy of chemistry the creation of really suitable subjects of observation must have been difficult, to a degree that we can scarcely realise today. One can scarcely understand how the activity of these ancient scrutinisers of nature could have led to the discovery of the principal chemical phenomena, if they had not been stimulated, as the illustrious Berthollet [24] has indicated, by limitless hopes based on chimerical notions of the composition of matter.

The complex and equivocal nature of the phenomena, and the difficulty of exploring them, suffice to explain the tardy and incomplete positivity of chemical conceptions, in comparison with all other conceptions of inorganic nature. Now that we have seen how imperfect is the study of mere physical phenomena, and how radically defective in more than one respect is the scientific character of physics, we naturally expect a still greater degree of inferiority in the much more difficult, as also more recent science that establishes the laws of the composition and decomposition of matter. Under whatever aspect we view it, whether speculatively or practically, that is, in respect to the nature of its explanations or the predictions it is able to make, we have here obviously the least advanced branch of inorganic science. Prediction above all, which I have recommended as the most rational, the most exact and the least equivocal criterion of perfection in speculative knowledge, shows chemistry scarcely meriting at present the name of science in the greater part of its research, since that research hardly ever leads to certain prediction. If we introduce into a chemical action which has already been well explored a few specific modifications, even though these be slight and few, it is seldom possible to predict exactly what changes they will produce. Yet without such prediction there is no *science* properly so called; there is only *erudition*, whatever be the number and importance of the facts collected. To think otherwise is to take a quarry for a building.

The extreme imperfection of our chemistry no doubt results from the complex nature of the science and the fact that it has only developed recently; it would be unrealistic to hope that it could ever attain as satisfactory a state of rationality as that of sciences relating to simpler phenomena, especially astronomy, that true, eternal type of natural philosophy. But it seems to me indisputable that its present inferiority must also be attributed to the faulty philosophy which determines and guides its research, and to the defective education of most of its devotees. There is every reason to believe that a judicious philosophic analysis might contribute directly to an early improvement in this so important science. Such is the conviction I would wish to create in your minds by the brief sketch of chemical philosophy I shall now give, treating it in all its various aspects. Although from the nature and limits of these lectures I cannot develop this outline in a way that would ensure its effectiveness, perhaps I shall be able to convey to at least one of the eminent men who today cultivate chemistry, the necessity of rethinking its fundamental conceptions.

First of all we must exactly define the object of this final section of inorganic philosophy.

However vast and complex the subject of chemistry, the clear indication of its aim, and the strict delimitation of its domain of research, in a word, its definition, present far less difficulty than we have experienced in dealing with physics. We have had to define the latter in contrast with chemistry, so that the preliminary work is already done. Besides, it is easy to characterise chemical phenomena as associated with a more or less complete, and always observable modification of the inner constitution of the bodies concerned, in other words, associated with composition and decomposition, generally both, if we take into consideration all the substances participating in chemical action. And so at all periods of scientific development, at least since chemistry separated itself from the art of pharmaceutical preparation and became a subject of speculative study, chemical research has been distinguished by a high degree of originality, and could never be confused with any other part of natural philosophy: this has been far from the case with physics, which right up to modern times has generally been entangled with physiology, as scientific language itself bears witness.

Through the character of its phenomena, chemistry is clearly distinguished from physics, which precedes it on our encyclopaedic ladder, and from physiology, which follows it; the comparison tends to bring out its proper nature. These three sciences may be regarded as having for their object the study of the molecular activity of matter in all its modes. Each corresponds to one of the three principal grades of this activity, grades which are distinguished from one another by profound and natural differences. Chemical action evidently has something more than physical action, and something less than vital action, in spite of the vague approximations which hypothesis may establish between these three orders of phenomena. The only molecular disturbance that physical activity can produce in bodies is in the arrangement of particles; such modifications, usually slight, are as a rule also temporary: in no case is the substance changed. Chemical activity on the contrary, besides these changes in the structure and state of the aggregation, always brings about a profound and lasting change in the composition of the particles; the bodies that have contributed to the phenomenon have usually become unrecognisable, so much have their properties been disturbed. As for the physiological phenomena, they exhibit an activity of matter raised to a far higher degree of energy: as soon as a chemical combination is effected, the bodies become completely inert, while the vital state is characterised, apart from the physical effects and chemical operations which it always possesses, by a more or less rapid, but always continuous double movement of composition and decomposition, calculated to maintain within certain variable limits the organisation of the body for a more or less considerable time, while constantly renewing its substance. It cannot be denied therefore that we have here three fundamental grades of molecular activity, never to be confused in any sane philosophy.

Two secondary considerations must be added to complete the notion of chemical phenomena, one on the nature of the chemical phenomenon, and the other on its conditions.

Every substance is doubtless subject to more or less varied, and more or less dynamic chemical activity; for this reason chemical phenomena have been rightly classed among the general phenomena, of which they are the last in the order of increasing complexity: thus they are clearly distinguished from physiological phenomena, which by their nature are proper to certain substances only, substances organised in certain ways. Nevertheless it is undeniable that chemical phenomena, especially in contrast with physical phenomena, present something specific in each case, or, to borrow Bergmann's[25] energetic expression, something *elective*. Not only does each of the different elements produce chemical effects that are entirely peculiar to it, but it is the same with their innumerable and diverse compounds, of which even those most analogous to one another will always manifest, from the chemical point of view, fundamental differences, often the only means of identifying them. Thus while physical properties, in one body or another, only present distinctions of degree, chemical properties are specific. The former constitute the foundation of all material existence, the latter, that of individuality.

In the second place, among the extremely varied conditions attendant on the development of the different chemical phenomena, it has always been noted that the fundamental condition common to them all, not an all-sufficing condition but certainly an indispensable one, is that of immediate contact between the antagonistic particles, and consequently that one at least of these should be in a fluid state, either gaseous or liquid. When this condition is not present naturally, it must be artificially produced, by liquefying the substance either by fire or by some solvent. Without this previous modification a combination would not take place, in accordance with the celebrated aphorism which dates from the infancy of chemistry.* Up till now there has not been a single well-attested example of chemical action between two solid bodies, at any rate where the temperature had not risen to a degree where it would be

* (Translator's note) Heraclitus: 'All things are an exchange of fire.'

difficult to estimate the true state of aggregation of the bodies. And it is when both substances are liquid that chemical action manifests itself with most energy, if a slight difference of densities allows complete intermingling. Nothing shows more clearly that chemical effects are essentially molecular, especially in contrast with physical effects. In this respect they are even essentially distinguished from physiological effects, though not so definitely, as the production of the latter requires a co-operation of solids with fluids.[26]

All of which may be summed up in the definition of chemistry as having for its aim *the study of the laws of composition and decomposition resulting from the specific molecular action of various natural and artificial substances on one another*.

There is every reason to fear that it will be long before this science, in view of its extreme imperfection, can receive a more strict or more exact definition, characterising the data and the unknowns of any chemical problem. Nevertheless, the better to indicate the true spirit of chemistry, it will no doubt help to consider the most rational, and so to speak the most mathematical definition that can be given to it, although far from corresponding to its actual state.

With this in view, and as always associating *science* with *prediction*, I affirm that in any piece of chemical research, considered from the philosophic point of view the aim must be, given the properties of substances, simple or compound, placed in chemical relation to one another in well-defined circumstances, to determine exactly in what their action will consist, and what will be the principal properties of the new products. Logically the problem, however difficult, is certainly now determined, and nothing of this could be suppressed without its ceasing to be so, so that there is nothing superfluous in this statement. But one can see that if such solutions were ready to hand, the three fundamental applications of chemical science, to vital phenomena, to the natural history of the earth, and to industrial operations, instead of being as today the almost accidental irregular result of the spontaneous development of science, would *ipso facto* be rationally organised, since in any one of these three departments a question would immediately fall under our abstract formula, the data of which would be furnished by the circumstances proper to the case. Such a manner of conceiving the chemical problem fulfils therefore all the essential conditions. However superior it appears to the real state of the science—which only proves the imperfection of that state—it must be allowed to be the real end towards which the efforts of chemists ultimately tend, since, on their own admission, the few simple questions in which up till now this result has been attained are regarded as the most advanced parts of chemistry; whence we may conclude it to be the goal of the whole science.

On closer examination this definition will be seen to admit of an important transformation, for if the method were repeatedly applied and properly guided, all the fundamental data of chemistry could be reduced to the essential properties of simple bodies, which would lead to a knowledge of the various immediate principles, and consequently to the most complex and remote combinations. As for the study of the elements themselves, evidently this could not be reduced to anything else; it must be a direct experimental operation, divided into as many distinct and independent parts as there are undecomposed substances at any time. The only rational thing to be done, apart from a few more or less plausible analogical inductions to which certain observed resemblances might lead, is to discover the relations between the chemical properties of each element and the whole of its physical properties. But although certain facts seem to confirm the principle, philosophic in itself, of a certain necessary proportion between these two orders of properties, it seems to me that at no time will it be possible for this proportion to be so clearly revealed as to make up for the direct exploration of the chemical characteristics of each element. Thus, instead of aspiring to an imaginary perfection, we must always regard the chemical study of the various simple bodies as to be pursued through a series of direct observations. But once this general basis has been obtained from experiment, all the other chemical problems, despite their immense variety, should be capable of rational solution by applying a small number of invariable laws established by the genius of chemistry for the various classes of combination.

As for the combinations, they lend themselves to two general modes of classification, both of which must be taken into consideration: 1. The simplicity or greater or less degree of complexity of the immediate principles. 2. The number of elements combined. Now, according to general observation chemical action becomes more difficult between substances as the order of their *composition* rises: most compound atoms belong to the two first orders;[27] beyond the third order combination seems almost impossible. As to the second mode, combinations rapidly lose their stability as the elements in them multiply; generally we have to do with a binary, and there is almost no body that is more than quaternary. Thus the number of chemical classes to which these two distinctions may give rise cannot be very extensive; for each of them there should be a corresponding law of combination, which when applied to various specific cases would reveal, by elementary data, the result of each collision. Such, no doubt, would be a truly scientific state of chemistry. The distance that separates us from such philosophising is to be attributed to the radical weakness of our intelligence, and to the wrong directions it has taken, much more than to the nature of the subject itself. Yet however difficult of attainment it may appear, it is now beginning to be partially realised in a very important though secondary category of chemical research, the study of proportions. Here with the aid of a chemical coefficient, empirically evaluated for each simple body, we succeed in determining in many cases with considerable exactitude in accordance with a small number of general laws, the proportions according to which the previously known principles unite to produce each new product. Why should all other chemical studies not exhibit the same perfection? We may then, to sum up, define chemistry as having for its ultimate aim: *given properties of all simple bodies, to find those of the compounds they form.*

This end is rarely attained in the present state of the science, but a continual consideration of it would be none the less useful, even today, for it would put our research habits more in the way of progress, and give them a more philosophic character. There is no science that is not more or less inferior to its definition: but the use of a precise and systematic definition is for any doctrine the first symptom of scientific consistency, at the same time as it is the best means of measuring its progress in each epoch. From these motives I have insisted on this important matter of definition, which will perhaps earn for me some gratitude from philosophic chemists.

The fundamental law that I have established of the necessary proportion between the degree of complexity of the diverse orders of phenomena and the extent of our means of exploring them, is verified in chemical science especially, if we compare it to the sciences preceding it, and especially to physics. Here the first of the three modes of investigation which we distinguished in natural philosophy, *observation*, begins to reach its full development. Up till now observation has played but a limited part. In astronomy it has been necessarily confined to one of our senses; in physics hearing, and above all touch, are added to sight; but taste and smell remain inactive. In chemistry on the contrary all our senses participate in the analysis of the phenomena. The additions this convergence brings to our means of investigation can only be estimated, if we ask ourselves what would become of chemistry should we renounce our sense of smell or taste, which quite often furnish us with the sole means of recognising and distinguishing the effects produced. But what the philosopher must particularly note is that this connection is in no wise accidental or empirical. For in sound physiological theory the senses of taste and smell, contrary to the other senses, are seen to act in a thoroughly chemical manner, and consequently the nature of these two senses is peculiarly adapted to the perception of the phenomena of composition and decomposition.

As for *experiment*, there is no need to insist on the dominant role it plays in chemistry, since most of the present chemical phenomena, and above all the most instructive ones, are artifically produced. However, impressive though this may be, I persist in my belief that the real part played by experimentation in chemical discovery has been exaggerated. Indeed the natural or artificial character of the phenomena is not the point if we are considering experimentation as an improved mode of observation; its real character consists in the institution, or what amounts to the same thing, the choice of circumstance for the phenomenon, so as to secure a more illuminating and decisive exploration. Now from this point of view it seems to me that the experimental method is less appropriate to the nature of chemical research than to that of physical research. For chemical effects usually depend on too many influences acting at once for it to be easy to illuminate the production of these effects by experiment, that is by instituting two parallel cases exactly identical in all their circumstances except the one that we wish to estimate; this after all is the fundamental condition of any true experiment. Here for the first time though in a lesser degree owing to the greater complexity of the phenomena in physiology, we come into contact with the type of obstacle that the nature of physiological researches opposes to the purely experimental method, rendering its use almost always delusive. Yet it cannot be doubted that experimentation has considerably contributed to the advance of chemical science, quite apart from the new objects of observation it has produced. It seems to me undeniable that the superiority of physics over chemistry in this regard does not depend today on the respective natures of the two sciences alone (although this is the principal cause), but also on the fact that physics has reached a more advanced stage of development than the second. When chemistry comes to be cultivated in a more rational manner, experiment will no doubt be better understood and applied to it. From the early days of this difficult science the immortal series of experiments of Priestley[28] and above all of the great Lavoisier[29] have offered admirable models, almost comparable to the most perfect ones that physics has to show, models which alone would suffice to demonstrate that the nature of chemical phenomena does not oppose insurmountable obstacles to luminous and extensive employment of the experimental method.

Finally, with regard to the third mode of rational exploration, *comparison*, the least general of all, it is important to note that even although, by its nature, it is specially adapted to physiological investigation, it may well prove effective in chemical research. Essential to the method is the existence of a sufficiently extensive series of analogous yet distinct cases, in which one common phenomenon is more and more modified by successive and almost continuous simplifications or degradations. From this statement alone it can be seen that such a procedure is completely suited only to the analysis of vital phenomena. Only in this context, therefore, has this mode of observation produced important results up to the present; here alone can it be studied to any effect. However, now that I have given an abstract formulation of the procedure, I cannot help thinking that even if it is radically inapplicable to astronomy, and of not much use to physics, chemistry has totally different conditions, much like those that appear in their completeness only in physiology. Of this we need no other proof than the existence in chemistry of natural families, today admitted by every philosophic mind concerned with this science, although a classification corresponding to this principle is still far from being established. But the recognised possibility of such a classification implies the possibility of the comparative method, as both these things are based on the recognitions of the uniformity in a long series of different bodies, of certain outstanding phenomena. Between these two orders of ideas, indeed, there is so close a connection that the construction of a natural system of chemical classification, so much needed today, is impossible without considerable use of the comparative method, in the sense in which it is understood by the physiologists; and conversely, comparative chemistry cannot be regularly cultivated so long as there is not even a rudimentary natural classification to serve as a guide. At any rate these considerations of high chemical philosophy appear to me to prove beyond a shadow of doubt that the comparative method is peculiarly adapted, and will be applied in the not too distant future, to the advance of chemical knowledge. Perhaps in indicating this important relationship I have gone too far ahead of the present state of the science which, it must be confessed, offers no real example of this type of procedure except in a very small number of researches, and even in these its influence is difficult to assess. But we must not forget that chemistry is still in its infancy; consequently we should not think it strange that on the whole its methods do not emerge very clearly from a haphazard development. It is only by going a little beyond the natural phases of this development that the special study of the philosophy of the sciences, as I conceive it and endeavour to promote it, will notably hasten progress.

Whatever be the direct or indirect means employed in chemical exploration it must be observed that their use can be tested, in a manner very appropriate to the nature of this science, although not peculiar to it. The test consists in the confrontation of the two procedures, *analysis* and *synthesis*.

Every body that has been decomposed must, obviously, be considered as capable of being recomposed, though this may be difficult, and sometimes almost impossible. If the inverse process reproduces the original substance exactly, the chemical demonstration will *ipso facto* be recognised as certain. Unfortunately the considerable extension of the powers of chemistry which we have witnessed in our century has involved the analytical faculties much more than the synthetic ones; so that these two approaches have not preserved a balance.

To define those cases where such a balance is indispensable to the establishment of absolute certainty, it is necessary to distinguish between two very different kinds of chemical analysis: preliminary analysis, consisting in the simple separation of immediate principles, and final analysis, leading to the determination of the *elements* properly so called. Although final analysis is always a necessary accompaniment of chemical investigation, preliminary analysis is in a great number of cases and especially with regard to practical applications, more important and of greater scope. Now one can easily understand that elements analysis may strictly speaking dispense with synthetic verification. For if the operation is initiated with precision and pursued with care, one can always deduce quite certainly from the composition of the reactives employed the unknown composition of the proposed substance, whose various elements have been separated in some kind of a way. The impossibility of recombining them to reproduce the original body would evidently not throw any doubt on the reality of the solution; unless, as can only happen very rarely, there are serious motives for calling in question the simplicity of one of the elements involved. Synthesis in such a case therefore can only add a useful and illuminating confirmation to analytical demonstration, but in no sense an indispensable one. It is quite another matter when the sole aim of the research is to determine the immediate principles. As the elements of which they are formed would be necessarily capable of producing various combinations of a different order among themselves, one can never be absolutely certain, in this kind of analysis, that one or several of the immediate principles obtained does not owe its origin to the reactions caused by the analytic operation itself. Synthesis alone will be capable, by reconstructing the proposed substance with the material produced, of finally deciding the issue beyond any doubt; unless the low energy of the reactives employed, and the power of analogical induction suffice, which often happens, to remove any doubt from the results of the analytical operation. In very complicated immediate analyses, even when the agreement of several analytical procedures strongly confirms the conclusions obtained, one can almost never count on true chemical demonstration without a synthetic confirmation. The analysis of mineral waters, and especially of organic substances, abound in noteworthy instances of this maxim of chemical philosophy.

To complete our account of this principle, we note the existence of a certain concord between the possibility of applying the synthetic method and the obligation to apply it; although of course we do not claim that this correspondence of means to ends will leave nothing to be desired. The concord in question is the result of a law mentioned above in another context, that combinations become less tenacious in proportion as the order of composition of the particles rises. Now the facility of recomposition should correspond to that of decomposition. Thus elements analysis, the only analysis which, for the reasons given above, can dispense with the synthetic countercheck, is precisely the analysis which leads to the most difficult, often impossible recompositions, if the elements are at all numerous, because of the energetic reactions it has usually been necessary to employ, as chemical experiment demonstrates every day: while the cases of immediate analysis, requiring on the contrary only weak antagonisms, oppose no great obstacles to synthetic operations, which have thus become almost indispensable.

VII

Philosophic Considerations on Biological Science[30]

The study of man and the study of the external world will always be the dual occupation of philosophy. Each of these two orders of speculation may be imposed on the other, may even serve as its point of departure. Hence arise two entirely different ways of philosophising, radically opposed to one another, according as one proceeds from the consideration of man to that of the world, or on the contrary from the knowledge of the world to that of man. Although, when arrived at full maturity, true philosophy must inevitably tend to conciliate these two antagonistic methods, their contrast is that of the two great philosophic paths, the theological and the positive, which our intelligence follows successively. The true spirit of theological or metaphysical philosophy consists in adopting as a principle, for the explanation of the external world, our immediate feelings touching human phenomena, while on the contrary positive philosophy is always characterised by the subordination of the conception of man to that of the external world. Whatever be the manifest incompatibility of these two philosophies, as evidenced by the fact that one has succeeded the other, this incompatibility has no other origin, nor any other basis, than a simple matter of order between two equally indispensable mentations. By giving precedence to the consideration of man over that of the world, as the human mind had of necessity to do in the beginning, it was inevitably led to attribute all phenomena to *wills*, first natural, and then supernatural, and this is the theological system. The study of the external world was alone able to produce and develop the great idea of the laws of nature, that indispensable basis of the positive philosophy, which gradually extended itself to phenomena of ever greater irregularity, and in the end attained to complete generalisation by being applied to man and to society.

The various theological and metaphysical schools, in spite of the innumerable profound disagreements by which they cancel one another out, are all agreed on this one point, that the primary consideration is that of man, and in relegating to second place that of the external world, which they generally neglect. In the same way there is no more outstanding characteristic of positivistic study than its tendency to base the real study of man on a previous knowledge of the external world.

This is a question of high philosophy which we cannot treat here, but it was necessary to give a general view which would at once reveal the spirit of positive philosophy, and indicate at the same time its chief imperfection as it is at present scientifically constituted. If it were a question of any other science, what we have said would only affect its place on the encyclopaedic ladder, not its essential nature. But where physiology is concerned, a general subordination to the science of the external world constitutes the very foundation of positivity. This long time past people have been vainly accumulating a multitude of facts, more or less well analysed, in the study of man; whereby the primitive style of philosophising has been necessarily maintained, from the very fact that this study was always looked on as isolated from inorganic nature. Physiology began to acquire a truly scientific character, and to extricate itself thoroughly from theological and metaphysical domination at the time —almost in our own day—when vital phenomena came to be regarded as subject to general laws, of which they are simply the modifications. This revolution is now irreversible, if incomplete, however unsuccessful have been recent attempts to render positive the study of the most complex and peculiar physiological phenomena, and especially that of the nervous and cerebral functions. The so-called independence of general laws attributed to living bodies, and still loudly proclaimed at the beginning of this century by the great Bichat himself, is no longer openly maintained except by metaphysicians. There are the beginnings of a feeling for the true speculative point of view from which life must be studied, but they are still so feeble that they have not brought about any real change in the ancient system by which biology is cultivated, especially not in the preliminary studies which continue to be as a rule independent of mathematical and inorganic philosophy, those true sources of the scientific spirit, and only solid foundation for an entire positivity in the study of life.

Thus there is no fundamental science for which the philosophic enterprise of these lectures can have so much meaning as for biology, for they will define its nature, up till now uncertain, and never the subject of open and rational discussion.

To remove the study of living bodies from the various metaphysical influences by which essential conceptions continue to be so greatly distorted, is not our sole purpose. We have another no less important duty, that of protecting the scientific originality of this subject, continually exposed as it has been in the past to the encroachments of inorganic philosophy, which tends to make it a mere adjunct of its own scientific domain. For almost a century biology has been trying to establish itself within the hierarchy of the fundamental sciences, and has been pulled hither and thither between metaphysics endeavouring to retain it, and physiology tending to absorb it, between the spirit of Stahl[31] and that of Boerhaave.[32] This tug of war, which is still in evidence, though fortunately greatly mitigated, can only cease when the character of biological science is examined in the light of the highest positive philosophy, whose rule alone will ensure that the study of living bodies follows unhesitatingly the path marked out for it by its true nature.

The extreme complexity of physiological phenomena compared with those of inorganic nature, sufficiently explains the relative defects of biological research, if we add the fact, itself a consequence of the complexity, that this class of research is quite recent. The complexity, as we showed in our prolegomena, removes the hope of biological science ever at any time achieving progress equal to what can be realised in the simpler and more general departments of natural philosophy. At the same time candour compels us to admit that in spite of its present sad state the study of living bodies is already farther advanced than one might expect from the irrational state of mind that generally prevails with regard to it. The pronounced influence that metaphysical or even theological philosophy continues to exercise on the popular mind in relation to this class of ideas too often leads to the search for those absolute and unverifiable notions which the human spirit has wisely given up this long time past as far as less complex phenomena are concerned. With singular, but entirely natural inconsistency, the same intelligence which when concerned with the simplest natural effects, recognises the inanity of any speculation on first causes and on the mode of production of phenomena, does not hesitate to raise these vain questions in the complex study of living bodies. For almost a century the best minds have agreed that physics should be excused from penetrating the mystery of weight, and content itself with revealing the laws by which it works; but that does not prevent sound physiology from being daily reproached with teaching nothing on the inner essence of life, of feeling and of thought. It is easy to see how through this metaphysical tendency the real imperfection of present day biology will come to be exaggerated. If we bring to the examination of this great science the same philosophic outlook as to previous parts of natural science, we shall recognise, I think, that though biology is of necessity more backward than any other science, it possesses on the subjects of positive research rational notions of very great value; in a word its scientific character is far less inferior than we supposed to that of the preceding sciences. Our estimate of these other sciences, as previously set forth in these lectures, will make it possible for us to determine the relative degree of perfection of biological science, when we come in the natural course of our analysis to make the comparison.

After this preamble, let us consider biology under the same philosophic aspects as the other fundamental sciences. We must determine its object precisely, and delimit, as strictly as possible, the field of its research.

It is the spontaneous development of our intelligence no doubt which tends to decide without any other motive the passage of each branch of our knowledge from the theological and afterwards the metaphysical state to the positive. But our speculative faculties, even in the most eminent minds, are generally too sluggish for such progress to be anything but extremely slow, were it not fortunately accelerated by an external, permanent and unavoidable stimulus. The entire history of the human mind shows not a single example at all important of this decisive revolution being really accomplished by the only rational means: the logical sequence of abstract conceptions. Among the auxiliary influences which speed up the natural progress of human reason, the impetus given by the need to apply science should be noted as the most general, the most direct and the most effective. For this reason most philosophers have said that every science was born of a corresponding art, an exaggerated maxim, no doubt, but which contains a good deal of truth, if we restrict it to the separation of science from the universal primitive system of theological or metaphysical philosophy, that product of the first spontaneous flight of our intelligence. It is very true that in every department of knowledge the formation of the true sciences has been, if not determined, at least accelerated by the reaction of the arts on them, either by reason of positive data with which they furnish them involuntarily, or in virtue of their tendency to draw speculative research in the direction of real and verifiable problems, and to bring out forcefully the radical inanity of theological or metaphysical conceptions.

But although the link between sciences and arts has long been of prime importance for the sciences, and although it continues to influence their daily progress much for the better, the irrational way in which this relationship has almost always been handled has tended to slow down the advance of speculative knowledge once that knowledge has achieved a certain development, through the subjection of theory to an over-close connection with practice. However limited be human capacity for speculation, it has a wider range than the capacity for action, so that it would be quite absurd to constrain the first to following in the wake of the second; it should be the other way round. The rational domains of science and art are quite distinct, though philosophically connected; to the first belongs knowledge, and therefore prediction, to the second power, and consequently action. In its nascent positivity, no doubt, every science derives from an art, but it is quite as certain that it cannot acquire the speculative condition suitable to its nature, nor achieve a consistent and rapid development until it is understood in itself and freely cultivated, quite apart from any idea of art. This is an indefeasible necessity, as can easily be verified in the case of every one of the fundamental sciences whose nature we have defined. The great Archimedes felt this necessity keenly when, in his naïf sublimity he excused himself to posterity for having momentarily applied his genius to practical inventions. But as regards the mathematical sciences and even astronomy the proof that science must be separated from art is little appreciated today, as the formation of these sciences is so far back in the past. As for physics, however, and above all chemistry, the birth of which we might be said to have witnessed, everyone feels that their relation to the arts has been essential to their first steps, and at the same time that their subsequent separation from the arts contributed to the rapidity of their progress. It is to the labour of art that we owe, for example, the first series of chemical facts: but the immense development of chemistry during the last half century must certainly be attributed in great part to the purely speculative character it has assumed, in complete independence of any art.

These considerations apply particularly to physiological science, and would tend to correct its present philosophical constitution. There is no science whose progress has been more tied to the development of the corresponding art than history shows biology to have been, linked as it was to the medical art; the extreme complexity of the science, and the overwhelming importance of the art easily explain this intimate connection. It is in virtue of the growing needs of practical medicine, and of the data that medicine necessarily accumulated on the principal vital phenomena that physiology began to detach itself from the common trunk of primitive philosophy, and to form itself more and more in accordance with positive ideas. Thus had it not been for an art's powerful and fortunate influence, physiology would probably still be at those academic dissertations, half literary, half metaphysical, with here and there a few scattered observations of a purely episodic nature, of which it consisted scarcely more than a century ago. The great importance of this relationship for the effective development up to the present of physiology cannot be called in question. Nevertheless there is reason to believe that biological science today has arrived—like the other sciences before it—at the period of full maturity when, in the interest of further progress, it must soar into pure speculation, freed from adherence either to the medical or to any other art. The rational co-ordination of the system of human knowledge imposes such a condition, without which our fundamental conceptions would necessarily have a bastard character, greatly hindering their natural development. Only, when all the speculative sciences have definitely acquired the abstract character proper to each of them, it must be understood that philosophy will be concerned to attach the system of arts to that of the sciences, in accordance with rational conceptions specially adapted to this purpose, and whose nature has not yet fully emerged. The operation would be premature at this date, as the fundamental sciences are not yet completely formed. With regard to physiology, our principal care must be to isolate it from medicine and to establish the originality of its scientific character, by laying down the conditions of organic philosophy, as a sequel to inorganic philosophy. Since Haller[33] this important separation has been visibly taking place, above all in Germany and France, but it is far from being so complete as to enable biology to launch itself into the free realm of abstraction. Not only does its prolonged connection with medical art give to physiological research a character of immediate and specialised application tending to narrow it, and even to prevent it from acquiring the generality that it needs if it is to assume its true rank in the system of natural philosophy; but it also prevents biological science from being cultivated by the intelligences most capable of guiding it. The result is that except for a few brilliant exceptions, this important study has hitherto been abandoned to the doctors, whom the absorbing nature of their principal occupation and as a rule the great deficiency in their education must render unfit for such a task. Although the scientific world is in general far removed from the rational constitution it could quite easily acquire, the first condition of its existence has been sufficiently fulfilled in the case of the other fundamental sciences, of which each one is specially consigned to minds that devote themselves to it exclusively. Physiology alone is still an exception to this law: it has not even a definite place in the best constituted scientific bodies. Its great importance and its overwhelming difficulty make it impossible to believe that such inconsistency is normal and permanent. Those who would reject as absurd the idea of entrusting astronomy to navigators will in the end find it strange that biological study should be the leisure occupation of doctors; one is not more unreasonable than the other. An organisation of research so fundamentally defective bears undoubted witness to the uncertain notions we have today on the nature of physiological science, and at the same time it must contribute to prolonging the uncertainty which has produced it.

The only excuse for such confusion is the fear that theory, given over to its own free impulse, would lose sight of the needs of practice, and that its separation from practice would slow down improvement in the latter. But any person of good sense would see that science could contribute still less to the progress of arts if these clung to it, and opposed its true development. Besides, the striking and unanimous experience of the other fundamental sciences must in the end dissipate any serious misgiving. For it is since each one of them has been entirely consecrated to the most complete discovery possible of the laws of nature, without any intention of meeting our needs, and has thus been able to make important and rapid progress, that they have brought about great improvements in the corresponding art, which if they had been sought directly would have stifled its speculative enterprise. The relationship of theory and practice which has long been quite striking in astronomy, has become in our day very perceptible in physics, and above all in chemistry which, after it was entirely separated from the arts, brought about more improvements in them than in all the time it was attached to them. Why should things be different in the sphere of vital phenomena? Nevertheless it is still important, in this kind of research as in any other, to organise more certain and efficient relations between science and art than those spontaneous reactions which always seem to have something fortuitous about them. But there can be no clear and rational relation except between previously distinct and independent conceptions.

The theory of philosophic classifications, designed not only to aid memory but to perfect scientific combinations, is employed by any and every one of the fundamental sciences, which all require the exercise of every faculty of our intelligence. With regard to this I have already established in my first volume,[34] that mathematical science, the prime source of all the other sciences, offers a decisive application of the true theory of classification in the grand conception of the illustrious Monge,[35] too little appreciated by the ordinary run of geometrists, that surfaces fall naturally into families according to their mode of generation, a conception in which one recognises not only the superior purity and perfection that would naturally be associated with mathematics, but the philosophical characteristics of sound zoological and botanical method. Yet however true these remarks of inorganic philosophy and especially of chemical science, one must admit that the principal development of the art of classification is reserved for biological science. Obviously each of our mental activities must be specially developed by the fundamental positive study that most urgently requires its use, and presents to it at the same time the widest field. Now no science favours the development of classifications as directly or completely as biology. First of all in none could the need of rational classification be felt so keenly, not only in view of the immense multiplicity of distinct yet analogous beings that biological speculation must embrace; but also through the necessity of organising the exact and systematic comparison between these beings which constitutes, as we have seen, the most powerful tool of investigation where living bodies are concerned, a tool whose application obviously demands a previously established biological hierarchy at least in its general features. Secondly, those same characteristics that render philosophical classification almost indispensable, tend also to facilitate it and evoke it. Minds that are strangers to biological philosophy will look on the number and complexity of the subjects to be classed as so many obstacles to systematic arrangement. But we should rather regard the very multiplicity of living beings with the extreme diversity of their interrelations as rendering their classification easier and more perfect, for it enables us to seize more spontaneous, extensive and verifiable scientific analogies. This philosophic law[36] is so sure that, precisely because of the great variety and complexity of animal organisms, which give the art of classification more of a hold, the classification of animals is very superior to that of plants. In mathematics, the as yet so imperfect classification of curves, and even of plane curves, contrasts with the perfect systematisation of the vast number of surfaces.[37] This is because the surfaces, by their multiplicity and complexity enable us to establish clearer and better defined comparisons, either geometrical or analytical, than those arising from the too restricted and above all too homogeneous material of curves and especially of plane curves. It can therefore be readily understood that the very nature of the difficulties peculiar to biological science must both demand and ensure a marked development in classification.

Here then is the source to which the philosopher must come if he would obtain an exact knowledge of this important art, nor can such knowledge be obtained in any other way, whatever be the subject to which one intends to apply it. Among the geometrists, astronomers, physicists and even chemists, those whose minds, however eminent, have never passed the bounds of their own studies are noted for strange aberrations with regard to fundamental conditions of classification, whether it be in the formation of natural groups, or in their co-ordination, the two aspects of the theory, and especially in the subordination of characteristics, which constitutes its essential tool. In these three important respects biologists alone among scientists usually have clear and positive notions. It is in their school that other positive philosophers can learn to cultivate the skill of classification with success, and introduce it into the other fundamental sciences, some of which need it in various ways. Chemists need it as an education in logic,[38] if they are to achieve the fundamental improvement necessary to the constitution of their science. Although the genius of Monge made instinctive use of the principle of classification in his chief mathematical conception, without his work's showing any trace of the indirect influence on his intelligence of biological considerations, I do not hesitate to say that his genius, a genius not exclusively mathematical, since he discovered in so original a fashion the true composition of water, was excited by this subject and even drawn to it by the great philosphical discussions on the question that had not ceased to echo round him on all sides, ever since the great work of Bernard de Jussieu[38a] and Linnaeus[38b] had made its tremendous impact.

Thus the positive study of living bodies leads inevitably to the art of classification and of comparison. These two activities ought to attract the attention of every philosophic spirit, even apart from the keen scientific interest excited by the important knowledge that biology brings. It may be affirmed without exaggeration that any intelligence unacquainted with biological study has received an imperfect education, since several of the fundamental faculties which together constitute the positivist power of the human spirit have remained idle. Thus it is a principle of my philosophy that the universal positive method, although always unchanging, cannot be truly known except by the attentive study of all the subjects of the scientific hierarchy, for each one of those subjects possesses the property of developing some one of the great logical procedures of which the method is composed. Although the simplest sciences are independent of the more particular and complex ones, which indeed are dependent on them, we see here unmistakably the logical reaction that the less perfect (but more complex) sciences can have on the more prefect (because simpler) sciences, contributing to the improvement of these through the rational faculties that they especially are called on to cultivate. This fact illustrates both the subordination that constitutes the true scientific hierarchy, and the general *consensus* from which the unity of the system derives. Once these notions have been properly gone into, it will be easy for me to demonstrate how profoundly irrational is the mode of isolation still governing our positive studies, a mode as harmful to their progress as to their collective action on the intellectual government of humanity.

It now remains to consider from the scientific point of view the philosophic properties of biological science, that is, the part it has to play in emancipating and developing human reason, not only through the positive method, but also the positive spirit, of which this great science is destined to be the indispensable ally.

Here we can verify and apply the general law that I established when examining the last two branches of inorganic philosophy, especially chemistry. This law is that the positive study of any order of phenomena tends directly to destroy all the essential conceptions of theological philosophy by two means, complementary to one another, the rational prediction of phenomena and their deliberate modification by man, the latter possibility becoming progressively wider in scope, while the former becomes less perfect, as the phenomena become more complex. Thus it is seen in an equally irrefutable manner, though by means of two different procedures, that the diverse events of the real world are not ruled by supernatural wills, but by natural laws. Biological science confirms the efficacy of this double approach.

Although its complexity must hamper the development of prediction, positive biology has its own way of manifesting its radical incompatibility with theological fictions and metaphysical entities. This emerges from the analysis of the conditions, organic or external, indispensable to each act of existence of a living body, an analysis which is the object of all anatomical or physiological study. The prima facie opposition of this kind of research to every theological or metaphysical conception is particularly noticeable today in the theories relating to intellectual and affective phenomena, where positivism is so recent, and which, together with the social phenomena that derive from them, are still the subject, in the mind of the vulgar, of a struggle between positive philosophy and ancient philosophy. These are phenomena whose regular incidence, because of their highly complex nature, demands the co-operation of a great variety of conditions, external as well as internal, so that the positive study of them makes obvious even to the rudest intelligence the sheer inanity of the abstract explanations emanating from theological or metaphysical philosophy: thus accounting for the aversion which this study is privileged to inspire in the different theological and metaphysical sects. The public could not but be struck by the vain efforts of the latter to reconcile the play of supernatural influences or psychological entities in the production of moral phenomena with the close dependence of these phenomena on the environment and the organism, as revealed or indicated by the work of modern anatomists and physiologists. Such are the services that the development of biological science has rendered to the establishment of universal positive doctrine, for it has put it in possession of that part of the intellectual domain where ancient philosophy had thought to find its surest support.

The tendency of sound anatomical and physiological studies to positivise our most complex conceptions becomes still more evident if we consider vital phenomena under the second philosophical aspect indicated above, that is, as eminently modifiable. The extensive co-operation of heterogeneous conditions which the actualisation of these phenomena requires, allows us to modify them, more than any others, by intervention, to which most of these conditions are by their nature accessible, whether they have to do with the organism itself, or with its ambiance. Now our capacity for upsetting these phenomena, for suspending and even destroying them is here so striking that it must immediately lead one to reject any idea of theological or metaphysical government. Like prediction, of which it is but a more individualised prolongation, this new capacity of positive biology is more pronounced as touching moral phenomena, the most modifiable of all organic phenomena. The most obstinate psychologist could not persist in maintaining the sovereign independence of his intellectual entities, if he reflected for example that merely to reverse for a moment his normal vertical stance would be enough to oppose an insurmountable obstacle to the course of his speculations.

In these two ways biological doctrine sufficiently compensates, antitheologically and antimetaphysically, for its necessary inferiority in the systematic prediction of corresponding phenomena. Yet although we must regret that this rational divination is so imperfect in biology, we should note that it need be very little developed to produce a philosophic effect. For when, though only in a few clear-cut cases, biological events take place in strict conformity with the predictions of science, as often happens even today, within the limits of variability proper to the nature of the phenomena, the good sense of the vulgar cannot help recognising that these phenomena are, like all the rest, subject to unvarying natural laws, whose necessary complication is the only cause of the failure, on other occasions, of scientific forecasts. Such a philosophic conclusion would be impossible only if scientific prediction were always at fault; and this the most radical detractors of anatomical and physiological science cannot now claim.

Apart from its philosophic influence, similar to that of the other fundamental sciences, only more marked in certain respects and less in others, the positive study of living bodies has carried on from the beginning a special struggle against the general system of theological and metaphysical philosophy, the issue of which has been to transform an ancient dogma into a new principle, as real as the dogma was vain, as fruitful as it was sterile. Each branch of inorganic philosophy has already manifested a similar activity in some more or less important aspect. Chemistry substitutes for the primitive idea of the creation and destruction of matter the idea of decomposition and recomposition.[39] Astronomy[40] shows us the order of the world as the interaction of the principal masses that compose it, thus utterly overthrowing the hypothesis of final causes and providential government. Biological science, of its nature in deeper philosophic harmony with astronomical science than is any other science, now arrives to complete the demonstration with regard to more specialised and complex phenomena. Attacking in its turn and in its own fashion the elementary dogma of final causes, it has gradually transformed it into the fundamental principle of the conditions of existence, whose development and systematisation belong to biology, although in itself this principle is essentially applicable to all orders of natural phenomena.

It is true that the irrational preparatory education of most anatomists and physiologists in our day leads them too often to employ this principle in a distorted form that resembles the very theological dogma it has replaced. The spirit of biological science would certainly lead us to believe that the very fact that such and such an organ is part of a living being means that it contributes in a definite, though perhaps as yet unknown, manner to the acts that make up the existence of that being: which amounts to there being no organ without a function, any more than function without an organ. Since the development of the exact correlation between ideas of organisation and ideas of life constitutes the typical aim of all biological research,[41] such an attitude is eminently appropriate and indeed indispensable. But it must be admitted that this tendency to regard every organ as necessarily exercising a certain action degenerates very frequently into blind, antiscientific admiration of the actual mode in which the various vital phenomena are produced. Such an attitude, obviously inherited from theology, is in direct opposition to every sound interpretation of the principle of conditions of existence, according to which, when we have observed any function, we are not surprised that anatomical analysis reveals in the organism a statical condition proper to securing the accomplishment of this function. An irrational and sterile admiration, by persuading us that every act of the organism operates in the most perfect way, tends to cramp biological speculation; it often leads to wonder and applause at complexities that are quite obviously harmful. Philosophers who have most insisted on these wonders have not noticed that they were going in the direction exactly contrary to the religious end they had proposed themselves, since they were assigning human wisdom as rule and limit to divine wisdom, which, thus challenged must inevitably find itself more than once decidedly inferior. Although our imagination is necessarily confined in all matters to the sphere of actual observation, and although in consequence it is impossible for us to imagine organisms that are really new, it seems to me that scientific genius is today, even in biology developed and emancipated enough for us to imagine, within the limits of biological law, organisms that differ notably from those that we know, and that might certainly be superior from a given point of view, without such improvements being balanced by equivalent imperfections. This potentiality seems to me so undeniable that I have not hesitated in the past to propose the systematic employment of such scientific fictions as capable of bringing about a real, though purely incidental improvement, in the elements of biological philosophy.

In spite of the blame that may attach on this head to the present habits of nearly all biologists, the basic aptitude of biological science for bringing out fully the philosophic principle of conditions of existence cannot be denied. No other science could make such extensive and decisive use of this great principle, for, of its nature, biological science is continually concerned to establish an exact harmony between means and end, besides which the inherent difficulty of the subject makes the assistance of that principle indispensable. Social science is, after biology, the science that allows and even demands the most complete and important application of it, and is destined to develop it fully, while at the same time demonstrating its efficiency. Future application is therefore an additional motive for pointing out here and now the philosophic origin of the idea. Moreover it applies to every order of phenomenon without exception, since none can exist in which is not realised the capital distinction established by M. de Blainville[42] between the statical and dynamical analysis of a subject. The philosophic principle of conditions of existence is simply the idea that there is necessary harmony between these two analyses. And if this principle is specially adapted to the nature of biological science, it can be for no other reason than the importance and character that this double analysis assumes in biology.

Such, then, from a doctrinal point of view, are the philosophic properties which belong specially and unequivocally to positive biology. From this cursory examination of them, we can see that the positive spirit cannot be completely developed, in all its essential aspects, in those who have not properly studied the new aspect that it assumes in the science of living bodies—quite apart from the direct disadvantages of such ignorance. Also, in view of the defects and lacunae of the present scientific education, even when it is least irrational, the spectacle so frequently met with of minds quite eminent on certain specific points, and almost puerile on a great many others not less important, should not surprise. Although several philosophers have attempted to erect this anomaly into a principle, there is no doubt that it is simply the result of the kind of intellectual interregnum induced by a slow and difficult revolution, that of humanity passing from theological and metaphysical philosophy to a homogeneous, complete and exclusive system of positive philosophy, whose universal dominion will finally eliminate such disparities.

VIII

Preliminary Considerations
on the Necessity of Social Physics
as suggested by the Analysis of the
Present State of Society [43]

In each of the five preceding parts of our study philosophic exploration
has rested on a truly scientific state of the sciences, pre-existing and unan-
imously accepted, whose constitution, although only more or less complete up to the present, even with regard to the least complex and most
closely studied phenomena, satisfies the conditions of positivity in all
cases, including the most recent and most imperfect, and needs only an
effort of rational appreciation, guided by incontestable rules, to desig-
nate the principal improvements yet to be made in order to detach real
science from every indirect influence of ancient philosophy. Unfortunately this does not apply to social phenomena, the theory of which has
not yet issued from the theologico-metaphysical prison, to which thinkers appear to condemn it, as a fatal exception, for all time. The philosophic enterprise that I have initiated, without changing its nature or its
goal, now becomes more difficult and more audacious, and assumes a
new character: instead of estimating and improving, our present task is
to create a whole order of scientific conceptions that no previous philosopher has so much as outlined, and which had never even been glimpsed
before as a possibility.

Such creation, even if happily accomplished, cannot at once lift this
branch of natural philosophy, dealing with the most complex phenomena, to the rational level of the various fundamental sciences, even of
those whose development is least advanced. All that we can attempt in
our day is to bring its foundations so far forward that intelligent people
will realise the possibilty of cultivating social science in the manner of
the positive sciences; we can also see to it that its foundations are solidly
established and its philosophic character defined. That will be sufficient
for our most urgent intellectual needs, and even for the most imperious
demands of social practice, especially today. Even when reduced to these

dimensions, the enterprise is still too vast to be properly treated in lectures concerned with the positive philosophy as a whole. The new science can only figure here as an indispensable element, whose importance, it is true, merits its eventual predominance. I shall later expound all my ideas on this great subject in a special Treatise on political philosophy[44], with all the necessary explanations, and not without due comment on possible applications to the present transitional state of society. Here I must necessarily confine myself to the most general considerations, adhering as scrupulously as possible to the strictly scientific point of view, and not aiming at any other effect than the reduction to order of our intellectual anarchy, true source of our moral and political anarchy —with which latter subject I shall not here be directly concerned.

But the extreme novelty of the doctrine would render these scientific considerations almost unintelligible, and certainly inefficacious, if my exposition did not become, with regard to a science I am endeavouring to create, much more explicit and more specific[45] than it needed to be in previous lectures,[46] where I could suppose the reader to be sufficiently familiar with the basis of the subject. That is why, before opening up the subject methodically, I must devote this chapter[47] to defining the significance of this philosophic departure, and the inanity of previous attempts at it.

The great and fundamental lacuna left in the system of positive philosophy by the deplorable state of prolonged infantilism in which social science still languishes, should suffice to demonstrate to any philosopher the necessity of an enterprise that will stamp the human mind, already prepared for it in so many ways, with the character of unity of method and homogeneity of doctrine, indispensable to its full speculative development and to the nobility and energy of its practical activity. But however weighty this enterprise, which in truth embraces all others, the point of view in politics today is too narrow and too superficial for even the best minds to be able to grasp its real meaning straight away and to derive from it sufficient motivation to endure the long and painful contention that its gradual accomplishment would involve. In its first stages no science can be cultivated or conceived apart from its corresponding art, as I showed in the seventh chapter,[48] where we learned that the more complex the order of phenomena, the more intense and prolonged is this connection. If biological science, in spite of its advanced state, still appears too closely attached to the medical art, should we be surprised that statesmen are inclined to regard as a mere intellectual exercise any sociological speculation that is not immediately linked to practical effect? However blind such an attitude, it will be obstinately persisted in as the best safeguard against vague and chimerical utopias, although experience has abundantly proved its uselessness in this capacity, for it has not been able to prevent a daily flood of the most extravagant illusions. But I must allow for what is at bottom reasonable in this puerile prejudice and will devote this lecture to preliminary explanations of the link between the institution of what I call *social physics* and the deplorable ills of present society, as manifest to every thinking mind. From these elucidatory remarks every real statesman will understand, I hope, that the great labour I have set myself, although it does not pretend to any special immediate application, is undeniably of the greatest utility, without which indeed it would not merit the attention of those who are rightly absorbed by the obligation in which they find themselves of resolving the frightening revolutionary tension of modern society, an obligation every day more pressing, and apparently every day more difficult to discharge.

From the lofty standpoint that we have now attained,[49] the social situation is seen in full light as characterised quite simply by the most widespread though temporary anarchy of the intellectual system, in an interregnum following on the increased decadence of the theologico-metaphysical philosophy, now in the last stages of decrepitude, coupled with the continuous but still incomplete development of positive philosophy, up till now too narrow, too specialised and too timid to take possession of the spiritual government of humanity. To this situation must be traced the origin of that vacillating and contradictory state of all the great social ideas which so disrupts moral and political life: but here we perceive also the system of operations, some philosophic, some political, which must gradually deliver society from its present fatal tendency to immediate dissolution, and lead it to a new organisation at once more progressive and more consistent than that which rested on theological philosophy. Such is the proposition which will emerge as proved, I hope, from the treatment that follows,[50] and of which I will give here a preliminary sketch, whose purpose is to demonstrate in the political schools most opposed to one another an equal impotence, and the absolute necessity of bringing to these sterile and stormy struggles a new spirit capable, once its ascendancy has been gradually established, of guiding our society towards the final goal of that revolutionary movement that has been developing within it for three centuries.

Order and progress, which antiquity regarded as irreconcilable, constitute, from the nature of modern civilisation, two equally necessary conditions whose combination is at once the principal difficulty and the principal strength of every political system. No real order can now be established, and above all can now endure, if it is not fully compatible with progress; and no great progress can be effected, unless it tends to consolidate order. Everything that reveals the exclusive preoccupation with one of these fundamental needs at the expense of the other, arouses instinctive repugnance in modern societies, as mistaking the nature of the scientific problem. Therefore positive politics will be characterised in practice by so natural an aptitude for fulfilling this double function that order and progress will appear as the two necessary inseparable aspects of the same principle, in accordance with an essential property gradually realised in the various classes of ideas that have become positive. The ensuing lectures will I hope leave no doubt as to the possibility of extending this general attribute of the scientific spirit to politics, for that spirit always presents the conditions of interconnection and advance as originally identical. For the present it will be enough to indicate rapidly the view that real notions of order and of progress must, in social physics, be as strictly indivisible as in biology are those of organisation and of life, from which indeed in the eyes of science they derive.

But the present state of the political world is still very far from this reconciliation. The principal defect of our social situation is the complete cleavage between the ideas of order and those of progress, thus seen as profoundly antipathetic. In the half century during which the revolutionary crisis of modern societies has been developing, one cannot disguise the fact that all the great efforts in favour of order have been guided by a retrograde spirit, and the principal efforts for progress by radically anarchical doctrines. In this respect the mutual reproaches of the extreme parties are unfortunately only too justified. This is the vicious circle in which modern society turns, and from which there can be no escape but in a doctrine equally progressive and hierarchical. The observations on this important subject that I am about to make are applicable to all the European nations, which have suffered a common, and even simultaneous disorganisation, although in different degrees and with different modifications, which moreover cannot be reorganised independently of one another, though they would be reorganised in a certain sequence. Nevertheless we should have French society particularly in view, not only because the revolutionary movement is here more completely and more obviously manifest, but also because, in spite of appearances to the contrary, French society is better prepared than any other for a true reorganisation.

Whatever be the variety at first sight existing between opinions that are politically active, analysis shows that on the contrary they are confined to a very narrow sphere, since they really all consist of two orders of radically opposed ideas, mixed in varying proportions, the second order being the simple negation of the first, without offering any new dogma of its own. The present state of society only becomes intelligible when one perceives in it the final stage of the general struggle during the last three centuries to demolish the old political system. Now we see that if for fifty years the inevitable decomposition of that system has made more and more inevitable the founding of a new system, the still undefined feeling of this need has not brought forth any really original conception appropriate to the grand design: so that theoretical ideas have remained very inferior to practical necessities, which in a normal state of the social organism they usually anticipate, thus preparing regular and peaceable satisfaction. Although the principal movement in politics has had to change its nature entirely, and from purely critical become distinctly organic, as an inevitable consequence of the immense philosophic lacuna it has continued to be directed by the ideas which had guided the various parties during the long-drawn-out previous struggle, and with which all minds had familiarised themselves. Defenders and assailants of the old system have alike attempted to convert their old weapons of war into instruments of reorganisation without suspecting their ineptitude for this task, the very nature of which rejects both kinds of principle with equal energy, as being the one too regressive and the other purely critical.

It cannot be denied that such is the deplorable intellectual state of the political world today. All ideas of order are borrowed exclusively from the antique doctrine of the theological and military system, especially in its Catholic and feudal form; a doctrine which, from the point of view of this course represents the theological state of social science: in the same way all ideas of progress continue to be deduced exclusively from that purely negative philosophy which, issuing from Protestantism, achieved its final form and full development in the last century, and whose social applications today constitute the metaphysical state of politics. The various classes of society adopt one or other of these two opposed directives according as they feel more keenly the need for conservatism or the need for reform. Hence the profound cleavage between the two different sides of the social question, as a result of which the moves of both sides cancel one another out. For as each fresh aspect of the need of our time is revealed by the march of events, one notes that the invariable reaction of the retrograde school is to propose as universal panacea the restoration of some corresponding part of the old political system; while the no less invariable response of the critical school is to attribute the trouble to what survives of this old system, with the inevitable corollary that all regulative authority should be suppressed. It is true that one rarely meets with either of these doctrines today in its pure and unadulterated form, which tends to survive only in speculative minds. But the monstrous alloy that people are attempting to make today of these two incompatible principles, whose varying degrees in the combination correspond to the different shades of political opinion, cannot possess any virtue other than the elements that compose it, and only tends to promote their mutual neutralisation. In the interest therefore of a clear and correct analysis, it is necessary to consider theological and metaphysical politics separately, and only afterwards their mutual antagonism and the vain attempts at combining them.

However pernicious theological politics be today, no true philosopher can ever forget that the formation and development of modern societies took place under its tutelage. But it is none the less true that for the last three centuries its influence among the most advanced nations has been essentially retrograde, in spite of the partial services that it has still been able to render. There is no need to spend time discussing this doctrine, whose total inadequacy discloses itself more and more with every passing day. Only the absence of any real views on social reorganisation can explain the absurd project of buttressing the social order with a political system which proved unable to maintain itself in the face of intellectual and social progress. The historical analysis[51] of the successive developments which gradually brought about the dissolution of the Catholic and feudal system demonstrates better than any argument that its decay is deep-seated and irreversible. The theological school seeks to explain the dissolution by almost fortuitous and quasi personal causes, out of all proportion with the immensity of the effects; or else, in its extremity, it has recourse to its usual subterfuge: supernatural explanation, turning that great series of events into a mysterious whim of Providence, which had taken it into its head to subject the social order to a period of trial, the time, duration and nature of which remain unexplained. The great modifications undergone by the theological and military system have tended to eliminate a regime to which the law of social evolution necessarily assigned a provisional, though strictly indispensable role. Obviously every effort to bring back this system, even if it has a momentary success, far from restoring society to a normal state, can only place it again in the situation that brought about the revolutionary crisis, obliging it to recommence still more violently the destruction of a regime which has long ceased to be compatible with its chief lines of progress. For these reasons I decline to enter into controversy on this subject, but I think it necessary to point out a philosophic aspect of the question that seems to offer the simplest and surest criterion of the value of any social doctrine, and is particularly decisive against theological politics.

From the merely logical point of view, the fundamental problem of our social reorganisation seems to me to amount to this one requirement: that of constructing a political doctrine of sufficient rationality to be always, in action, consistent with its own principles. None of the existing doctrines satisfies, even by remote approximation, this great intellectual condition. All include as indispensable elements numerous contradictions on the greater number of their important points. It is here that their inadequacy is most clearly discerned. It can be laid down as a principle that the doctrine which, on the various fundamental questions of politics, furnishes solutions in exact agreement, without the progress of practical application leading to any contradiction, ought to be recognised as fit to reorganise society, since such an intellectual reorganisation will primarily consist in re-establishing a genuine and lasting harmony in the profoundly troubled system of our social ideas. Even if such a regeneration were at first accomplished only in one single intelligence (and it must necessarily begin in this way), its speedy generalisation would be assured; for the number of minds does not augment the essential difficulties of intellectual agreement and can only influence the time necessary for its realisation. I shall take care to point out, as opportunity offers, the superiority of positive philosophy in this respect, for once it is applied to social phenomena it will necessarily bind together the various orders of humanistic ideas much more completely than has ever been possible by any other means. This is the chief rule that right from the beginning of my work on political philosophy has guided me in estimating my progress towards the conception of a genuine social doctrine.

It is from theological politics that one would expect to obtain the perfect fulfilment of this logical condition, whose fundamental difficulties seem completely removed for any doctrine that limits itself to reproducing the past, and co-ordinating a system so clearly defined by long use and so fully developed in all essential parts, that it would appear necessarily immune from every grave inconsistency. And so the retrograde school generally boasts of the perfect coherence of its ideas as its characteristic attribute, as opposed to the frequent contradictions of the revolutionary school. Theological politics is indeed, for reasons easily understood, less inconsistent than metaphysical politics, yet every day one observes its irresistible tendency to fundamental concessions directly contrary to its principles. Nothing certainly is more calculated to expose the profound inanity of this doctrine than the fact that it does not even possess the quality most directly corresponding to its nature. The old political system reveals itself as so much in ruins that its most devoted partisans have completely lost the feeling for it. One can easily observe this not only in practice, but even in the speculation of minds, however eminent, unconsciously affected by the irresistible movement of their time. A few outstanding examples will suffice to show how easy it would be to dilate on this theme.

If, as logic demands, we considered the retrograde doctrine first of all in its relation to the essential elements of modern civilisation, demonstration of our point would be too easy. There can be no doubt that the development and the propagation of science, industry and even the fine arts have been the root though latent cause of decline for the theological and military system, whose occasional losses might have appeared reparable but for that. It is the ascendancy of the scientific spirit which preserves us today and will forever more preserve us from any resurrection of the theological spirit, whatever the aberrations in which the train of events may momentarily involve society: in the same way, in secular matters, which every day grow in scope and influence, it is certainly the most efficacious guarantee against any serious return of the military or feudal spirit. Although the political struggle is not yet declared between these two pairs of principles, such is at bottom its real nature. Now, in spite of this antagonism, did there ever exist in the modern development of theological politics any government or even any school so fully retrograde as to attempt or even to conceive the systematic repression of the sciences, the fine arts and industry? Except for a few isolated gestures, a few cranks who every now and then unwittingly disclose the fundamental incompatibility in question, is it not obvious that every government thinks itself in honour bound to encourage their progress? Such is the first inconsistency of retrograde politics, annulling by its own spontaneous day-to-day acts its general plans for the reconstruction of a past about which all statesmen have ceased to have any real feeling. Although this is the least apparent contradiction it should be seen as the most decisive, precisely because it is the most universal and instinctive. Did not Bonaparte himself, the man who in our day most clearly conceived and most vigorously pursued the politics of regression, quite apart from his other inconsistencies, set himself up, like many other chiefs of the same school, as the declared protector of industry, and fine arts and the sciences? Nor do the pure theorists escape this irresistible movement, although it is much easier for them to isolate themselves from it. One has only to analyse, for example, the repeated attempts of distinguished, and even eminent minds during the last two centuries to subordinate reason to faith, as the theological formula has it; one sees at once the radical contradiction in these attempts, where reason itself becomes the judge of her own submission, whose earnestness and duration depend entirely on variable and none too rigorous decisions. The most eminent thinker of the modern Catholic school, the illustrious De Maistre, bore striking, though involuntary testimony, to this necessity when, renouncing all theological apparatus, he endeavoured in his principal work to base the re-establishment of papal supremacy on mere historical and political, though in certain repects quite admirable arguments instead of simply commanding as of right divine, the only mode that is in harmony with the nature of such doctrine, and which such a thinker would not have hesitated to adopt if the general state of human intelligence had not neutralised it even in his mind. After such an example nothing more need be said.

Now let us consider more superficial inconsistencies, less profound, but more striking, for they show a flagrant contradiction between different parts of the same doctrine. Of this an attentive examination of the past will yield plenty of proof, since the demolition of the old political system was brought about chiefly by the violent antagonism between its principal powers. But confining ourselves for the moment to the present epoch, one notes every day in the different sections of the retrograde school a fundamental opposition to some point in their common doctrine. The most important instance is the strange unanimity with which this school agrees to forgo the principal basis of the Catholic and feudal system, viz., the division between the spiritual and temporal power, or what amounts to the same thing, its acquiescence in the subordination of the former to the latter. This is perhaps the one great political concept on which all parties today are agreed, although sound philosophy must regard it as a fatal aberration, but one that is momentarily unavoidable. In this regard kings are no less revolutionary than peoples; and priests themselves, not only in the different Protestant countries, but also in the nominally Catholic ones, have voluntarily ratified their political reduction to the ranks, as it were, either in view of some ignoble interest, or in a vain spirit of nationalism. How then can any of them dream of restoring a system of which they are so profoundly ignorant? For this restoration surely the reunion of the innumerable sects engendered by the decadence of Christianity would be an indispensable preliminary measure. Now the various schemes that have been launched in this direction, especially in Germany, by a few statesmen have always foundered on the obstinate determination of the various governments to retain supreme authority over the theological power, whose centralisation thus became impossible. On this score the rude inconsistencies of Bonaparte, in the midst of his vain efforts to establish the old political system, have been but a livelier reproduction of an example already familiar to us from other princes. When after his fall the kings undertook to institute in 'concert'[51a] a high European authority against any further inroads of revolution, it did not even occur to them to allow participation to the ancient spiritual authority, thus completely usurping its most legitimate function. So thorough-going was this usurpation that the Supreme Council of Europe was composed in great part of heretic heads of state, led by a schismatic prince, thus rendering papal membership impossible in the sight of all, as M. de Lamennais[52] remarked very justly before his conversion to the revolution. No doubt it is not only in our time that kings and even popes have subordinated the application of their religious principles to the immediate interests of their temporal dominion. But such inconsistencies, besides being more numerous and more flagrant today, are also more significant, for they show how the fundamental thinking of the old political system has ceased to sway even those who have ardently undertaken to restore it, as we have seen recently on many occasions, in Greece, in Poland, etc.

The spirit of disunion and disruption in the retrograde school has been frequently remarked by good observers, and has shown itself under varied but equally significant forms, whether in the partial and momentary triumphs of theological politics, or in its reverses. For a party as proud of its cohesion, the possession of power[53] should have meant the drawing together of all shades of opinion with the single aim of putting into practice a doctrine vaunted for its consistency and homogeneity. But have we not seen on the contrary over the years, the most violent schisms declaring themselves between the ever more numerous subdivisions of this triumphant party? In spite of the close and obvious interconnection of their causes, have not the partisans of Catholicism and of feudalism violently separated? And among these latter, have not the champions of aristocracy and of royalty engaged in combat? In a word has not this short period reproduced in little measure but unmistakably the manifestations of those very principles of discord and dissolution that developed through the centuries and finally brought about the ir- reversible ruin of the theological and feudal system? If, contrary to all probability, the retrograde party were again to come to power, I do not hesitate to affirm that, in spite of past experience, much more profound divisions would declare themselves, and much sooner, as a result of the ever-increasing incompatibility of the present state of society with the old political system, the conception of which tends to fade more and more in the minds of its most zealous partisans. The more scope theo- logical politics has for its development and application, the more it engenders irreconcilable subdivisions, disguised by a vague consent to its general principles as long as they stay in the speculative state: which is the usual symptom of a theory incompatible with the facts.

Since the memorable upheaval of 1830[54] put the retrograde party into opposition, its ramshackleness has revealed itself in another equally deci- sive way, one that has been before in evidence, but never so blatantly. During the last three centuries this party, when reduced to the defensive, more than once had recourse to the principles of revolution, undeterred by the risks of so monstrous a self-contradiction.[55] For instance, there was the spectacle of the Catholic school invoking the dogma of liberty of conscience, on behalf of its coreligionists in England, and especially in Ireland etc., while continuing to demand an energetic repression of Pro- testantism in France, Austria, etc. When in this century the kings in coa- lition wanted to rouse Europe against the domination of Bonaparte, they rendered solemn and unequivocal testimony to the impotence of the retrograde doctrine and to the power of the critical doctrine, by forego- ing in that crucial juncture any appeal to the former, and invoking the latter, which they thus tacitly recognised as alone capable of influencing civilised populations, while still continuing to cherish as their ultimate aim the restoration of the old political system![56] But the self-confessed decrepitude of theological politics can never have been as complete as we see it today, now that the retrograde school, endeavouring to systematise for its own purposes the entire body of critical doctrine, undertakes before our very eyes the resurrection of the Catholic feudal system by the aid of those very principles that served to destroy it, and does not hesitate to ratify their most anarchical consequences: which topsy-turvydom appears to be motivated by nothing more than a change of royal person- nel[57] without the nature of the main political direction having been in any way modified. Those who engineer this singular metamorphosis are considered to be the best brains of the party, whose political abdication, yea, moral degradation they thus sign and seal.

Such are the facts, and in view of them it scarcely seems necessary to waste more time demonstrating the impotence of a doctrine which, while fundamentally antipathetic to modern civilisation, contains so many elements directly contrary to its own basic principles, and cannot even rally its various partisans either in good fortune or in bad, although it offers them a definite type in the past, the contemplation of which would, one might think, prevent any serious deviation. De Maistre[58] is known to have reproached the great Bossuet,[58a] quite justifiably as far as the Gallican church is concerned,[59] with seriously mistaking the political nature of Catholicism; it would not be difficult, as I noted above, to point out inconsistencies, perhaps not analogous, but at least equivalent, in the famous author of the *Pope*. And modern society is to be reorganised according to a theory so decrepit that it has been understood this long time past even by its most illustrious interpreters!

In subjecting metaphysical politics in its turn to scrutiny, one should never lose sight of the fact that its doctrine, though exclusively critical, has long merited the name of progressive, as having dictated the main political reforms of the last three centuries, reforms which perforce were negative. This doctrine alone could effectively destroy the system that had guided the first developments of the human spirit and of society, but tended to perpetuate its nonage. So the political triumph of the metaphysical school was bound to provide an indispensable preparation for the social advent of the positive school, which alone can bring to an end the revolutionary epoch, by founding a system as progressive as it is orderly. Taken absolutely, the dogmas of critical doctrine can only have an anarchical character. Such critical dogmas, at source, within the framework of the old system, against which they were evidently instituted, establish a necessary though provisional condition for the introduction of a new political organisation, until the appearance of which the dangerous activity of the destructive instrument cannot and ought not to cease.

Through an inherent necessity of our feeble nature the passing from one social system to another can never be continuous and direct; it always entails, for a few generations at least, a more or less anarchic interregnum, of which the character and duration depend on the depth and extent of the change to be brought about: actual political progress in that period consists in the gradual demolition of the old system, whose principal foundations have in any case been already undermined. Such an upheaval is not only inevitable from the sheer groundswell that leads up to it, but even indispensable, either to allow the elements of the new system, which had been slowly and silently developing, to take on institutional form, or to stimulate reorganisation through the experience of the inconveniences of anarchy. Besides these motives, which we can easily appreciate today, there is another consideration of a purely intellectual nature which I must indicate here, and which will render more evident the necessity of upheaval. Without such preliminary destruction the human mind could not rise to a clear conception of the system to be established.

The feebleness of our intelligence, and the shortness of individual life compared with the slowness of social development keep our imagination, especially as regards political ideas, which are very complex, entirely dependent on the milieu in which we actually live. Even the most declared utopians, who believe they have emancipated themselves from every condition of reality, undergo, all unconsciously, this necessity, and faithfully reflect in their dreams the contemporary social state. *A fortiori*, the conception of a political system radically different from the one that surrounds us is quite beyond the bounds of our intelligence. The state of infantilism and empiricism in which social science has languished up to the present has no doubt contributed to the strengthening of this natural bondage. Thus, to consider the intellectual conditions alone of social revolution, a far advanced demolition of the previous political system is an indispensable preamble to it, without which the most eminent minds would not be able to perceive clearly the true nature of a new system concealed by the foreground spectacle of the ancient organisation, without which also, even if this difficulty were overcome, the public mind would not be sufficiently familiarised with a new conception to help by participation in its gradual realisation. The greatest intelligence of antiquity, Aristotle, was so dominated by his time that he could not so much as conceive a society that was not founded on slavery, although its final abolition began a few centuries after him. Such an example makes one realise how general is this bondage, also manifested by many notorious cases in the history of science, in regard to ideas much simpler than political ones.

IX

Fundamental Characteristics of the Positive Method in the Study of Social Phenomena [60]

In every science conceptions relating to method are by their nature inseparable from those relating to doctrine, as I established at the beginning of these lectures. Apart from practical application, the soundest notions on method are little more than a few incontrovertible but vague generalities, quite useless for guiding research to any real success, because they leave undefined the modifications that these uniform precepts must undergo in relation to a subject. The more complex and specialised the phenomena, the less possible it is to separate method from doctrine, since modifications then acquire more intensity and more importance. If up till now we have avoided the vain and sterile separation of method from doctrine with regard to the least complex of phenomena, it could not be otherwise when the greater complexity of the subject and its present non-positive state actually dictate this course. Especially in the study of social phenomena the true notion of method can only result from a rational conception of the science itself, so that the same principles appear to relate alternately to method and to doctrine, according to the viewpoint. Such a situation considerably augments the difficulties of outlining a science, especially the present one, where everything must be created at once. Nevertheless the possibility of satisfying the intellectual condition of combined doctrine and method will become clear as we proceed, and might already have been predicted when my theory on the general progress of the human spirit was seen to be scientific and logical by turns in response to the different requirements, and that with equal efficiency.

It is plain that in sociology as elsewhere, and even more than elsewhere, the positive method can only be appreciated through its uses, as they emerge, so that there cannot be any question here of a preliminary treatise on method in social physics. On the other hand before proceeding to an examination of sociological science, we must characterise its general spirit, and the resources peculiar to it, as we have done for all the previous sciences:[61] its present imperfect state makes this all the more pressing. These are considerations that have to do with the science itself and its concepts, but they can also be related to method, since their object is to guide our intelligence in the study of this difficult subject.

In the course of this preliminary operation as far as the other fundamental sciences were concerned we have been gradually drawn into explanations the more elementary and explicit as the science was more complex and more imperfect. With regard to the simplest and most advanced sciences their more philosophic definition at once sufficed to convey their conditions and general resources, about which there can be no further uncertainty in any reasonable mind. But another procedure had to be adopted when more complex phenomena did not allow the true nature of a more recent and less settled study to emerge, except as a result of difficult discussions, which fortunately were uncalled for in the previous sciences. In biological science above all, elementary explanations such as would have seemed puerile in any other case appeared absolutely indispensable in order to protect from challenge the principal foundations of positive study, whose philosophy still excites profound disagreement among the most advanced spirits of the age. As a result of this progression a similar necessity was bound to make itself felt in the science of social development, which up till now has in no wise attained any real positivity, and which the best minds even today proclaim incapable of ever doing so. It is not surprising therefore if the simplest and most fundamental notions of positive philosophy, happily now a commonplace in less complex and less backward subjects through the natural progress of human reason, here demand formal discussion, of which the results will no doubt appear to the majority of enlightened judges as a bold innovation, although limited to conditions which are no more than the barest equivalent of those accepted without demur for any other type of phenomena.

When one considers without prejudice the present state of social science in that frankly positive spirit which sound scientific study must everywhere develop today, one cannot help recognising, both in the method and the doctrine, a combination of the various features that have always distinguished the theologico-metaphysical infancy of the other branches of natural science. In a word the general situation of political science today is exactly analogous to that of astrology in relation to astronomy, of alchemy in relation to chemistry, and the cure-all in relation to medicine. Theological politics and metaphysical politics, despite their practical antagonism, can be lumped together without any serious inconvenience, and so simplify investigation, because at bottom the second is but a modification of the first from which it does not differ except in being less extreme, as we have already observed in connection with other natural phenomena, and as we shall see still more with social phenomena. Whether phenomena are referred to a direct and continuous supernatural intervention or explained by the mysterious virtue of corresponding entities, this merely secondary difference between ultimately identical concepts in no way prevents a common production of the same characteristic attributes, indeed less here than in any other philosophic subject. The characteristics consist, as to method, in the preponderance of imagination over observation, and as to doctrine, in the exclusive search for absolute ideas, whence results, as the aim of 'science' the exercise of an arbitrary and indefinite action upon phenomena, which are not regarded as subject to invariable natural laws. In a word the general spirit of human speculation in the theologico-metaphysical state is ideal in its procedures, absolute in its conceptions, and arbitrary in its applications. Now it cannot be doubted that these are still the dominant characteristics of social thought. If we reverse the triple aspect of the theologico-metaphysical spirit, its imagination taking precedence over observation, its absolute conceptions, and its arbitrary applications, we shall have the intellectual attitude necessary for the creation of positive sociology, and which must afterwards guide its entire development.

Positive philosophy is first of all characterised, in any subject by that necessary and permanent subordination of imagination to observation which constitutes the scientific spirit, as opposed to the theological or metaphysical spirit. Although such a philosophy offers to human imagination the widest and most fruitful of fields, as we have seen from our examination of the fundamental sciences, it restricts its activity to discovering or perfecting either the exact co-ordination of the facts as they stand, or the means of undertaking new investigations. It is this habitual tendency to subordinate scientific conceptions to the facts—it being the sole function of these conceptions to demonstrate the interconnection of the facts—that must be introduced into social studies, where vague and ill-defined observation still offers no sufficient foundation for truly scientific reasoning, and is continually being modified by imagination under the stimulus of very lively passions. By virtue of its greater complexity, and incidentally its more intimate connection with human passions, political speculation more than any other was bound to remain sunk in this deplorable situation where it still languishes, whilst simpler and less stimulating studies have one by one been extricated from it during the last three centuries. We must never forget that up to a more or less recent past every order of scientific conception has been in the same state of infancy from which, the more complex and specialised its nature, the later it was emancipated; indeed the most complex have been emancipated only in our time. The intellectual and moral phenomena of individual life for instance—except by a few advanced spirits—are still studied most of the time in almost as anti-scientific a manner as political phenomena. Thus only a superficial judgement can regard as peculiar to politics that disposition to vague and uncertain observation by which sophists and rhetoricians interpret known facts according to the whim of their imagination. The same vice has prevailed in every subject of human speculation; the only thing that is special in this case is that the vice is more ingrained, as a natural result of the greater complexity of the subject, according to my theory of the development of the human mind. These reflections lead one to consider the extension to social studies of that philosophic regeneration which all other scientific studies have experienced not only as possible but as certain and imminent, were it not for the much greater intellectual difficulty that they present and the hindrances arising from more direct contact with the principal passions. But this should only stimulate the true thinker to greater efforts.

If instead of mode of procedure, we consider the actual scientific conceptions in positive philosophy, we see that in contradistinction to theologico-metaphysical philosophy it has a constant tendency to make all those notions relative which had been considered absolute. This transition from the absolute to the relative constitutes one of the most important philosophic results of each one of the intellectual revolutions that have brought various orders of speculation out of the theological and metaphysical state to the scientific state. From the purely scientific point of view, and setting aside all idea of utility, it seems to me we may regard the contrast between the relative and the absolute as expressing the antipathy between modern and ancient philosophy. Every study of the inner nature of beings, of their primary and final causes, etc. must obviously be absolute, while every investigation of the laws of phenomena is eminently relative, since it presupposes that the progress of thought is dependent on the gradual improvement of observation, exact reality being never, in any subject, perfectly disclosed: so that the relative nature of scientific conceptions is inseparable from the true notion of natural laws, just as the chimerical attachment to absolute knowledge accompanies the use of theological fictions or metaphysical entities. Now there is no need to insist here on the obvious fact that this absolute spirit still characterises social speculation. Its various schools, both theological and metaphysical, are dominated by the idea of an unchanging political type, more or less vaguely defined, but always conceived in such a manner as to prevent any radical modification of the chief political conceptions according to the state of human civilisation. Although such a notion, which could not possibly be based on rational thinking, must at once engender great philosophic differences, especially today, yet less pronounced differences than they appear, yet each one of the opinions of which this type is the subject preserves the immobility of the type throughout all modifications of social history. The absolute spirit inherent in contemporary political science, with all its disadvantages, has at least constituted up till now the only means of controlling individual extravagances, and of preventing a flood of different opinions. The various philosophers who, impressed by the danger of this intellectual absolutism, have sometimes endeavoured to free themselves from it, but have not had the strength to rise to the conception of truly positive politics, have incurred the blame, still more grave, of presenting all political ideas as being by nature radically uncertain and even arbitrary, for they have destroyed the foundation of their present stability, without substituting a firmer basis. These ill-conceived attempts have even cast general discredit on any attempt to regenerate the spirit of politics. By losing its absoluteness it seems today, in the eyes of many respectable men in the various political parties, to have necessarily lost its stability, and consequently its morality. But these fears, although very natural, will easily be dissipated in the mind of anyone who appreciates the character of positive sociology, and considers the development of the previous branches of natural philosophy, where one certainly does not observe that in ceasing to be absolute, and becoming relative, scientific ideas have become in any way arbitrary. On the contrary it is clear that by this transformation these ideas have acquired a consistency and a stability very superior to their vague primitive immutability, each one of them being gradually involved in a system of relations of constantly increasing range and strength and tending more and more to prevent any serious aberration. Thus there is no risk at all of falling into a dangerous scepticism by destroying once and for all the absolute spirit that characterises so deplorably the prolonged infantilism of social science, provided this destruction is but the natural result of the passage of this science to the positive state. Operating this transition, positive philosophy will not fail to display its usual characteristic of never suppressing a means of intellectual co-ordination without immediately substituting another means, more wide-ranging and more efficacious. Is it not apparent that the transition from the absolute to the relative offers today in politics the only means of arriving at conceptions capable of eliciting unanimous and lasting assent?

The two attitudes that I have just examined constitute, the one for method, and the other for doctrine, the condition of any future positivity in social science. Yet study of them is not what is best calculated to impress the public of today with the signs of the philosophic transformation. That is because of the too close connection that exists in this domain more than in any other between theory and practice, in consequence of which anything purely speculative and abstract, however important, excites very little interest. The close adherence of theory to practice, or rather the almost total confusion of the two, is the necessary result of a defective social science, which in turn, as I have explained,[62] is the result of the extreme complexity of that science. If the scientific principles therefore are to be really brought out, I had better consider the contemporary political attitude to application rather than to the science itself.

The present spirit shows itself still intent on exercising unlimited action on phenomena; it is an aberration now confined to social phenomena, but which, as I have often shown, used to dominate, in a practically equivalent manner, although to a less marked degree, all the orders of human conceptions, as long as they remained subject to metaphysical or theological philosophy. While the real power of man to modify phenomena at will can only result from a knowledge of their natural laws, the infancy of human reason has always coincided with the pretension to exercise practically unlimited influence over phenomena. What we might call the great primitive illusion results from ignorance of the fundamental laws of nature, combined with the hypothesis that an undefined arbitrary power exists in supernatural agents, and after that in metaphysical entities: for as the vain ambition we have spoken of manifests itself precisely at the epoch when man really has least influence on his surroundings, he cannot attribute to himself this authority save through the agency of mysterious forces.

The general history of human opinion clearly shows the existence of this aberration with regard to astronomical, physical, chemical and even biological phenomena. It will be readily understood that the longer, in proportion to their complexity, the formulation of natural laws is delayed for the various orders of natural phenomena, the longer will the illusion last. Still another influence should be noted as powerfully reinforcing this obstacle to the development of human reason, namely, that at the same time that they become more complex, the different phenomena become also more modifiable. The cause of more extensive modification is also the cause of greater complexity; it is the decreasing generality of the various orders of phenomena. All of which tends to perpetuate the primitive aberration on the power of man, which has become more difficult to detect, and consequently more excusable. The two conditions of complexity and modifiability must have affected the study of social phenomena, which has been subject, more thoroughly and for a longer time than any other study, to certain illusions. But in spite of these disadvantages in this study, it was important to show that, as with ideality and absoluteness, this illusion of power is not peculiar to this order of phenomena, and has always characterised the infancy of human reason, in every possible type of speculation, even the simplest: the similarity is as valuable as it is undeniable, since it permits the hope that it will be possible to get rid of this aberration in political ideas, as in other subjects of research. However that may be, the aberration survives today only in social phenomena, except for a few analogous illusions in connection with intellectual and moral phenomena, from which progressive spirits have now emancipated themselves. In politics it is obvious that, in spite of the undeniable tendency today to a sounder philosophy, the prevailing disposition of statesmen and even of publicists, both in the theological and in the metaphysical school, is to conceive social phenomena as arbitrarily modifiable to an indefinite extent, and to suppose that the human species is without any innate inclination, and is always ready to undergo passively the influence of the legislator whether temporal or spiritual, provided he be invested with sufficient authority. In this respect as in every other, theological politics shows itself less inconsistent than its rival, since it at least explains, after its own fashion, the disproportionately immense effects attributed to exiguous causes, by making the legislator nothing but the organ of an absolute supernatural power: which however leads all the more inevitably and irresistibly to the infinite domination of the legislator, who has only to borrow his principal authority from on high. The metaphysical school has recourse to the device of Providence in a much vaguer and less specific way, without ceasing to base itself on the same hypothesis, and habitually introducing its unintelligible entities into these vacuous political explanations, especially the great entity of *nature*, which today embraces all the rest, and which is nothing but an abstract derivative of the theological principle. Disdaining even any subordination of effect to cause, it attempts to elude the philosophical difficulty by attributing to chance the production of observed events, and sometimes, when the inanity of this procedure becomes too glaring, by exaggerating to the point of absurdity the influence of individual genius on the course of human affairs. Whatever the mode adopted, the result in both schools is always to represent the political action of man as essentially indefinite and arbitrary, exactly as in the past biological, chemical, physical and even astronomical phenomena were believed to be, during the more or less prolonged theologico-metaphysical infancy of these sciences. The aberration is in my eyes the outstanding characteristic of the infancy, which still persists in the order of social ideas. It indicates in the most unequivocal manner a systematic refusal to see political phenomena as subject to natural laws, the application of which would necessarily impose, as in all previous cases, limitations on action, by annihilating once and for all the vain pretension of governing according to our fancy this kind of phenomena, necessarily as independent as any other kind of human or superhuman caprice. It is this pretension, together with the tendency noted above to absolute ideas from which it is inseparable, that must be seen as the principal cause of the present social unrest. The human species finds itself delivered up without any logical protection to the disordered experimentation of the various political schools, each of which seeks to make its own immovable type prevail. As long as the dominance of the old political system forbade free examination of social questions these abuses were necessarily controlled, and a certain intellectual discipline could exist, as a result of external pressure, in spite of the theological nature of political philosophy. But the natural course of individualistic extravagance could only be contained for a while, and the philosophic irruption was bound to take place as the gradual ascendancy of metaphysical politics brought with it the right of free inquiry. Metaphysical political philosophy was thus allowed to develop with all its dangers to the utmost, up to the point of calling in question the utility of the social state itself, since eloquent sophists, as we know, did not hesitate to preach the superiority of the life of savages, as they imagined it. Having reached this height of absurdity and eccentricity, the metaphysico-theological utopias now rightly recognise the absolute impossibility of establishing any stable and accepted idea in politics as long as people continue to pursue this search for the absolutely best government, apart from any particular state of civilisation, or, to put it in scientific terms, as long as human society is conceived as marching under the arbitrary guidance of the legislator, without any impulse of its own. Thus in political philosophy from now on there can be no order or agreement possible, except by subjecting social phenomena, like all other phenomena, to invariable natural laws that will limit in each epoch, without the possibility of serious doubt, the extent and character of political action: in a word by introducing once for all into the general study of social phenomena the same positive spirit as has already regenerated and disciplined all other kinds of human speculation, whose state used to be no more satisfactory than is today that of social science. Apart from this and if we preserve the present mode of philosophising, there is no means of arriving at a proper degree of stability and agreement except by re-establishing sufficient intellectual repression—a project which happily today has become as fantastic as it is dangerous. Not less important is the fact that the true scientific basis of human dignity, in the political order, is a spontaneous social movement regulated by natural laws, since the principal tendencies of humanity thus acquire an imposing authority which must always be respected, as the main basis of society by any rational legislation. While the present belief in the infinite power of political combinations seems at first to increase the importance of man, it ends by conferring on him a kind of social automatism, passive under the supreme and absolute guidance either of Providence or the human legislator—a paradox also to be observed in relation to the other classes of phenomena. The rectification therefore of this third aberration—the notion of arbitrary power over nature—is the crux in the regeneration of political science, which so presented becomes comprehensible to an epoch whose prevailing intellectual habits scarcely permit the formation of social concepts except from a practical rather than a scientific point of view, still less from a logical one.

We may usefully conclude these preliminary indications of the conditions that positive sociology must fulfil by one final consideration that embraces them all; I refer to rational prediction, which I have so often presented as the most irrefragable criterion of scientific positivity when I treated previous departments of natural philosophy. The difficulty is to conceive social phenomena as capable of scientific prediction like any other phenomena, within the limits of exactitude set by their greater complexity, according to our general rule. This way of looking at our philosophic renewal recalls very forcibly the three characteristics that I have been examining in this lecture, which all relate, in different but equivalent ways, to the subordination of social concepts to invariable natural laws, without which obviously there can be no prediction of political events. The very idea therefore of rational prediction presupposes that the human mind has definitely quitted the region of metaphysical idealities in politics, in order to take its stand on the firm ground of observed realities through a systematic and constant subordination of imagination to observation; with no less authority it demands that political conceptions cease to be absolute and become relative to the constantly varying state of human civilisation, in order that theories, being allowed to follow the natural course of the facts, should permit a real prediction of facts; finally it implies the limitation of political action in accordance with exactly defined laws, for if it were otherwise the general series of social events, continually exposed to disturbance by the intervention of a legislator whether divine or human, could not be foreseen with any certainty. Thus, to facilitate our philosophic inquiry, we might summarise the various conditions of positive philosophy in this one attribute of rational prediction. Concentration on this attribute is the more indicated, as in this subject, just as in all the others, and today even more than in the others, in view of the greater urgency of social regeneration, it serves to distinguish the new social philosophy from the old. Indeed, events ruled by supernatural will may well allow for prophecies, but they are totally incompatible with any kind of scientific prediction, the very idea of which is sacrilege. And it is the same when the direction of events belongs to metaphysical entities, except for prophecy, which would be *ipso facto* excluded were metaphysical concepts not at bottom a mere modification of theological ones. Nothing is more apparent today than the lack of prediction with regard to political events, in face of which both theological and metaphysical doctrine can offer nothing as a rule but blind and sterile acceptance: their strange modes of explanation would usually apply equally well to directly contrary events, nor can their vain formulae ever lead to any indication of what the social future will be. If none the less in every epoch a great number of secondary political facts have generally been regarded as predictable, this simply confirms what I said at the beginning, that theologico-metaphysical philosophy could never be universally applied, and has had to be more or less tempered with a weak and incomplete positivism, strictly subordinate, but indispensable to the movement of the human spirit and of society. But although this confirmation of our thesis be particularly notable as regards political phenomena, it does not prevent the continuous subordination of these phenomena to theological or metaphysical concepts from rendering them incompatible with any truly scientific prediction, except in an entirely secondary and incidental manner, a kind of popular prediction that does not rise above the level of empiricism as unsure as it is rudimentary, provisionally useful no doubt but which cannot disguise the fundamental need of regeneration in political philosophy.

In the present state of vague and confused irrationalism in social studies, all the preliminary conditions which I have just finished explaining might well pass, with a little artifice, for a first realisation of the great philosophic renewal, which, forsooth, only needed to be duly defined: in a subject as ill-conceived as this one has been up till now, simple statements have often, with less justification, been magnified into real solutions. But minds properly prepared by long familiarity with scientific concepts will be proof against such an illusion; they will immediately recognise that the conditions defined in the course of this lecture have to do with fundamentals in political philosophy, and cannot therefore suffice to put us in the way of execution. What we have is an important preamble, that may guide us in formulating the scientific goal we must attain, and even in exactly estimating the gradual progress towards that goal. We must now proceed to an exposition of the general spirit of social physics, of which the essential conditions are now sufficiently defined. It is however above all through the continual exemplification of it in the course of the following lectures that that spirit will become known and appreciated.

As the philosophic principle of this spirit can be summed up in the concept that social phenomena are subject to natural laws and associated with rational prediction, what we have to decide is the subject and character of these laws. With this in view we must extend to social phenomena a scientific distinction that is truly fundamental, and applicable by its nature to any phenomena, above all to those of living bodies: that between the *static* and the *dynamic* state of every subject of positive study. In biology, i.e. in the study of individual life, this dichotomy gives rise to the distinction between the anatomical point of view, which relates to organisation, and the physiological point of view, which is proper to life: in sociology the splitting up must be effected in a similar manner, and not less definitely, by distinguishing in every political subject between the conditions of existence of a society and the laws of its movement. The difference is sufficiently marked for its natural development to give rise perhaps eventually to two sciences within social physics, which might be called social statics and social dynamics, as essentially distinct from one another as anatomy and physiology for the individual. But it would be certainly premature to attach any importance to this classification at the very moment when the science is being founded. It is also to be feared that so clear-cut a division of social science might introduce a grave defect, characteristic of modern scatter-brains:

that of neglecting the combination of the two points of view, as it is seen in biology, where the popular division between anatomy and physiology is tending to disappear entirely. At any rate any split in sociological work would be inopportune, and even stupid, so long as the whole has not taken shape. But this point does not affect in any way either the truth or the necessity of our fundamental distinction between the static and the dynamic state of social phenomena, provided that instead of being made the source of a harmful or pedantic division, it is applied solely to the analysis of every social theory, which will always be found to have this double aspect.

The better to characterise this dichotomy and show at once its practical importance, let me say here that it corresponds perfectly to the double notion of order and progress in politics, which we can now regard as accepted in public life. Obviously the study of the static social organism coincides at bottom with the positive theory of order, and this can only consist in a just harmony of the various elements of human society; in the same way we see that the study of the dynamic life of humanity yields the positive theory of social progress, which by thrusting aside all vain thoughts of absolute and unlimited perfection, reduces itself to the simple idea of development. This parallel of the static and dynamic states in society with the static and dynamic in science, by lending more interest and clarity to speculations and more nobility and consistency to practicality, seems to me to manifest quite plainly at the very beginning of the new philosophy the continuous correspondence between science and applied science. Statesmen will thus be able to judge if what we are dealing with is a vain intellectual exercise, or philosophic principles that can actually permeate our political life. They will begin to feel, I hope, that I am keeping my promise of building a social science that will satisfy the twofold intellectual need of modern societies, since I am establishing on unshakable foundations the twofold notion of order and progress,[63] which thus finds itself embodied in the entire system of social concepts and even in the entire system of positive theories. The permanent subject of science may thus be considered in political philosophy to be essentially similar to that of art, as the same system of interrelations is viewed from two quite distinct, but equivalent points of view, different as the abstract differs from the concrete, and speculation from action. A science which has constantly in view the positive study of the real laws of order and progress, cannot be taxed with speculative temerity by men of action with any intellectual vision if it claims to be alone capable of providing the rational basis for satisfying the double social need: and this necessary correspondence of order and progress will come to be recognised as analogous to the harmony, admitted in principle though imperfectly developed in practice, between biological science and the arts that relate to it, especially the medical art. The prime philosophic conception of positive sociology has the virtue of linking indissolubly the two equally fundamental ideas of order and of progress, whose mutual hostility is today a chief symptom[64] of the profound disturbance at the heart of modern society. It cannot be doubted that these two fundamental notions, separately consolidated, will by their fusion acquire an unassailable intellectual consistency, for they will become as inseparable as are in biology the ideas of organisation and of life, whose scientific dualism proceeds from exactly the same principle of positive philosophy. The properties and qualities which I have just indicated will naturally develop as time goes on, and as positive philosophy manifests its spirit both of organisation and of progress in the rational study of social phenomena, instead of spreading abroad the perturbing or depressing influence with which too often it is credited. Here I have briefly indicated the scientific root of these important qualities.

Defining according to this conception the static laws of the social organism, we shall find that their philosophic principle is a general consensus, such as characterises any and all phenomena of living bodies, and which social life manifests in the highest degree. Thus understood, the social anatomy which constitutes static sociology must have as its permanent object the positive study, at once experimental and rational, of the various parts of the social system in their action and reaction upon one another, abstracting for the time being as much as possible the movement which is always modifying them. Sociological predictions, founded on the exact knowledge of these interrelations, are thus destined to derive the various static indications on each mode of social existence in conformity with further observation, in a manner analogous with what takes place habitually in individual anatomy. This first aspect of political science therefore presupposes that, contrary to present philosophical habits, each of the numerous social elements, ceasing to be regarded as something absolute and independent, is always conceived as relative to all the others, to which it is bound in fundamental solidarity. It seems to me that there is no need to insist on the utility of such a sociological doctrine; it must obviously serve as the basis for the study of social movement, which if rationally conceived must have the continual intention of preserving the organism; but besides, this doctrine can be immediately used, at least provisionally, as a substitute for direct observation, which in many cases cannot take place with regard to certain social elements, whose condition may however be deduced from the scientific relationship with other elements already known. The history of science at once gives an idea of the importance of this method. The erudite twaddle on the astronomical knowledge of the ancient Egyptians was silenced even before scholarship had dealt with it, by the simple reflection that the general state of astronomical science is linked to that of abstract geometry, which was then in its infancy. It would be possible to cite a multitude of similar cases. But lest we exaggerate, it should be noted that these necessary relations of the different social aspects to one another cannot of their nature be so simple and precise that the observed results would only proceed from one single mode of co-ordination. Such a belief would be too narrow in biology, and essentially contrary to the more complex nature of sociological speculation. But clearly the exact estimate of the limits of variation, both normal and abnormal, is here, at least as much as in individual anatomy, an indispensable complement of any theory of static sociology, without which the indirect exploration in question might often lead to error.

As we are not writing a special treatise on political philosophy, it is not necessary for me to demonstrate the fundamental solidarity of all possible aspects of the social organism, as to which, in principle at least, there is little disagreement among people of any intelligence. Take any social element you please; it will be a useful scientific exercise to make out its contacts, mediate and immediate, with all the others, even those that appear most independent of it. The continuous dynamic development of civilised humanity no doubt yields still more interesting proof of the social consensus, as it shows the universal reaction, either immediate or eventual, to every particular modification. Such indications can always be preceded, or followed, by static confirmation, for in politics, as in mechanics, the communication of movement proves at once the existence of interconnection. Quite apart from the intense solidarity of the branches of any art or science, are not the different sciences, and almost all the arts, so interconnected socially, that if the state of one single part is sufficiently defined, the corresponding state of every other part can be predicted with philosophic certainty, in accordance with the laws of harmony? Looking farther afield, we see the continuous interrelation of the systems of sciences and of arts, if we allow for the solidarity becoming less intense as it becomes more indirect. It is the same with the totality of social phenomena, not within one nation, but among the various contemporary nations, whose influence on one another cannot be denied, especially in modern times, though here the consensus will as a rule be less pronounced, and decrease gradually with the diminishing affinity of the cases and number of their contacts, to the point of disappearing altogether, as for instance between Western Europe and Eastern Asia, whose societies have appeared up till now to be practically independent of one another.

Without dwelling any longer on ideas that are so little open to question, I will here treat the one single case where the fundamental solidarity is still, if not denied in principle, at least misunderstood, and even ignored. This case is unfortunately the most important of all: it is that of social organisation, the theory of which continues to be conceived as independent of any corresponding civilisation, although social organisation can only be one of the elements of a civilisation. Such distorted thinking is today almost equally characteristic of the most opposed political schools, theological or metaphysical. One and all they carry on their abstract discourse on the political regime, without giving a thought to correlative civilisation, and generally end up making the ideal political model of their vain utopian dreams coincide with some more or less infantile state of the human race. In order to grasp what this ingrained aberration amounts to and all that it implies, we must, by exact historical analysis, trace it to its philosophic source, which in my view is none other than the famous theological dogma that human civilisation developed through an original fall of man. By this dogma, which all religions reproduce in one form or another, and of which the domination has been still further fortified by the natural inclination to admire the past, we are taught to see the spread of civilisation as synonymous with the decadence of society. When theological philosophy gradually passed into the metaphysical stage, this primitive dogma tended to transform itself into the celebrated hypothesis—still the principal basis of metaphysical politics—that there is a state of nature superior to the social state, from which we are more and more separated by the development of civilisation. It is impossible to ignore the extreme gravity, both for philosophy and for politics, of an aberration so rooted in the scientific constitution of the various existing doctrines, and which, though it has ceased to be directly formulated and maintained, continues to dominate social speculation, often without the knowledge of the participants.

Yet it cannot be possible for this prime irrationalism to survive philosophic discussion in this day and age; it is in obvious contradiction with many ideas of political philosophy which, although not yet scientifically established, are gradually gaining intellectual ascendancy, whether through the enlightenment that proceeds from the natural course of events, or the development of public understanding. Thus all enlightened publicists now recognise that there is a certain solidarity of political institutions, by which some are mutually exclusive, while others maintain one another and even necessitate one another: this must have been a first step towards a notion of the consensus of these institutions and their specialised systems with the total system of human civilisation. The evidence of this correlation for certain subjects at once justifies its extension to all the subjects known to be in harmony with these, and this must tend to multiply, as also to simplify, the means of demonstration in political philosophy. I can even point out an intellectual attitude that is still closer to the spirit of social statics: the realisation by the most advanced thinkers, of France and Germany especially, that there is a constant and necessary solidarity of political power and civil power, which means, in positive language, that the predominant social forces become in the end also the ruling forces, as I affirmed in my System of Positive Politics in 1822.[65] But however interesting these insights for the sociological education of the public mind, we should certainly be guilty of underestimating the difficult and imperious demands of the true scientific method if we thought that such lucky gropings dispensed with the direct rational conception of general consensus in the social organism; they are but a preparation for the ultimate dissemination and acceptance of the idea. A decisive example will show, I think, that these vague isolated hints, more literary than scientific, can never fulfil the real philosophic requirements: Aristotle, and even most philosophers before him, harped on the aphorism that laws are subject to manners, yet this first element of sane political philosophy did not prevent them during twenty centuries from treating systems of institutions as essentially independent of contemporary states of civilisation, however flagrant the contradiction. In conformity with the natural course of human things, intellectual principles and philosophical opinions, as well as social manners and political institutions, continue to exist in spite of their known decrepitude and recognised disadvantages, once they have really taken possession of minds, merely giving rise to more and more serious inconsistencies, until the development of human reason produces new principles, equally general and more rational. In the intellectual order not less than in the material order, man feels more than anything else the need of a superior direction, which by calling forth all his strength makes him capable of sustained effort. Thus, without undervaluing the various attempts of political philosophy that I have just indicated, I do not hesitate to regard them as non-existent, as far as the development of static sociology is concerned, for they do not promote an understanding of how the political regime as a whole participates in the general consensus of the social organism.

The continuous application of this fundamental idea[66] would be still more efficacious than any methodical demonstration could be in dissipating completely real doubts as to the solidarity between the system of political powers and institutions and the corresponding state of civilisation. But decisive as the historical proof is, if social science is to be properly constituted, we must attach extreme importance to the rational explanation of this great correlation, as I shall undertake to show later on in my Treatise of Political Philosophy.[67] In it every scientific means will be combined to establish once for all this fundamental conception, from which proceeds the true spirit of social statics, and which annihilates, more quickly than any other sociological theory, the absolute character of our various political schools. The scientific principle of this relationship is the harmony which must always reign between the whole and the parts in the social system, whose elements cannot avoid being combined in the end in the manner conformable to their proper nature. Clearly not only are political institutions and social manners on the one hand, and on the other manners and ideas, necessarily interdependent, but in addition the whole system is attached to the corresponding state of development of humanity, with all its modes of activity intellectual, moral and physical, whose ordered advancement towards their predetermined goal cannot but be the sole aim of any political system temporal or spiritual. Even in revolutionary epochs, with their insufficient realisation of this fundamental harmony, it continues to make itself felt, for it could not be entirely dissolved except with the dissolution of the social organism itself, of which it is the principal attribute. In these exceptional times, except for a few occasional anomalies, which cannot in the nature of things leave any deep traces, one can continue to regard the political regime as being ultimately in necessary and complete conformity with the corresponding state of civilisation, since the breaks or disturbances which occur in the one arise from corresponding disorders in the other. The immense social revolution in the midst of which we live only confirms the sociological law which was explained in our eighth lecture, that contrary to the current opinion, the present deplorable state of the political regime results primarily from our intellectual, and secondarily from our moral situation; it is with this that every rational solution must attempt to deal, while the stormy attempts to regenerate directly the political system can have no appreciable effect.

In vulgar estimation the legislator has the power to break up the harmony we are considering, if only he possesses sufficient authority: which amounts to a complete negation of the solidarity we are considering. But it is easy to see that this opinion represents the vicious circle resulting from illusions on the sources of political power, where the symptom is taken for the cause. Without attempting to establish at this point the positive theory of authority, we can say that according to the nature of the social state any power whatsoever is constituted by the assent, spontaneous or considered, explicit or implicit, of the various individual wills which have decided in accordance with certain convictions, to co-operate in a common action, of which the said power is first of all the instrument, and afterwards the regulator. Thus authority derives really from co-operation, and not co-operation from authority, except of course through an inevitable reaction; so that no power can be constituted except from the dominant forces in a society, and when nothing dominates, any power that exists is necessarily feeble and uncertain, this correlation being the more inevitable as the society is more extensive. Current theory, by interverting this relationship, produces a strange situation, familiar to metaphysical conceptions, in which the source of the political power to which a mysterious social influence is attributed is not known, and a supernatural origin for it is supposed, as also happens in theological politics, though more consistently. It is true, no intelligent person can deny the great influence plainly exercised by a political regime on a system of civilisation: influence of political institutions, measures or events, sometimes bad, sometimes good; influence even on the direction of the sciences and the arts, in every age of the civilisation, but above all in its infancy. But there is no need to linger on this aspect of the question, since no one denies it. The usual mistake is to exaggerate it beyond all reason, to the point of giving precedence to reaction over action. At any rate it is clear that by their correlation government and society emphasise the fundamental consensus of the social organism, which is the philosophic principle of static sociology, and an idea that is only difficult as regards the correspondence of the political regime and the contemporaneous state of civilisation. There will be many occasions for returning to this last subject from new points of view, apart from historical analysis, in considering the limits of political action, and also social statistics.[68]

The essentially relative point of view from which the political system will always be considered in this first sketch of social science has now been sufficiently stressed. The relative point of view, substituted for the absolute conceptions of current theories, is the principal scientific feature of positivity in political philosophy, as I have shown at the beginning of this chapter. Thus a political regime is never to be considered except in its continuous relation, sometimes general, sometimes special, to the corresponding state of civilisation, apart from which it cannot be properly judged, and by the gradual pressure of which it is produced and modified. If, on the one hand, this conception shows every idea of political good or evil to be necessarily relative or variable, without being for that reason in any way arbitrary, since the relationship is always rigorously determined, on the other it furnishes the rational basis of a positive theory of order in human societies, such as has been already vaguely glimpsed, under some subordinate aspects, by metaphysical politics in what is called political economy. And as the value of any political system consists in its harmony with the corresponding state, we now see that it is impossible for such a harmony not to establish itself in the natural course of events, without any calculated intervention.

Such a philosophy might, of course, lead momentarily to a dangerous optimism, as I have already warned, but only in those unscientific minds which native lack of precision, increased by defective education, renders unsuitable for the cultivation with any real success of so profoundly difficult a science as sociology. But every mind that is properly organised and rationally prepared, in a word worthy of such a destiny, will know how to avoid confusing the scientific notion of order with the systematic apology for existing order. With regard to any phenomena whatsoever in their relation to man, positive philosophy always teaches that in accordance with the natural laws of the phenomena a certain necessary order invariably establishes itself; but never claims that such an order does not offer numerous disadvantages that can be modified to a certain extent by wise human intervention. The more complex the phenomena become through increased specialisation, the more these imperfections are aggravated and multiplied, so that biological phenomena, for example, will be inferior in this respect to those of inorganic nature. By virtue of their still greater complexity, social phenomena must therefore be the most imperfect of all, and at the same time the most modifiable—which is far from being a compensation. If one has a notion of natural laws it will involve the idea of natural order, and this is always a concomitant of harmony. But the consequence is not more absolute than the principle from which it is derived. Completing the principle of the natural law by the consideration of increasing complexity in the phenomena, according to the scientific hierarchy which I established at the beginning, one completes also the conception of order, by that of a simultaneous increase in imperfection. Such is the true spirit of positive philosophy. You can see how profoundly it differs from the systematic tendency to optimism, of which the origin is obviously theological, since the hypothesis of a providential guidance ever present in the course of events, must necessarily lead to the idea of an inevitable perfection in accomplishment. Nevertheless we must recognise that in the development of human reason, the positive conception itself is originally derived from the theological dogma which it regenerates, as historical analysis would confirm, in essentially the same manner as the principle of conditions of existence derives originally from the hypothesis of final causes, and the philosophic notion of mathematical laws, from the metaphysical mysticism of the power of numbers: the analogy is perfect in all three cases. It arises from that tendency of our intelligence to keep to its usual modes of reasoning, at whatever age in the past they were discovered, and to adapt them gradually to new modes of activity by means of a few transformations that preserve the full value of these precious primitive inspirations of human genius, and even augment it by purifying it. But in any and every case the differences that separate the new principle from the old dogma will be immediately perceptable to anyone with the slightest philosophic insight. In the case we are now considering it is clear that positive philosophy, while indicating that there must have been a natural conformity of every political regime to a corresponding civilisation for that regime to have been able to establish itself and above all to endure, teaches also that the natural order must be most of the time very imperfect, owing to the complexity of the phenomena. Far from rejecting human intervention in this case, positive philosophy calls for it to be wisely and actively applied, and to a greater degree then for any other class of phenomena, since it sees social phenomena as being by their nature the most modifiable of all, and the most in need of modification according to the rational prescriptions of science. Only it reserves to itself the right to direct this necessary intervention, and to mark its limitations whether general or particular. While not exaggerating the utility of intervention, it never forbids its use save in those cases where it would involve a useless expenditure of resources, in accordance with a rule of economy applied to all natural phenomena without any consideration of prestige, human or divine. The extreme novelty of such a political philosophy may well lead people to mistake its real character, and to reproach it with those very peculiarities that are most antipathetic to it. It is even to be feared that owing to the weakness of our nature, which causes the life of feeling to triumph continually over the life of reason, once this philosophy is in the ascendant it will be systematically accused of social and political lukewarmness by those who feel constantly impelled to turbulent material activity, for men of speculation need expect little appreciation from men of action. From the moral point of view positive philosophy could only reply to such recriminations by pointing to the results, in themselves significant enough, of its day to day application. As for philosophic discussion, anyone can judge, from the preceding examples, how it will be carried on. In order to bring out the full irrationality of the accusation of political optimism, it will be enough to point out the flagrant inconsistency of such an accusation apropos of the most complex phenomena, while no one dares to formulate it apropos of the simpler ones, which are nevertheless represented by positive philosophy as necessarily better regulated and less modifiable. And it might well happen that the same people who reproach it with optimism in politics, reproach it at the same time with the opposite fault, that of crying down providential government with regard to the rest of the economy of nature!

Two motives compel me to insist on the fundamental notion of consensus in the social organism: first its extreme philosophic importance as the mother of social statics, which is destined to be the basis of the new political philosophy, and second its spirit, as being that of static sociology, which must be characterised in advance as subsequently we shall perceive it only indirectly. Apprehended in its entirety, that is, including the correlation of society and government, the positive conception of social harmony furnishes the scientific basis of a sound elementary theory of political order, whether spiritual or temporal. For it leads to the consideration of the artificial and voluntary order as a prolongation of the natural and involuntary order towards which all human societies naturally tend in all their aspects, so that every truly rational political institution, if it is to have real and lasting social efficacy, must rest on a preliminary exact analysis of the natural tendencies which alone can furnish its authority with firm roots: in a word, order is to be considered as something to be perfected, not created, for this would be impossible. From the scientific point of view, the primary idea of universal social solidarity is the inevitable consequence and complement of an idea we have already established as proper to the study of living bodies. From a strictly scientific point of view, this notion of consensus is not peculiar to sociology, but presents itself as common to all phenomena, with immense differences of intensity and variety, and therefore of philosophic importance. It may be said that where there is system, there is solidarity. Even astronomy, with its purely mechanical phenomena, gives us the first notion of it, at least if we set aside the idea of the universe, and confine ourselves to that of the world, here the only completely positive idea: certain irregularities of a star can sometimes seriously affect another star, modifying its gravitation. But we must recognise that the more complex and the less general phenomena become, the more complete and pronounced is the consensus. And so, in accordance with my scientific hierarchy, we find the study of chemical phenomena, in this respect as in every other, forming a kind of bridge between inorganic and organic philosophy. In accordance with this principle, as also with current belief, the scientific notion of solidarity and consensus, despite its universality, belongs essentially to organic systems by virtue of their greater complexity. It is here that the notion of solidarity, which up till now has been incidental, becomes the actual basis of positive conceptions; and the more composite the organisms and the higher and more complex the phenomena, the more marked becomes its dominance. Thus animal consensus is much more complete than vegetable consensus; and develops with the progress of animality to its maximum in man; the nervous system of man, more than any other, becomes the principal seat of biological solidarity. Pursuing this philosophic line with the aid of all our positive knowledge, we find that this great idea was bound *a priori* to acquire, in the study of the social organism, a scientific preponderance still greater than that attributed to it by the best minds in biology, by reason of the additional complexity of this order of phenomena. Now as the present attitude in political philosophy is on the contrary to disregard persistently the fundamental solidarity of the various aspects of society, it was supremely important to clear up this philosophic anomaly, as I think I have managed to do, although only briefly. These considerations were as necessary to the proper coordination of social physics with other sciences as to the proper constitution of the science itself.

The conception of social consensus is chiefly important as giving rise to one of the principal characteristics of the sociological method, that is, the radical modification of the method in accordance with the nature of phenomena. Since social phenomena are closely interconnected, their study cannot be undertaken separately, hence the necessity of always considering the various aspects of society simultaneously, whether in social statics or in social dynamics. Each of these aspects may, it is true, become the subject of particular observation, and this is necessary up to a point, as a means of acquiring material for the science. But this preliminary necessity applies only to the present epoch, during which the science is in course of shaping itself, and is forced to employ, with the necessary precautions, the disjointed data of previous random investigations. When the foundations of the science are sufficiently well laid, the correlation of phenomena will no doubt be the principal guide in exploring them, as I shall show presently. No social phenomenon by whatsoever means it has been explored, as long as it is viewed in isolation —apart from the peculiar mode of observing it—can be introduced into the science, not only from the point of view, where social harmony is always a direct consideration, but also from the dynamic point of view, where consensus, though it is less immediate, is no less predominant. Thus every isolated study of social elements is from the very nature of social science quite irrational, and will remain sterile, as would always be the case of political economy, even if it came to be more intelligently cultivated. Therefore those who endeavour today to sectionalise still more the system of social studies, aping the methodical fragmentation of the inorganic sciences, are falling into the error of regarding an intellectual procedure radically antipathetic to a subject as an essential means of its improvement. No doubt social science will one day be subdivided to some advantage, but we cannot possibly know now what these subdivisions will be, for their principle can only result from the gradual development of the science, which at present can only be founded on comprehensive study; I have already proved that there would be a real philosophic danger in endeavouring to establish a permanent division of labour for the static and dynamic conditions, however rational and constant the distinction between them. At any period of this science the partial researches that may be necessary cannot be selected and formulated except in relation to the progress of the entire study; it is the entire study that indicates the special points whose elucidation can really contribute to the advancement of the subject. Any other way, one would only get a conglomeration of sterile investigations, ill-conceived and ill-pursued, better fitted to hinder the formation of true political philosophy than to furnish it with useful material—which is what we see today. Only comprehensive concepts and studies can contribute to the foundation of positive sociology, whether static or dynamic; work must descend only gradually towards specialisation, the study of elements being constantly dominated by that of the system which, as its general idea clarifies, will do most to illuminate each partial aspect. It cannot be denied that the necessity of observing this procedure, in view of the solidarity of all social phenomena, greatly augments the difficulties already created by its complexity for this new science. The most intense and sustained concentration is necessary if none of the numerous simultaneous aspects that must be embraced is to escape. But these conditions are so clearly a part of the science that they must simply be seen as one more reason for reserving so transcendent a study to the best scientific minds, which are better prepared than any others by wise and arduous study to sustain continued speculative effort, and can apply themselves without respite to the seconding of soaring thought by an ever more perfect subordination of passion to reason. One can realise therefore how contrary the propensities, both moral and intellectual, at present in vogue and even sometimes systematically advocated, are to the accomplishment of this great philosophic enterprise, destined to serve as a basis for the social reorganisation of modern peoples. It would seem that the more difficult of attainment the aim the less one prepares oneself properly! There can be no doubt that the deplorable discrepancy between means and end greatly contributes to the prolongation of our social unrest, whose true source is intellectual.

The better to appreciate the comprehensive character of sociological method, we must see it as not confined to social physics, where it is merely most in evidence, but as belonging to all sections of the study of living bodies, which is thus sharply distinguished from that of inorganic bodies. An empirical aphorism which has been turned by modern metaphysicians into a dogma tells us to proceed constantly, in every possible subject, from the simple to the composite; at bottom there is no other reason for this than that such a procedure is suitable to the nature of the inorganic sciences, whose simpler and more rapid development and greater perfection made them a type for the precepts of universal logic. But there is no logical necessity common to all varieties of speculation except the obvious one of going from the known to the unknown, certainly an inescapable necessity, but one that imposes no direction. Clearly that obvious rule will prescribe going from the composite to the simple, or from the simple to the composite, according to which is better known and more immediately accessible. Now as to this, there is a fundamental difference between inorganic and organic philosophy. In the first, where solidarity is very little marked, and has little influence on the study of the subject, it is a matter of exploring a system, which is almost always better known in its elements than as a whole, the elements being indeed usually alone directly observable, so that one does proceed habitually from what is less to what is more composite. But in the second, where man and society are the principal object, movement in the opposite direction is generally indicated by the same logical principle, since the whole of the subject is certainly much better known and more immediately approachable than the various parts which will be distinguished later on. In the study of the external world it is the whole that escapes us, and that will always remain more or less unintelligible.[69] The idea of the universe cannot of itself become positive, that of the solar system is the most complex one that we can clearly conceive. But in biological philosophy it is the details that are inaccessible, if one wishes to take up specialised study. In this second half of natural philosophy, the more complex and the higher the entities are, the less unknown they are, so that for example the general idea of 'animal' is certainly clearer than the less composite notion of vegetable, and becomes ever clearer as it approaches man, the principal of all biological units, the notion of whom, though the most composite of all, is the point of departure of speculation in this field. Thus, comparing these two great halves of natural philosophy we certainly see that in the one case the extremely composite entity, and in the other the extremely simple entity, escapes scrutiny: hence the mutual inversion of procedure. Sociology is therefore not the only science where it is necessary to proceed from the whole to the parts; biology also in no equivocal manner, has shown a like character for the same reasons. Perhaps, because of its too recent origin, biological philosophy has indulged in too much empirical imitation of the previous sciences, and has not yet manifested its true spirit; I am inclined to think so, and to predict that as its true nature emerges the regular movement from the more to the less composite will become more definite and decided than is yet the case. But from the nature of its phenomena social physics necessarily presents the most complete and incontestable development of this great logical modification, without for that reason impairing the unity of positive method. Indeed the innate solidarity of this subject is so much greater than that offered by biology that any isolated study of a partial aspect must be judged as completely irrational and sterile, serving at the most as a preliminary exercise and means of acquiring scientific material, and even then subject to revision. But to avoid as much as possible idle and puerile discussion, which is always ready to break out today, let it be said here and now that positive philosophy always subordinates ideality to reality, and can never tolerate those vain logical controversies engendered by metaphysical philosophy on the absolute value of such and such a method, apart from scientific application: its preferences being purely relative, the result of an observed harmony between means and end, would change at once without any obstinacy and also without any philosophic inconsistency, if practice revealed an inferiority in the method adopted; which is certainly not to be feared in the case under discussion.

Now that we have sufficiently characterised the spirit of static psychology, there remains to consider what philosophic concept should guide the dynamic study of human societies. As this second subject is less imperfectly understood and more familiar than the first, a greatly curtailed discussion will suffice, especially after the explanations we have been giving which will have cleared away the greatest difficulties in view of the close link that exists between the static and the dynamic, the theory of existence and that of movement, the laws of order and those of progress, this last from the political point of view.[70]

The static conception of the social organism must constitute the basis of all sociology, but social dynamics is the part of most direct interest, especially today; also it gives to the new science its most outstanding characteristic, it brings to the fore the idea that most distinguishes sociology from biology, the idea of the continuous progress, or rather of the gradual development of humanity. In a methodical treatise of political philosophy, no doubt, we should have to analyse the individual impulses that are the elements of progress, and relate them to the fundamental instinct, made of a number of concurrent tendencies, that pushes man to improve his condition in all its aspects, in other words, to develop ceaselessly his physical, moral and intellectual life, as far as circumstances will permit. We may however consider this idea to be sufficiently clear today to most intelligent minds, and at once proceed to the conception of social dynamics, that is, we can begin to study of this continuous movement as seen in the whole of humanity. To grasp the idea let us, by scientific abstraction, after the model of Condorcet, construct a hypothetical people which undergoes consecutively all the social modifications that are observed in different peoples. This fiction is far nearer to reality than we usually suppose, for the true successors of such and such peoples are certainly those which, utilising their primitive efforts, prolong their social progress, whatever be the country they inhabit, or even the race from they spring; in a word it is political continuity which ensures sociological continuity, although community of fatherland must greatly influence such continuity, in the majority of cases. But without going into this, which will form the subject of a special treatise in which the idea of nation or people will be subjected to positive analysis, it is sufficient for our purpose to employ the said hypothesis, as a scientific device of known utility.

In the true spirit of dynamic sociology, each of the consecutive social states is seen as the necessary result of the preceding one, and the necessary cause of the following one, according to the axiom of the great Leibnitz: *The present is big with the future.* To discover the laws of this continuity becomes the aim of science, for it is the continuity that determines the direction of human development. In a word, social dynamics studies the laws of movement, while social statics seeks out those of co-existence: the former applies itself to furnishing practical politics with a true theory of progress, while the latter provides a theory of order: there can therefore be no doubt whatsoever that it is this combination that will satisfy the twofold need of modern society.

So defined, social dynamics has a purely scientific nature which eliminates the idle yet still raging controversy over human progress. Once in possession it will put an end to these sterile discussions—as much as one can ever put an end to a metaphysical discussion—by shifting the ground from ideality to reality. If there were not a danger of lapsing into puerile affectation, and of appearing to elude the difficulty that positive philosophy at once dispels, it would be easy, in my opinion, to treat the whole of social physics without once using the word *progress*, replacing it always by the scientific expression *development*, which designates without emitting any moral judgement an incontestable fact. Obviously this abstract idea is not peculiar to sociology; it already exists in the study of individual life where biologists use it continually, and where it leads to the comparative analysis of the different ages of the organism, especially the animal organism. This scientific parallel, by showing the idea as it were in germ, also indicates the speculative intention that must preside over its use, as all idle and irrational controversy over the respective merit of the various consecutive states is put aside, and only the laws of their succession to one another are studied. But it must be recognised that the necessary succession of the different social states constitutes in political philosophy an overmastering concept as it does not in biological philosophy with its sequence of ages only in the individual. The great idea of the social series has as its equivalent in biology both as science and as method not the analysis of ages but the conception of the organic series, as I shall explain it at the end of this lecture.

As we have already demonstrated the existence of sociological laws in the most difficult and most uncertain case, the static condition, there is no need to insist on the much more readily appreciable necessity of dynamic laws. At all times and in all places notable modifications have been seen taking place in the social state, even in the brief lifetime of the individual. The most ancient descriptions of human existence bear testimony to these changes, though without explanation. It is the slow and gradual but continuous accumulation of these successive changes that constitutes the social movement of which each generation marks a step, for it is by the constant renewal of adults that the most notable variations in politics are brought about, the variations represented by the same individual being generally scarcely perceptible. In an age in which the average speed of this progression seems notably increased, whatever moral opinion one may have about it, one cannot deny its reality, felt even by those who wish it to hell. Controversy therefore only arises over the subordination of these great dynamic phenomena to invariable natural laws; that this is so will not be disputed by anyone who has the point of view of positive philosophy, a condition, it is true, still too rarely fulfilled. But if our observation is at all complete, we shall realise that, from whatever angle one regards society its successive modifications are always subject to a definite order, of which the explanation, in terms of human nature, is possible in a sufficient number of cases for us to expect it to be confirmed in those that remain. This order has a remarkable fixity, and can be seen in the parallel developments of populations quite distinct and independent of one another. Since on the one hand the existence of the social movement is undeniable, and since on the other the order of succession of the various states of society is never arbitrary, we must certainly regard this great continuous phenomenon as subject to natural laws not less positive, though more complex, than those of any other class of phenomena, unless we introduce the theological machinery of a permanent providence, or have recourse to the mystic virtue of metaphysical entities. There is no intellectual alternative; and so it is in the domain of social phenomena that the struggle which has been going on for three centuries between the positive and the theologico-metaphysical spirit is destined to end. Banished from all the other classes of human speculation in succession, theological and metaphysical philosophy hold their own today in social studies: from that domain also they are to be expelled: a result to be brought about by the concept of social movement as subject to invariable natural laws, not ruled by arbitrary wills.

The fundamental laws of social solidarity are seen in operation in the state of movement, but this phenomenon, despite its inevitable unity, can be decomposed for the convenience of observation, into the various elementary aspects of human existence, and regarded alternatively as physical, moral, intellectual, or political. Now from whatever point of view one regards the total movement of humanity, from the most ancient historic times right up to our own day it can easily be seen that the various steps have followed one another in a fixed order.[71] Here I will confine myself to the example of intellectual evolution, the clearest and most irrefutable of all, as it has been less hindered and more advanced than any other, and for that reason has played the role of guide. The principal part of this evolution, that which has most influenced general progress, is the development of the scientific spirit, from the primitive researches of the Thales and the Pythagorases to those of the Lagranges[72] and the Bichats.[73] Now no enlightened mind could doubt today that in this long succession of efforts and discoveries, the human mind has followed an exactly determined course, so that, with previous knowledge of this course, it would have been possible to predict before it was realised, the progress marked out for each epoch, according to the genial insight of Fontenelle[74] at the beginning of the last century. In all that we have said historical conditions have only been incidentally referred to, but our hearers will have noted numerous examples of necessary sequence, more complex but not more arbitrary than any other natural law, both in the development of each science, and in what concerns the influence of the various branches of natural philosophy on one another. The principles that we laid down in advance on the course followed by the intelligence and on the general hierarchy of the sciences, have greatly facilitated such observations, and above all have conferred on them a high degree of rationality. Thus in a variety of important cases the progress of each epoch, and even of each generation, has been seen to result from the state immediately preceding: men of genius, to whom this progress has been exclusively attributed, were but the organs of a predetermined movement which, if they had not been there, would have found other outlets; this history confirms in the most striking manner, for it shows us several eminent minds about to make the same discovery at once; the discovery therefore must have had but one single organ. The same could be said of all parts of human evolution, although they might be more complex and not so observable. It would serve no purpose to pause here and point out briefly the same situation in the arts, whose natural progress, whether individual or collective, is today quite evident. As for the part of this great movement which seems today the least amenable to natural laws, the political movement, which we still look on as governed arbitarily by people of sufficiently strong will, everyone will be able to recognise with the same certainty at least as in any other case, that the various political systems have succeeded one another historically in an exactly determined order, which I have no hesitation in declaring to be still more inevitable than that of the general and special states of the human intelligence.

If you wish to develop the feeling for the positive laws of social dynamics in all its aspects, you will be greatly helped if you consider the fundamental solidarity between social elements in the static state. All the more reason then for the solidarity to exist in movement, for without it movement would bring about, as in mechanics, the break-up of the entire system. Now the fact of this intercommunication at once simplifies and strengthens the demonstration of the necessary dynamic order, for it is enough to have observed this order in one connection to be able to extend it to all the other aspects; thus are linked up the partial proofs that one acquires piecemeal of its reality. In the choice and use of these various proofs you should note first of all that from the nature of the subject the more extensive the populations concerned, the more perceptible the laws of social dynamics will be, for secondary disturbances will exert less influence.[75] In this connection let us also note as more specifically dynamic, that fundamental laws necessarily become more irresistible, and therefore more observable with the advancement of civilisation, since social movement, which is at first vague and uncertain, becomes more marked and more consolidated as it prolongs itself, surmounting with increasing energy all accidental influences. The twofold consideration of extent and age, applicable to all aspects of society, will I hope serve as a guide to my hearers in the preliminary work which I must now indicate, and from which I cannot excuse them, if they are to follow the rest of these lectures. And my hearers must be warned, in connection with the philosophic co-ordination of these preliminary partial proofs, of which the combination is not at all indifferent to science, that the fundamental evolution of humanity, studied comparatively under its various social aspects, is the more subject to stringent natural laws as the phenomena are more composite, for then irregularities arising from individual influences are naturally effaced. How irrational then is the belief that while the scientific movement is subject to positive laws, the political movement is entirely arbitrary, seeing that the latter by reason of its greater complexity overrides individual disorders, and therefore must be more predetermined than the former, where personal genius must personally hold more sway as we shall presently note in treating of the limits of social action. However paradoxical this principle may appear, I do not doubt that it will be finally confirmed on further investigation.

As I have indicated, people are now coming to see quite definitely the possibility of defining the true spirit of dynamic sociology by limiting themselves to the study of the development of humanity, which is the real scientific subject, without pronouncing one way or another on the famous question of human progress. It would be easy for me to continue on this path, paying no attention to the heated controversy that today, as the result of the irrational preoccupations of our political philosophy, seems destined to furnish the basis of the entire system of social concepts: this would-be important discussion would then be judged once for all, though indirectly, by simply carrying out a complete study of human evolution without any consideration of 'progress.' But however useful such scientific stringency—a stringency which should indeed prevail in a methodical treatise—I must here, in what is really a first sketch, attach some importance to elucidations of principle demanded by the present state of philosophy, even although they may appear from a purely scientific point of view secondary and incidental. Which is why I think it would be useful to examine this celebrated philosophic debate, object of such puerile awe and reverence; it will be a natural transition to the analysis of the limits of political action.

The relative spirit of all the ideas of positive politics is destined to eliminate once and for all the vain and idle metaphysical controversy on the increase of human happiness from age to age of civilisation: which means eliminating the only part of the question on which it would be impossible to obtain real and permanent assent. Since the happiness of each individual demands a harmony between the development of his faculties and the system of circumstances which dominates his life, and since on the other hand such an equilibrium tends always to establish itself naturally, there can be no means of comparing positively either by feeling or by reason social situations which can never be commensurate with one another, as far as individual happiness is concerned: one might as well propound the question of the different degrees of happiness of the different animal organisms, or of the two sexes of each species.

Now that we have got rid of this text, or rather pretext for puerile declamation and sterile dissertation, positive analysis of the vague notion current today under the name of human progress leaves us with nothing but the eminently scientific idea of human nature's many-sided development, in continuous harmony and according to the invariable laws of evolution. Now this conception, without which there cannot be any veritable social science, has a most undeniable reality, even in the light of the brief explanations we have given: no dialogue is possible with those who deny it, any more than in any science with those who reject its primary axioms, as for instance in biology, with those who would deny organic series, of which the sociological series constitutes the philosophic equivalent. It is therefore obvious that humanity develops ceaselessly throughout the course of its civilisation, especially in physical, moral, intellectual and finally political fields, those of the higher faculties of our nature; that is to say, those faculties, latent and comparatively numb at first, little by little, by more and more extensive and regular exercise, come finally into full play, within the limits imposed by the human organism. The question is then if we are to consider the two ideas of development and improvement, the one theoretical, the other practical, as equivalent, in other words if this development is to be regarded as necessarily accompanied by an amelioration of some sort, by a progress. Now although science could easily abstain from resolving this question, I do not hesitate to affirm that this continuous amelioration, this constant progress, seems to me as irrefutable as the development from which it derives: as long as one does not cease to regard it as subject, like the development itself, to limits, both general and particular, which science will later be able to define at least in the most important cases, so that the fanciful extravagance of unlimited perfectibility does not enter into it. It must also be understood that it is the whole of humanity, and not an isolated people that is considered as improving. That being granted, human development seems to me to bring about a twofold amelioration: in the human condition—which today would scarcely be denied; in human faculties, which is far less appreciated: the term 'perfectibility' really applies in particular to this second aspect. With regard to the first there is no need to dwell on the obvious improvement that social evolution has brought about in the externals of our living conditions, through wisely directed action on the environment thanks to the progress of science and arts, and through increasing mildness of manners, or the improvement of social organisation. As regards this last, which is most disputed in our time, there can really be no doubt, despite the political regression attributed to the Middle Ages in which, contrary to the prevailing prejudice, progress was principally political.[76] One undeniable fact is sufficient refutation of all the sophistical declamation to the contrary: the constant increase of human population over the entire surface of the globe, as a consequence of civilisation, although individuals are finding better satisfaction for all their physical needs. Such a tendency to improvement in the human condition must certainly be spontaneous and irresistible, since it has persevered in spite of the misdemeanours, especially the political misdemeanours, that at all times have absorbed or neutralised the greater part of our energies. Even in these revolutionary times, and in spite of the growing gap between the political system and the state of civilisation, there is no doubt that the improvement is continuing, not only in physical and intellectual terms, which is obvious, but also in moral terms, although temporary disorder must disorientate evolution in that sphere more than in any other. As for the second aspect of the question: a certain gradual improvement in human nature, within very narrow limits which will later on define themselves though at present they are very little known—it seems to me impossible, from the point of view of biological philosophy, not to admit up to a point the principle of the great Lamarck,[77] in spite of his exaggerations, namely, that a homogeneous and continuous practice must exercise an influence on an animal organism, especially that of man, so as to produce an organic improvement which can gradually become fixed in the race, if it has persisted long enough. It is a ticklish problem, but take the most obvious case, that of intellectual development: we can scarcely shut our eyes to the fact, although experiment has not yet fully confirmed it, that there is greater natural aptitude for intellectual operations among the very civilised peoples, independently of culture, or, which is the same thing, less aptitude among the backward peoples. The comparison, of course, must always be made between individuals of a similar cerebral organisation, and of average intelligence. The intellectual faculties must be the chief ones to be modified by social evolution; nevertheless their low intensity relatively to the human constitution as a whole seems to authorise the conclusion, *a fortiori*, from their amelioration, that more prominent and not less exercised aptitudes are proportionately improved also, though this philosophic view will eventually have to be tested scientifically. Especially with regard to ethics, it seems to me undeniable that the gradual development of humanity must bring about the preponderance of the noble inclinations. Our worse instincts continue to subsist, modifying only their mode of expression, yet a less sustained and more restricted exercise of them must gradually tend to weaken them, and their increasing regulation leads to their contributing involuntarily to a good social system, especially for the less individualised organisms, which are the immense majority.

These considerations should make it clear that the continuous development of humanity can always be considered as a gradual amelioration within the proper limits. Therefore we have the right to admit in sociology the equivalence of the two terms, development and progress, as is habitually done in biology, in the comparative study of the animal organism. Yet I think I should continue to employ for preference the first expression, which has not yet been spoilt by irrational usage, and which appears peculiarly suitable to science. And my preference is further motivated by the fact that the word *development* has the advantage of defining what *progress* for humanity consists in; it indicates a spontaneous unfolding, gradually seconded by an appropriate culture, of the fundamental faculties that have always existed and that make up the whole of our nature, without any introduction of further faculties. The second expression has not the same aptness, because of its erroneous use today, and we shall have to avoid it, without pedantic affectation, as much as possible, while using the first with all its philosophic significance, both scientific and practical, as we have defined it.

To complete the conception of human development, which is the proper subject of dynamic sociology: it leads to regarding a social state, in all its aspects, as being as perfect in each epoch, as the corresponding age of humanity permits, in combination with the circumstances that accompany the evolution of that state. This philosophic attitude, without which history becomes incomprehensible, is the complement of an analogous intellectual attitude that we established for static sociology; the one is to progress what the other is to order, and both derive from the same principle, that of the relative prevailing over the absolute point of view, which is the distinguishing mark of any subject in positive philosophy. As the various social elements cannot fail to observe the harmony which is the first principle of order, so also each of them, or all together cannot avoid in every epoch being as advanced as the total system of influences, internal and external, that have actualised them. Not more in the one case than in the other have we to do with final causes, or providential guidance. In movement, as in existence, we have to do with the simple sequence of natural order resulting from natural laws, which applies to all possible phenomena, but must manifest itself in a less regular way by reason of their greater complexity in regard to social phenomena, whether static or dynamic. The principle of relativity · here also rules out any senseless accusation of optimism, about which I have already said enough apropos of social statics, and which is not less strange in social dynamics. To attribute social progress to political measures would certainly be to endow them with a totally incomprehensible power, and one totally contrary to observable facts. Since real progress results from the spontaneous development of humanity, how could it in any epoch be anything else than what it is from the situation as a whole?

But this rational development does not at all exclude the possibility, and even the necessity, of individual aberrations, voluntary or involuntary, more marked than with any other type of phenomena, although confined within certain limitations imposed by the conditions of the subject and without which the phenomenon of continuous progress would become inexplicable. This philosophic caveat merely leads to a kind of scientific indulgence which disposes one to understand better and even to detect more easily the historical chain of events, without excluding severe censure where circumstances demand, nor the idea of active human intervention.[78]

We now come to the examination of the last main aspect of social dynamics, one that more than any other exemplifies the true philosophic character of positive politics. I refer to the principle of the limits of political action, a notion that immediately dissolves the spirit of absolute and infinite idealism that still dominates social speculation thanks to the influence of metaphysical philosophy. No man of sense can deny today the necessity of such limits, quite apart from actually being able to fix them, if we are not to carry on with the ancient theological hypothesis that represents the legislator as the organ of a continuously active providence, to whose influence no limits are admissible. Our age no longer needs to refute such a conception, which has even ceased to be really understood by its most determined partisan, although the intellectual habits contracted under its prolonged domination are still with us. Human action being always necessarily very limited in any order of phenomena, in spite of the most extensive assistance, directed by the most ingenious artifice, there would be absolutely no reason why social phenomena should alone be excepted from such restriction, which is the inevitable accompaniment of natural law. Whatever the illusions of human pride, any statesman, after having exercised political authority for a time will from personal experience be entirely convinced of the reality of the limitations on political action imposed by the combination of social influences to which he must fain attribute the failure of the majority of his cherished projects, and perhaps this feeling will be all the stronger, though disguised, the greater his power, for the impossibility of struggling against the natural laws of the phenomena will then have become all the more apparent, unless perhaps intelligence has intervened to resist the intoxication so frequently induced by power. Further insistence on this principle without which social science could not exist is unnecessary, except to point out that the new political philosophy is singularly adapted to the task of determining definitely, as a result of its own scientific development, with all the precision compatible with the subject and sufficient for real needs, in what the said limits consist, whether general or special, permanent or temporary.

For this purpose we must first of all note how the steady progress of human development may be affected by any cause of variation whatsoever; secondly we shall examine what is the relative importance, among the various possible modifiers, of the voluntary and calculated action of political combinations. Such is the order prescribed by the nature of the subject, the first part being much more important than the second, and being indeed the only part fully available to science.

To proceed with the first part: social phenomena, by reason of their high degree of complexity, must be seen as the most modifiable of all, as I have demonstrated in the two preceding lectures. Thus sociological laws have wider limits of variation than even biological laws, *a fortiori*, than chemical, physical and especially astronomical laws. If therefore, among modifying causes, human intervention occupies a corresponding rank in influence, as it is natural to suppose, its influence must be much more considerable in sociological phenomena than in any other. But although the modifications produced by any causes are necessarily greater with political phenomena than with simpler phenomena, neither there, nor anywhere else, can they ever rise above their nature of modifications, that is to say they remain subordinate to the fundamental laws, whether static or dynamic, that regulate the harmony of the various social elements and the chain reaction of their variations. There is no intrusive influence, either inanimate or human that can make antipathetic elements coexist in the political world, or alter, from whatever cause, the natural laws of the development of humanity; provided of course that in the positive study of social solidarity and human evolution every constant cause, both internal and external that produces these phenomena has been taken into consideration. The inevitable preponderance, however gradual, and however imperceptible at first, of continuous influences, is today admitted with regard to all natural phenomena; it must also be applied to social phenomena, as soon as the same manner of philosophising is extended to them. In what then do these undeniable modifications consist of which the political organism is eminently capable, if nothing can alter the laws of harmony or of sequence? This rather stupid question leaves out of account the fact that a modification is something that affects only the intensity of phenomena and their secondary mode of accomplishment, and does not affect either their nature or their sequence, for that would be to raise the disturbing cause above the fundamental cause, and would at once destroy the economy of the subject's laws. Applied to the political world this principle of positive philosophy demonstrates that as regards the statics of the situation, the different possible variations can only consist in the greater or less intensity of the different tendencies proper to the whole of a social situation, without anything being able either to prevent or to produce these tendencies, or to alter them: in the same way, as regards the dynamics of the situation, the evolution of humanity must be regarded as modifiable to a predetermined degree, as far as its speed is concerned, but without any possible reversal of the order of development, and without any important intermediate stage being completely omitted. One can get an idea of the true nature of these variations by comparing them to analogous ones in the animal organism, which are exactly parallel as they are subject to similar conditions both static and dynamic, with this difference only that social modifications can and must become more extensive and more varied than mere biological modifications, on condition of course that there is a constant milieu and a constant organism. As a sound theory of these limits remains to be established in biology, ever since the work of Lamarck who indicated its principle, one cannot expect sociology to be more advanced in this matter. But it will be enough to have defined its general spirit, as we are doing here, both in social statics and social dynamics. From either point of view, if we consider the principle that I have just laid down, it will be impossible to dispute it, in the context of general political observation. In the intellectual order, which is more easily grasped today, there is no accidental influence or individual superiority that can transfer to one epoch the discoveries really reserved to a later one, in accordance with the advance of the human mind, or vice versa. The history of science proves quite definitely the close dependence of the most eminent genius on the contemporary state of human reason; it would be superfluous to quote the innumerable examples, especially in what depends on the improvement of the methods of investigation, either rational or experimental. This is truer still of arts, especially those in which mechanical means aid human action. Nor is there any more reason to doubt this principle in regard to the moral development of our nature, which is certainly regulated in each epoch by the corresponding state of social evolution, whatever be the voluntary modifications derived from education, and even the involuntary modifications brought about by particular organisation. Each one of the modes of social existence determines the system of morals, whose general aspect is easily perceived in all the individuals, whatever be their characteristic differences: there is for example a state of humanity in which the best natures necessarily contract habits of ferocity, from which very inferior natures, living in a more advanced society, free themselves almost without effort. It is the same thing in politics. In short, if one were to report all the facts and the reasoning which establish the existence of these necessary limits of variation of which I have just laid down the logical principle, one would find oneself reproducing all the reasons why social phenomena are subordinate to invariable natural laws, for the principle in question is but a strict application of this philosophic concept.

So much for the scientific limits of social modification, from whatever source. But I cannot be expected to treat the question from the second point of view, that is, the classification of the various modifying influences according to their respective importance. Such an investigation would be premature, since the general theorem of which it can only be a corollary has not yet been fully worked out, nor even sufficiently examined in biology, a much less difficult case. Thus the three general sources of social variation appear to me to be: (1) race, (2) climate, (3) political action, in the widest scientific sense: there can be no question of discovering at this point if their relative importance really corresponds to this order or to any other. Even if such a decision were not evidently out of place in the first stage of our science, the laws of method would demand that its direct enunciation be postponed till after the examination of the principal subject, so as to avoid a confusion between fundamental phenomena and their various modifications.[79] Besides, a classification of this type has less practical interest today, as of the three modifiers political combinations alone are sufficiently accessible to our intervention, and so attention is directed towards them—though it would be a serious scientific blunder to suppose that for that reason they have the greatest importance, thus prejudging the result of a comparison to be effected later, and so yielding to a superficial impression. While recognising that such a comparison is not yet properly prepared, we must also recognise that it is not at all important at the present moment as far as the institution of the positive spirit in politics is concerned. The scientific principle that I have set up, defining and delimiting the modifications compatible with the nature of social phenomena, whatever be the source of these modifications, is enough. If in this connection I have appeared to have political action principally in mind, this is only because of the quite illogical importance generally attributed to it, which tends to obscure any notion of sociological law. In addition to what I have already said, I will merely indicate here the source of the illusion that maintains this sophism, even in those who believe themselves to be completely emancipated from the theological philosophy that has given birth to it. This illusion arises from the fact that the various political operations temporal or spiritual have had a social effect when they were in conformity with the corresponding tendencies of humanity, and therefore seem to a prejudiced or unreflective spectator actually to have produced what spontaneous but almost imperceptible evolution alone had determined. Proceeding from this mistaken supposition one forgets the numerous decisive cases with which history abounds in which little trace has remained of the most energetic and persistent action on the part of the most far-reaching political authority, for the sole reason that this authority was exerted in the direction opposite to the general movement of contemporary civilisation, as witness the examples of Julian the Apostate,[80] Philip II,[80a] Bonaparte[80b] etc. More decisive still for science are the opposite cases, unfortunately much more rare, where political action, sustained by powerful authority, and pursuing premature reforms has aborted, in spite of certain progressive tendencies in its favour: intellectual history as well as political history offers incontestable examples. Ferguson[81] has shrewdly remarked that even the action of one people on another whether by conquest or otherwise, although the most intense of all political forces, could only realise modifications in conformity with native tendencies, whose development it would slightly accelerate or expand. In politics as in science, timeliness is the first condition of any great and lasting influence, whatever be the personal value of the distinguished man to whom the majority attribute a social action of which he was only the instrument. Any power of the individual over the species is subject to these general limitations, even if it is only a question of effects to be produced, for good or for evil. In revolutionary epochs, for example, those who attribute to themselves with such strange pride, the merit of having developed anarchic passions in their contemporaries, do not perceive that their ghastly triumph was due to a natural predisposition determined by the social situation as a whole, which produced a provisional and partial dissolution of the general harmony: as can easily be verified today with regard to the principal social aberrations derived from moral licence, resulting from intellectual anarchy; it has been the same at all times. Besides, now that we have recognised, for so many reasons, the existence of limitations to the variation of social phenomena, and especially to the modifications dependent on systematised political action, temporal or spiritual; now that we have at the same time established the scientific principle which will delimit and qualify such modifications, it is obviously for social science as it develops to determine the influence and the bearing of this general principle on each case, as the principle in no way dispenses with the need to estimate a particular situation. Intuitive insight into these matters operating entirely empirically has hitherto guided those men of genius who have really exercised a profound influence on humanity for any reason: only by taking cognisance of contemporary trends have they been able to rectify the illusory or fallacious findings of the irrational and chimerical doctrines that informed their reason. In every sphere, as I proved at the beginning of these lectures, foresight in the true source of action.

The vagueness that still prevails in political philosophy may lead to underestimating the practical importance of a new science that destroys once for all even in its speculative basis the illusion of the unlimited action of man on civilisation: therefore social physics must expect to be blamed sometimes for reducing us to simply observing passively human events, without intervening in any considerable way. It is certain that on the contrary the principle of the limitation of political action establishes the only true and exact point of contact between social theory and social practice. Thanks to it the art of politics can at last begin to assume a prudential character, and cease to be guided by arbitrary principles tempered by empirical impulses; in a word it will experience a transformation analogous to that which is taking place today in the medical art, to which it is most nearly akin by the nature of its phenomena. For since political intervention can effect nothing either for order or for progress except by basing itself on the tendencies of the political life or organism, so as to assist by well-chosen means its spontaneous development, it is necessary to know as exactly as possible the natural laws of harmony and sequence that determine in every epoch and for every aspect of society what human evolution is ready to produce, and even indicate the principal obstacles to be removed. In a word, as I showed in the work published in 1822,[82] civilisation does not advance in a straight line but by a series of movements oscillating unevenly around an average motion which always tends to predominate and a foreknowledge of which will permit of its being regularised in advance by diminishing the oscillations and the more or less pernicious trial and error corresponding to them. Certainly we should be exaggerating the practical importance of this art, even if it were cultivated with all possible intelligence and applied as widely as possible, if we attributed to it the property of preventing in every case the violent revolutions that burst the bonds imposed on the natural movement of human evolution. In the social organism, because of its great complexity, maladies and crises are in many ways still more inevitable than in the individual organism. But even if true science is forced to recognise its momentary impotence in the face of profound disorders or irresistible movements, it can serve to mitigate, and above all to curtail the crises through an exact appreciation of their nature, and a rational foreknowledge of their ultimate result, and may even intervene judiciously, unless such intervention has been recognised to be impossible. Here, as elsewhere, and even more than elsewhere, it is not a question of governing phenomena, but only of modifying their spontaneous development, which of course demands that one knows their real laws.

These notions, first static and then dynamic, sufficiently characterise the true spirit of the new political philosophy and determine the logical position of sociological questions. Without either admiring or cursing the facts, and seeing in them as in any other science simply subjects for observation, social physics considers every phenomenon from the two-fold viewpoint of its harmony with coexisting phenomena and its link with the previous and subsequent state of development; it endeavours on both these heads to discover as much as possible the true interrelations of all social facts; each of them appears to it to be *explained* in the scientific sense of the term, when it has been attached either to the corresponding situation or to the preceding movement, all vain and impossible research into its intimate nature and mode of production being carefully avoided. As a promoter of social feeling to the highest degree, this new science, according to the celebrated formula of Pascal,[83] now fully realised, represents men in the mass as constituting in the present, past and future, both in place and in time, one immense social unit, whose various individual or national organs, in their intimate and universal solidarity, necessarily contribute each according to its mode and degree to the evolution of humanity. This supremely important and quite modern conception is destined to become the rational basis of positive morality. Political science, leading like any other science to an exact and systematic prediction of the events that must result either from a given situation or from a given group of antecedents, as exact as is compatible with the complexity of the phenomena, furnishes to political art not only the necessary foreknowledge of the natural tendencies it must foster, but also a general indication of the principal means it can employ to avoid as much as possible vain or ephemeral, and therefore dangerous action, in a word any aberrant assistance to nondescript forces.

Now that we have characterised the spirit of the new political philosophy, which was much more difficult than it would have been for a science that was already constituted, we must proceed as in previous chapters to the consideration of the various means, suitable to its nature and aim, to be employed in sociological science. According to a philosophical law established in our fifth, sixth and seventh chapters, we must expect to find in sociology, because of the greater complexity of the phenomena, a system of research tools both direct and indirect, more varied and more developed than in any other branch of natural philosophy, not excepting even biology. This law continues to function in the present case, which indeed exemplifies it to the full, although the extension of means cannot compensate for the greater imperfection of the science in proportion to the complexity of its phenomena. The extreme novelty of the subject must render the extension of means much more difficult to prove than in any other science, and although I must here draw attention to it, explaining it briefly in passing in its principal aspects, I can scarcely hope for it to be sufficiently recognised before the gradual development of the science produces confirmation of it with a certain amount of logical force, in reality derived from the nature of the study.

As social physics must necessarily be subordinate to the system of fundamental sciences related to the successive classes of more general and less complex phenomena, according to the social hierarchy that I have established, two principal types of research tool are at its disposal: the one, direct, consists in the various means of exploration belonging to the science; the other indirect, but no less necessary, results from the necessary relations of sociology to the system of the previous sciences, which furnish it, for many reasons, with valuable indications all the time. I must finish this lecture with a summary appreciation of the first order of research tool.[84]

In sociology, as in biology, scientific exploration employs concurrently the three fundamental modes which I have already noted:[85] observation, experimentation, and finally the comparative method, essentially adapted to any study of living bodies. We must now see what is the import and character of these three procedures, in relation to the nature and the aim of our new science.

As regards observation, current notions are very imperfect and even fallacious as to what it can and must be for sociology.* The anarchic

* (Translator's note) While writing the volume of the *Cours de Philosophie Positive* in which this lecture appears (Volume IV) Comte invents the term 'sociology' to replace social physics.

influence of the metaphysical philosophy of the last century has extended itself from doctrine to method, and has tended, through sheer blind destructive instinct, to prevent any intellectual reorganisation, ruining in advance the only scientific bases of scientific analysis by an absurd theory of historical Pyrrhonism which even today exercises its deleterious influence, although the principle of it is no longer openly maintained. Sophistical theory both voluntary and involuntary exaggerates wildly the difficulties common to any kind of exact observation, and above all the special difficulties raised by the complex social phenomena, without taking into account the various precautions, experimental and logical, that guard against these; it has often gone so far as to deny outright any certainty in social observation, even direct observation. The explanation given at the beginning of these lectures (the second lecture) on the distinction that it is necessary always to make between certainty and precision in any subject at once disposes of these sophistries, on which I will not insist, and which, if given the scope which cannot consistently be denied them, would tend to destroy also the simplest and most complete sciences, as much as those of society, by a common metaphysical influence. Now that this aberration is no longer openly professed, systematic scepticism, withdrawing from immediate to mediate observation, has entrenched itself in the fundamental uncertainty of human testimony, in order to continue denying the positive value of historical knowledge. Some geometrists have even pushed their naïveté or servility so far as to attempt, according to the illusory theory of probability ponderous and ridiculous calculations of the necessary increase in this so-called uncertainty through the mere lapse of time: and this, besides being a source of grave social danger, because it supports harmful errors by investing them with an imposing air of rationality, has more than once discredited the mathematical spirit in the eyes of many sensible men, lacking the knowledge to judge it directly, but scandalised by these abuses. Philosophers less preoccupied with sophistical declamation against the scientific value of testimony have nevertheless been sufficiently impressed to set up a division of the sciences into testimony and non-testimony sciences, which clearly proves the unfortunate prestige still enjoyed by these sophistries, even with intelligent men, who have not sufficient command of the whole domain of the intellect. The above-mentioned distinction between certitude and precision will dispel the confusion of ideas that is the main source of these palpable errors, against which common sense has always rebelled. And there is an inconsistency in confining the application of this paradox to social studies only, for once it is accepted, it would apply to every department whatsoever of our knowledge, if the human mind could ever be completely consistent in the application of insane principles. It is obvious that contrary to the illusory division that I have cited, all sciences, even the simplest, require what are called proofs of testimony, that is, they need to admit, in working out their most positive theories observations which it has not been possible for those who employ them to make, or even to repeat, and whose reality rests only on the faithful testimony of the first searchers; which does not prevent them from being used constantly, concurrently with immediate observations. Such a necessity is too obvious, even in astronomy, and *a fortiori* in more complex and less advanced sciences, to require an explanation: even mathematical science is not as free from it as is generally supposed, and the kind of exception that mathematics represents in no way refutes this necessity. What science could ever emerge from infancy, what real division of intellectual labour could ever be organised, if everyone were only to employ his own personal observations? So no one dares to maintain such a principle, even among the most systematic partisans of historical Pyrrhonism. Whence comes it then that the paradox is only applied today to social phenomena? Fundamentally because it is an integral part of the philosophic arsenal, constructed by the metaphysics of revolution, for the demolition of the old political system. Many uncultivated minds would believe themselves almost obliged to put their necks again under the yoke of Catholic philosophy, which they had too recently and too incompletely shaken off, if they admitted the authenticity of the Bible tales, the methodical denial of which was the original motive of the logical aberration we are discussing: and such is usually the disadvantage of any antitheological attitude that does not rest on a sufficient preliminary development of the positive spirit.

To these aberrations, already sufficiently harmful, are added today errors less palpable, but almost as vexatious, in connection with the systematic empiricism that people endeavour to impose on social and above all historical observation, outlawing, under the pretext of impartiality, the employment of any theory. It would be difficult to imagine a dogma more radically opposed to the true spirit of positive philosophy, as also to the character it must assume in the study of social phenomena. In any order of phenomena whatsoever, even the most simple, no real observation is possible except as it is guided and in the end interpreted by some theory; it is this logical need, indeed, that first launched theological philosophy, in the infancy of human reason, as I showed at the beginning of these lectures. Far from dispensing with this condition, positive philosophy does nothing but develop it and satisfy it more and more in the process of multiplying and perfecting the relations between phenomena. We now know that from the scientific point of view any isolated, entirely empirical observation, is essentially idle and even uncertain; science can only employ observations that are attached, at least hypothetically, to some law; it is this connection that constitutes the principal difference between the observations of scientists and those of the common man, although they embrace the same facts, the only distinction being the point of view; observations made otherwise can only serve as provisional material, requiring as a rule some kind of revision. And the more complex the phenomena become, the more stringent is this logical requirement; without the guidance of a previous theory, the more realistic the better, the observer would not know what he should look for in what is taking place before his eyes; thus it is by the link with preceding facts that he learns to see the following facts. There can be no doubt about this if we consider astronomical, physical and chemical studies, and above all the various biological studies in which, by virtue of the extreme complexity of the phenomena, good observations are so difficult and still so rare, precisely because of the incompleteness of positive theory. Pursuing this analogy, we see that social observation, whether static or dynamic, relating as it does to the highest degree of complexity in natural phenomena, must demand more than any other type of observation, the continuous employment of fundamental theories directed towards linking facts in process of accomplishment with those already accomplished, contrary to the irrational precept so magisterially propounded in our day and age, the application of which floods us with perfectly useless descriptions. The more we reflect on this subject, the more we shall see that as the links established between known facts increase in number, so also does our appreciation, nay perception of facts as yet unexplored. I admit that this logical requirement in relation to such phenomena augments the difficulty, already considerable, of founding positive sociology, for one is obliged in some sort to create simultaneously both observations and laws in a kind of vicious circle, out of which one breaks only by using ill-prepared material and ill-conceived doctrines.[86] Obviously it is the absence of any positive theory that renders social observation today so vague and so incoherent. There is no lack of facts, certainly, since, in this order of phenomena, more than in any other, the most well-known ones are necessarily the most important, in spite of the puerile pretensions of the collectors of private anecdotes:

but they remain sterile, and even unperceived, although we are immersed in them, for lack of the intellectual attitudes and speculative signposts indispensable to their scientific exploration.* In view of the excessive complexity of the phenomena, static observation of them cannot become efficient unless directed by an at least rudimentary knowledge of the laws of social solidarity; and this is still more obviously true of dynamic facts, which would have no fixed sense, were they not attached, if only by provisional hypothesis, to the fundamental laws of social development. Thus a grasp of the whole is indispensable in social physics, not only in order to conceive and propound the proper questions, so as to secure the true progress of the science, but also to direct investigation, so that it acquires and retains its rational character, and fulfils the hopes it has kindled. Only thereby can that midnight oil so often wasted on the labours of conscientious but sterile erudition, become truly of use in the development of sound social philosophy, bringing honour to its devotees, who under the guidance of positive theories of sociology will know at last what they ought to look for in the facts they collect, and to what use they should put their investigations. The new political philosophy, far from proscribing true erudition in all its aspects, will stimulate it and nourish it with new and big subjects, unexpected points of view, a nobler destiny, and as a consequence greater scientific dignity. It will exclude only aimless work, work without any guiding principle or character, and tending to encumber science with idle and puerile dissertations or wrong-headed and incoherent views, just as physics today condemns the compilers of purely empirical observations; yet it will do justice to the zeal of those who in the past, although guided by unreal conceptions, maintained the habit of laborious historical research with instinctive obstinacy, in the face of philosophical disdain. No doubt that with this as with any other kind of phenomena—and even more than with any other, because of the greater complexity—there is a danger

* It is often thought that social phenomena must be very easily observed, because they are very common, and because the observer usually is more or less involved. But it is precisely this commonness and this personal involvement that combine with complexity to render difficult this type of observation, by making impossible of attainment the attitude of mind proper to a truly scientific inquiry. One only observed well as a detached spectator, and only the impact of some theory, especially a positive theory, can produce and maintain, with regard to social phenomena, this reversal of the natural point of view. And I am only speaking of pure speculation without considering the near hallucination which the passions naturally produce in this subject and which cannot be prevented or dispelled except by the intimate familiarity and practice of positive theory.

that continuous use of scientific theories may distort real observation, reading into it the confirmation of speculative prejudices that have no real basis. But this disadvantage can be avoided in every important case through the precautions that the true culture of science will always suggest, and also by subordinating the first tentative results to correction later, by further assembly of facts. If this danger were to be taken for a motive of re-establishing the dominion of empiricism, it would only mean substituting for the results of more or less rational theories that can be rectified, the notions of essentially metaphysical doctrines, of which the application would mean the end of any stability; for the absence of a guiding concept would necessarily lead to sheer fantasy. By transferring our intelligence from the domain of ideality to that of reality, positive theories must of their nature expose the observer less than any others to reading into facts what is not there. As the chief characteristic of positive theories is the continuous and systematic subjection of imagination to observation, the exclusive use of them puts the observer habitually on his guard against the inclination to read into facts what is not there, and though the weakness of our intelligence gives no guarantee that he will always be able to resist this inclination successfully, the habit of positive theories is the best prophylactic against such a speculative menace, which tends to alter the entire system of science in its very basis. It would certainly be very strange if the consideration of this peril were to motivate in our day the maintenance of the metaphysical method in political philosophy, for it is the metaphysical method that exposes our intelligence constantly to it, holding out the hope of some vague historical confirmation of irrational conceptions and preoccupations.

We see then that from the very nature of social science, observation needs to be subordinated, more than in any other case, to positive speculation on the laws of solidarity and sequence that hold good for these complex phenomena. No social fact can have any real scientific significance unless it is immediately associated with some other social fact; isolated, it necessarily remains in the sterile state of mere anecdote, capable at the most of satisfying a vain curiosity, but incapable of meeting any rational need. Such subordination must certainly increase the fundamental difficulty of social observation, and make good observers still more rare, at the present moment, although in the end it will multiply them as true science develops. This condition is imposed by the nature of the subject, and only serves to confirm, what already has been abundantly proved, that the cultivation of the social sciences should only be entrusted to the best minds, prepared by the most thoroughly rational education. This logical precept is nothing but the consequence and complement of the obligation, in social studies, of making the spirit of the whole predominate, by always proceeding from the system to its elements. And this same precept in my view confirms the widening of the means of investigation, which, as I have noted, is an *a priori* characteristic of sociological science. For social phenomena, if they are explored with due regard to their solidarity and sequence, imply means of observation more varied and more extensive than all other less complicated phenomena. Thus it is not only an inspection or description of events, but also the consideration of apparently insignificant customs, of various kinds of monuments, the analysis and comparison of languages, etc., and a host of other more or less important subjects, that can offer useful means of positive exploration to sociology. In a word, any rational person who has received an adequate education will, after sufficient practice, be able to convert the impressions he receives from almost every event in social life into sociological data, through the points of contact that he will perceive with the most elevated scientific conceptions, by reason of the universal interconnection of all social aspects. If this characteristic interconnection is at first the primary source of the difficulties peculiar to social observation, ultimately, by a kind of near compensation, it tends to extend and to vary to the utmost the procedures available for scientific exploration.

The second mode of the art of observation, experimentation, appears at first sight to be excluded from the science we are founding; which would in no way prevent it from being fully positive. But on closer inspection we shall see that our science is not really totally deprived by its nature of this tool of research, although it is far from being the main one that it employs. We must distinguish between direct and indirect experimentation. We have already seen[88] that the true philosophic characteristic of the experimental mode does not consist in the artificial institution of circumstances for the phenomenon, although to the majority of scientists this appears to be the principal attribute of this kind of exploration. Whether the case be natural or artificial, we know that observation will merit the name of experimentation every time the normal accomplishment of the phenomenon experiences a definite change, nor will the spontaneity of this change impair in any way the scientific significance of the modification of the habitual circumstances of the phenomenon, for the understanding of the production of that phenomenon. It is in this sense that the experimental mode belongs to sociological research. In biological research because of the complexity and solidarity of the phenomena direct experiment by artificial means must generally be so difficult of initiation and so ambiguous in interpretation that its habitual use cannot reasonably be counted on. That complexity and that solidarity are much more notable in sociology, and it is obvious that such experiment has no place there, even if it were morally admissible and physically practicable. As an artificial disturbance of any one of the social elements must necessarily, by the laws of harmony or sequence react on all the other elements, experiment, apart from the fact that its possibility is wholly imaginary, would be devoid of any important scientific value, owing to the impossibility of sufficiently isolating any of the conditions or results of the phenomenon: that this mode of investigation becomes in a sociological context impossible is therefore no cause for regret. In biological philosophy pathological cases, for the reason that they are involuntary, constitute the true scientific equivalent of pure experiment, in that although indirect, the natural experiments they offer us are eminently suited to the study of living bodies considered under some particular aspect, and all the more as the phenomena become more complex and the organisms rise higher in the scale. Now these same considerations are *a fortiori* applicable to sociological study, and must lead to similar conclusions for still better reasons, in respect to the superiority of pathological analysis as an indirect mode of experiment suitable to the highest organisms and the most composite phenomena. Here pathological analysis consists in the examination of cases, unfortunately only too frequent, where the fundamental laws of harmony or of sequence experience disturbances in the social state from accidental or momentary causes, either specific or general, as we see especially in revolutionary epochs, above all today. These disturbances, of whatever kind they are, constitute for the social organism the exact parallel to the diseases of the individual organism: and I do not hesitate to affirm that the more this philosophic analogy is subjected to analysis in depth, the more correct it will be seen to be, due allowance being made for unequal complexity of organs. In both cases we make a noble use of human reason when we apply it to revealing the true laws of our nature whether individual or social by the scientific analysis of the disorders that necessarily accompany its development. But if in biological research pathological exploration has up till now been ill-applied, it will readily be understood that it is still more defective in sociological research, where indeed no benefit of any importance has been derived from it, although material abounds. Such ineffectiveness stems from the fact that any kind of experimentation direct or indirect is even less than observation in a position to dispense with subordination to rational concepts, if it is to have any real scientific utility. The motives of this indispensable subordination we have discussed, it would be superfluous to reproduce them here; every day we have a glaring confirmation of them in social practice. Do we not see, especially in our time, the most disastrous political experiments tried and tried again, with modifications as insignificant as irrational, although the first time should have sufficed to show the ineptitude and the danger of the measures proposed? I know, in this connection, how great is the part played by human passion, but we forget that the absence of rational analysis must be one of the principal reasons why the lessons of social experiment have remained fruitless; if the course of these experiments were better observed, doubtless it would become more instructive. People think, it is true, that cases of social disturbance are incapable of revealing the fundamental laws of the political organism, which they see as destroyed or suspended in this situation. This is the same error as for the individual organism; it is more excusable, since the normal state itself is not yet sufficiently understood as subject to laws. But at bottom the principle established especially by the work of Broussais,[89] which is destined to permeate the philosophic spirit of positive pathology, is by its nature as applicable to the social as to the individual organism. In both, pathological cases cannot be seen as the violation of the fundamental laws of the normal organism, for the phenomena of the organism are modified in varying degrees, but can never be modified in their nature or relations. Social disturbances are necessarily of the same order as modifications brought about in the complex of social laws by different secondary causes whose influence I have circumscribed within its necessary limits in these lectures: there is no real distinction to be made except between the discontinuity of social disturbance and the continuity of modification, this does not alter the principle. Since, then, the fundamental laws continue to exist in any state of the social organism, there is ground for drawing rational conclusions, with the necessary precautions, from the scientific analysis of disturbances, on the positive theory of normal existence. Such are the philosophic reasons for utilising this kind of indirect and involuntary experimentation to reveal the true system of the social body in a more efficient manner than by simple observation, of which, as in other subjects, it constitutes the necessary complement. Of its nature this procedure is applicable to all orders of sociological research, whether they concern existence or movement, the physical, intellectual, moral or political aspects, and at every stage of social evolution, where unfortunately disturbances have been lacking. As for the scope of the method, it would be premature to measure it at this point, since it has not yet been really applied to any research in political philosophy, and will not become current practice until the new science I am endeavouring to found is developed. But it was necessary to draw attention to it and characterise if briefly, as one of the basic means of exploration physics.

Coming to the comparative method, we see it has primacy in any study where living bodies may become the subject, and the more complicated the phenomena and the higher the organisms, the more evident and indisputable this primacy. Blind imitation of comparison as used in biology would mean ignoring the true analogies between the two sciences, for the comparison of the various parts of the animal hierarchy, which in biology is the principal feature of the comparative method, can only have secondary importance in sociology. The reason is that at bottom, as we shall soon see, the animal hierarchy is not for sociology the true type of the organic series. Nevertheless I am convinced that the prolonged preponderance of theologico-metaphysical philosophy in this order of speculation excites unjustified disdain for every scientific comparison of human society with any other animal society. When social studies come to be properly guided by the positive spirit, people will soon recognise how useful, and even how necessary it is to introduce, up to a point, the sociological comparison of man with other animals, and above all with the higher mammals, at least after animal societies, which are still so little known, have been better observed and better understood. The motives for such a comparison are very similar to those that make it highly recommendable in the study of individual life, and its intellectual and moral phenomena, of which social phenomena are the necessary consequence and the natural complement. After having long ignored its importance in biology, intelligent men are beginning to realise it: it will be the same in sociology although here it will not be so essential. The principal defect of this type of comparison in sociology will be, doubtless, that it is confined by its nature to the static aspects of the subject, and can never attain to the dynamic ones, and these, especially today, must constitute the prime subject of this science. This limitation results from the fact that, without being so immutably fixed as is believed, the social state of animals has undergone, since the full development of man's domination, only imperceptible variations, not at all comparable to humanity's continual progress, even at the slow rate of the primitive stage. But confined to social statics, the scientific utility of such a comparison seems to me to be undeniable, if we are to seize the more elementary laws of social solidarity, and see them manifested irrefutably in the most imperfect social state, so as sometimes to suggest useful conclusions on human society. Nothing is more calculated to bring out the naturalness of the principal social relationships, which so many sophistical brains think they can transform according to their fancy: they will cease, no doubt, to regard the principal ties of the human family as factitious and arbitrary, when they find that they are essentially the same in animals, and that the higher the organism, the nearer to the human species, the more pronounced are these ties. In a word, in all that concerns the primitive germs of social relationships, those first institutions that established the unity of the family or the tribe, in that elementary part of sociology which almost merges into intellectual and moral biology or at least into the natural history of man, of which it seems to be merely a prolongation, not only will there be great scientific advantage in the judicious use of comparison between human society and other animal societies, but real philosophic necessity for it; as some philosophers have already suspected, above all Ferguson,[90] who has been the first to seize its importance. Perhaps also it will be as well not to confine oneself to those animal societies where the co-operation is voluntary, like that of human societies, although the consideration of them will, for that very reason predominate, the scientific spirit extending this mode of inquiry to its utmost logical limit, may well find some profit in the examination of these strange societies, peculiar to the lowest forms of animal life, where involuntary co-operation is the result of indissoluble organic union, whether of mere adherence, or of genuine continuity.* Even if we suppose that science would not derive any immediate advantage from this development of sociological comparison, the same cannot be said of method, which would gain in homogeneity as a result of greater similarity to biological procedures. The habit of comparing man scientifically, both as a social and as an individual entity to the other animals is bound to diminish that absolute spirit which is the principal vice of our time in political philosophy. And it seems to me—to descend to practicalities —that the insolent pride that makes certain castes regard themselves as in

* Collectively humanity has sometimes been compared to a kind of immense polyp covering the entire globe. But that pedantic metaphor, which endeavours to define a very well-known phenomenon by likening it to another that is much less known, betrays an imperfect understanding of out social solidarity, and above all extreme ignorance of the kind of existance proper to polypiers. It leads to the assimilation of a voluntary association to an involuntary and indissoluble participation; a system whose various elements, in spite of their individuality always affect one another, are thus assimilated to a system exactly the opposite, where the parts, although inseparable, never exercise any direct action on one another, so much so that some perish while others are born, without the remainder being in any way affected.

some sort another species than the rest of humanity, has some affinity with the disdain of any comparison between nature and the other animal natures. However whatever be the scientific importance of these considerations, their real place would be a methodical treatise of social philosophy, which I have already promised, and in which they will have all their due weight. But here, in this first sketch of the new science, when I must, for reasons already explained, have mainly social dynamics in view in which this type of comparison is almost unusable, I cannot make any important application of it, at least directly. For that very reason I have had to single out this part of the comparative method, lest it pass unnoticed, for that would have grave scientific consequences. Logical procedures regularly in use are as a rule sufficiently understood by their practical application for a preliminary account of them to be confined to their fundamental properties.

In accordance with the ascending order of importance of the principal forms taken by the comparative method in sociology, I now mention the chief mode of all, which is the comparison of the various coexistent states of human society on the different parts of the earth's surface, especially of populations quite independent of one another. Nothing is better calculated to give a clear idea of the various phases of human evolution,[91] seeing that they can be simultaneously studied and their principal characteristics defined. There is necessarily only one progress of humanity as a whole, but it is an incontestable fact that, from a combination of social causes, which for the most part have been very little analysed, quite considerable and very varied populations have attained to varying degrees of development below the general level, so that as a result of this inequality the various early states of the most civilised nations, with only secondary variations, are to be found with contemporary peoples distributed over the globe.* Like observation, of which it is the most natural ramification, the comparative mode has first of all the obvious advantage of being equally applicable to the two orders of sociological speculation, the static and the dynamic, so that it verified equally the laws of existence

* Within one single nation it would be possible to compare the principal phases of human civilisation by considering the social state of the different classes, which are 'contemporary' in very varying degrees. The capital of the civilised world nourishes in its bosom more or less faithful representatives of almost all the previous stages of social evolution, especially in an intellectual sense. But in spite of their apparent facility such observations are by their nature too indecisive ever to acquire real scientific importance, by reason of the influence exercised by the all pervading spirit of the epoch, which rules out any exact analysis except by means of a very advanced sociological theory, if serious error is to be avoided.

and the laws of movement, and even furnishes sometimes valuable conclusions touching these laws. In the second place it extends today to every possible stage of social evolution, whose every feature can now be the subject of immediate observation: from the unfortunate inhabitants of the Tierra del Fuego to the most advanced peoples of Western Europe, there is not a single variety of social existence that is not present at some point of the globe and even almost always in several quite separate localities. Certain interesting, though secondary phases of social development, of which the history of our civilisation has left no appreciable trace, can only be known by comparative investigation: and these are not, as one would think the most inferior stages—as recognised today —of human evolution. Even for quite historical phases there are numerous intermediaries that are available only to this indirect mode of observation. Such are the principal properties of this second part of the comparative method, destined to be of such excellent service in verifying the data furnished by historical analysis, and even in filling in its gaps. The general use of this sociological method is quite logical, since it rests directly on the principle that I have established of the necessarily identical development of all humanity, in view of the common type of human nature which prevails over the diversities of climate and even of race, such differences only affecting the rate of evolution.

But now that we have appreciated the virtues of this method, it is important to guard against any exaggeration by pointing out the grave scientific dangers that are associated with it, despite its advantages, and that do not admit of its being entrusted with the direction of sociological observation. Its first defect, at once the most serious and the most unavoidable, is that it does not take account of the sequence of the social states, and tends to present them as co-existent. Too exclusive or even too habitual a use of this mode of exploration could thus obscure the order in which the different stages of human evolution have resulted from one another; and indeed would so obscure it, if that order were not securely established by a better scientific method: now we know how fundamental this idea is in sociology, which shows how serious is the disadvantage of obscuring it. The better to understand its importance, we should realise that the disparity proper to comparative sociological observations does not allow us when employing them by themselves to perceive the interconnection of the various systems of society, even supposing that the positive order of these is already known. On both these counts it would be easy to cite numberless examples of error, even in the work of the most distinguished philosophers; but as the present course is essentially dogmatic, I abstain from critical remarks, which my hearers will easily supply. Still confining myself to precept, I must point out, finally, another and not less characteristic disadvantage of the comparative mode, which is a tendency to estimate erroneously the cases observed, taking secondary modifications for principal phases of social development. This is how people have been led to the most mistaken notions on the political influence of climate, attributing to its effect social differences that should have been referred to the degree of evolution; sometimes, but more rarely, the mistake has been the opposite: clearly when this method is used, nothing indicates to which of the two classes, causes or results of development, the difference belongs. The same tendency is seen, to a greater degree, in what concerns the different human races. Such sociological comparisons must often be made, especially in important cases, between populations belonging to distinct varieties of the human species; and this physiological modification seems to have been on many occasions one of the causes, if not the principal cause, of the varying rate in that evolution which is common to the whole human race. Thus one is in danger of confusing the influence of race and that of social age, either exaggerating or denying the one or the other. It must be added that climate introduces a third means of interpreting comparative phenomena, alternatively agreeing with, or contrary to, race and development respectively, and this increases the chances of sociological delusion, rendering the comparative analysis from which one had expected illumination almost impracticable.

Now that we have examined briefly but precisely the two sides of comparison, for and against, we must confirm what has already been noted with regard to observation and experiment: the impossibility of employing the method without both its elementary application and its final interpretation being constantly guided by a conception, general but fully positive, of the development of mankind as a whole. Nothing can do away with a philosophical necessity that has reappeared in various guises in our attentive examination of the nature of sociological research. Only under the guidance of this conception can the grave dangers of the comparative mode of exploration be averted, and its splendid advantages developed. We thus see how absurd and how dangerous, both for theory and for practice, both for science and for method, are the sophistical declamations of the partisans of systematic empiricism, or the blind belittlers of social speculation; it is as they become more general and more elevated that the notions of political philosophy become more real and more efficacious. Illusion and sterility are reserved for the conceptions, both scientific and logical, that are too narrow and too specialised. It follows that this first sketch of general sociology, which must guide the use of the different modes of investigation that we have just been analysing, itself rests on the use of a new method of observation, whose logical character, better adapted to the nature of the phenomena, is exempt from the grave dangers presented by the other methods. So it is, and we have at last reached the point of considering the last part of the comparative method, which in sociology I must distinguish by the name of *historical method*, in which dwells the sole basis on which can rest the system of political logic.

The historical comparison of the various consecutive states of humanity is not only the principal scientific tool of the new political philosophy: developed, it will prove to be the very basis of the science, at least in its most distinctive aspects. It is here that sociological science distinguishes itself sharply from biological science. The necessary influence that one generation exercises over another, a cumulative influence that soon becomes the predominant consideration in the study of social development, is the principle of the distinction between biology and sociology. As long as this predominance is not immediately recognisable the positive study of humanity must appear as a natural prolongation of the natural history of man. But this type of science, while very well suited to the first generations of mankind, soon begins to fade when social evolution begins to show itself more, and must in the end transform itself, once human progress has truly begun, into something quite different, something peculiar to sociological science, where historical considerations must prevail. Although such analysis seems to belong exclusively to dynamic sociology, it really extends to the entire system of the science, without any distinction of parts, because of the solidarity of those parts. Although social dynamics is the ultimate object of sociological science, we know, and I have already pointed out, that social statics is inseparable from social dynamics, in spite of the distinction between them being very useful, since the laws of existence manifest themselves above all in movement.

It is not only from the scientific point of view that sociology is characterised by the predominant use of the historical method: it is also from the logical one. By the creation of this new branch of the comparative method, sociology will at the same time have completed, in a mode reserved for it alone, the whole positive method, to the common advantage of the entire body of natural philosophy, and in a manner of which the scientific meaning is only glimpsed today by the best minds. From now on we can point to this historical method as offering the most natural proof and the most extensive application of that characteristic trait of sociological method, which is, to go from the whole to the parts. This indispensable condition of the rationality of social studies manifests itself unmistakably in all truly historic research, which otherwise would degenerate into the compilation of raw material, however skilfully presented. Since it is above all in their development that the different social elements are necessarily interdependent and inseparable, it follows that no partial system isolated from the rest can have reality, and that any explanation of such a system, before it is permitted to be special, must base itself on a general conception of fundamental evolution. The irrational spirit of narrow specialism that has today attained to such bad eminence would end by reducing history to an accumulation of detached monographs, where every idea of organic and necessarily simultaneous connection of events would lose itself in the multiplicity of description. Hence it is to social evolution as a whole that we must relate the historical comparisons of the various ages of civilisation, if they are to have a true scientific character, in conformity with the nature and destiny of this science; this is the only way in which we shall be able to attain to conceptions capable of guiding further study in the various specialised subjects: not that ill-conceived imitation of the procedure of inorganic philosophy, which is quite unfitted for organic philosophy and especially for social phenomena.

It should also be noted, in conclusion, and from a practical point of view, that the preponderance of the historical method in social studies has the advantage also of developing social feeling, for it is the continuous demonstration of the necessary interconnection of human events which inspires immediate interest today even in the most distant of these events, and is a continual reminder of the influence that they have exercised on the gradual emergence of our own civilisation. To quote the fine words of Condorcet, no educated man could today think of the battles of Marathon and of Salamis without at once realising their important consequences for the present destinies of humanity. There is no need to insist on this value. The hierarchy of the various social ages emerges plainly in history. Only it is important not to confuse the feeling of social solidarity with that sympathetic interest that all depictions of human life are bound to evoke, even those of fiction. The feeling that concerns us here is at once deeper, since it becomes in some sort personal, and more reflective, as springing from a scientific conviction; it does not develop through popular history, which has remained at the descriptive stage, but entirely through logical and positive history, history as a genuine science, arranging human events in co-ordinated series that show their sequence. At first reserved for an elite, this new form of social feeling may come to belong at a lower grade of intensity to all intelligences alike, as the results of social physics are popularised. It will complete the more obvious and elementary notion of solidarity between individuals and peoples which is common in our time by a more noble conception of human unity, showing the successive generations of humanity directed towards one final goal, whose gradual attainment had required from each one of them a definite participation. This disposition to see our co-operators in the men of all times barely manifests itself today with regard to the sciences, and that only for the most advanced: the preponderance of the historical method will develop it fully and extend it to every aspect of human life, so as to maintain, as the result of reflection, the fundamental respect for our ancestors that is indispensable to the normal condition of society, and has been shaken today by the metaphysical philosophy.

Now let us examine the procedure in this comparative method which has so many virtues. The spirit of the historical method seems to me to consist in the use of social series, that is to say, in the study of the successive states of humanity, showing from the historical facts the continual growth of each particular physical, intellectual, moral or political proclivity, and the corresponding decrease of its opposite, whence will result the scientific prediction of the final ascendancy of the one and the final decline of the other, as long as this conclusion is in full conformity with the general laws of human development, whose preponderance should never be forgotten. It is enough for me here to indicate the guiding principle of this type of investigation, which is as logical as it is useful. The movement of society and that of the human mind can be really foreseen to a certain extent in each particular epoch, and under each essential aspect, even in the things that appear to be most irregular, if we have previous knowledge of the direction taken by the modifications indicated in a good historical analysis, proceeding always according to the spirit of our science from the more composite phenomena to those that are less so. By a happy coincidence, scientific predictions are the nearer reality, the more important and general are the phenomena they deal with, for then continuous causes are more predominant in the social movement, and disturbances have less to do with it. The laws of solidarity will extend certainty to secondary and special aspects in accordance with their static relations to the important and general aspects, so as to compensate partially for the lesser degree of confidence suggested by the direct use of the mode of successive exploration. By striving to obtain the only degree of precision possible with such complex phenomena, affected by so many influences, some regular, some accidental, one may arrive at conclusions that suffice to guide the greater part of practice. The principal kinds of practice, those that concern the political art, will show a high degree of rationality, since the part of the movement on which they depend mostly is at bottom less disturbed than any other by the different irregular influences, as I have explained, in spite of prejudices to the contrary. If we desire to familiarise ourselves with this historical method, so as to be able to grasp and develop its spirit with skill and judgement, it is essential to apply it first of all to the past, seeking to deduce each well-known historical situation from all that has led up to it, while at the same time taking care not to look to a foreknown result. However paradoxical this order may seem, it is certain that in any science one only learns to predict the future after having in some sort predicted the past, for such is the first use of relations observed between accomplished facts, the previous discovering the future succession. Arrived at the modern epoch with all the intellectual authority derived from the gradual co-ordination of all the preceding epochs, the historical method, and the historical method alone, can analyse the modern epoch, estimating each element exactly for what it is, according to the sociological series to which it belongs. Vainly do statesmen insist on the necessity of political observation: as their observation is only of the present, or at the most of the recent past, the maxim they distil from it proves abortive on application. From the nature of the phenomena, observation of the present is radically insufficient; it acquires true scientific value, and becomes a source of logical prediction, only from comparison with the past, and the past in its totality. Isolated, the observation of the present would become a very powerful cause of political illusion, for it leads one to confuse principal with secondary facts, to overestimate noisy and ephemeral demonstrations in comparison with the fundamental tendencies which as a rule are not very noisy, and above all to regard powers, institutions and doctrines as in the ascendant which on the contrary are on the decline. Obviously the comparison of the present with the past is the principal means of investigation calculated to prevent or to correct these faults. Now such a comparison cannot be truly illuminating and decisive unless it embraces the whole of the past, seen in its stages. The nearer to the present the epoch beyond which it does not go, the graver the errors to which it is exposed. Today, especially, social elements, some about to triumph, others to disappear, are in such medley and confusion that most false political judgements are due to speculation not extending far enough back into the past, as almost all our statesmen in the various parties scarcely go beyond the last century, except the few abstract thinkers among them who venture sometimes into the preceding century, philosophers themselves rarely going beyond the sixteenth century: so that the revolutionary epoch as such is not even conceived by those who vainly seek to terminate it, although that epoch itself is but a transitory phase in the fundamental movement of humanity.

Yet whatever be the intrinsic superiority of the sociological method, like any other scientific procedure it can lead to serious errors in the hands of the unbalanced or the insufficiently educated. Mathematical analysis itself, so highly recommended, and with reason, has too often the fatal effect of taking signs for ideas; it cannot be denied, especially in our day, that it sometimes serves to disguise inanity of conception behind imposing verbiage. There is no scientific method, even amongst the best, that does not offer similar dangers, though their existence in no way detracts from the value of these logical tools, because such dangers can proceed only from an imperfect understanding or a faulty application of the method. This remark applies to all the sociological methods, especially to the historical method, which likewise cannot lead astray as long as it is properly understood and employed. Its only drawbacks are the great difficulty of this proper understanding and employment, by reason of the obstacles arising from the complexity of the subject. One cannot hope that the illusions it may induce can ever be entirely avoided, whatever the precautions taken, yet it may be of some use to indicate their character. It consists in taking a continuous recession for an approaching total extinction, according to the mathematical sophistry by which continuous variations of more or less are confused with infinite variations. A very striking example will suffice, by its very oddity, to show the danger of the method of historical series better than could any abstract explanation, and will indicate at the same time the way to prevent similar illusions, in the numerous cases where they would not be so blatant. If we consider social development under the very simple aspect of man's dietary regime, it cannot be denied that the tendancy is for civilised man to eat less and less. Compare savage with cultivated peoples, either in the Homeric epic or the tales of travellers; or contrast country with town usage; finally consider the difference between two successive generations. Everywhere comparative observation will confirm this conclusion, the effect of a more extensive sociological law. On the other hand such a recession is in perfect harmony with the fundamental laws of human nature, and the result of the growing preponderance of intellectual and moral activity as man becomes more civilised. Nothing then is better proved, either experimentally or logically. But would anyone venture to deduce from this undoubted and continuous recession, an ultimate extinction? Such an error, too flagrant in the case in point not to be immediately rectified, can take more specious forms and become almost inevitable in many other instances, because of their greater complexity. The preceding example suffices to indicate that recourse must be had to the constant laws of our nature, which being always in action throughout social evolution, continuously furnish sociological analysis with a means of verification.[92] Since the social phenomenon is at bottom nothing but the development of humanity, and creates no faculties, as I have already stated,[93] every disposition that sociological observation reveals must be found at least in germ in the primordial type that biology constructed for sociology, in order to set limits to its aberrations. Thus no law of social succession, even indicated with all possible authority by the historical method, can be definitively admitted unless it has been connected, directly or indirectly, but always indisputably, with the positive theory of human nature: induction that cannot pass this test will in the end under closer sociological examination be recognised as illusory, the result of either too limited or too curtailed observation. It is in this continuous harmony between the conclusions of historical analysis and the concepts of the biological theory of man that the force of sociological demonstration must consist. Thus one sees confirmed once again in every respect that philosophic preponderance of the whole over the parts which I have stressed in this chapter as the main intellectual characteristic of the new science.

Such then is the mode of investigation that is most appropriate to the true nature of sociological research. Its preponderance is equivalent to that of zoological comparison in the study of individual life. The necessary sequence of the various social states corresponds exactly from the scientific point of view, to the graded co-ordination of the various organisms, having regard to the difference of the two sciences: the social series, properly established, cannot be either less real or less useful than the animal series. When this new instrument has been used long enough for its properties to be clear to the enlightened, it will be recognised, I presume, as a modification of positive investigation distinct enough to take its place by the side of observation, experiment and comparison properly so called, as a fourth and last mode of the art of observation, destined to analyse, under the name of 'historical method' the most complex phenomena, and having its philosophic source in the mode immediately preceding, the biological comparison of ages.

In terminating this general appreciation of the historical method as the best mode of sociological investigation, I must call attention to the fact that the new political philosophy, consecrating as it does, from rational examination, the ancient landmarks of human reason, restores at last to history the entire plenitude of its scientific rights as the indispensable basis of all wise social speculation, in spite of the still too widely accepted sophistries of a vain metaphysics tending to eliminate in politics all broad consideration of the past. Thus in any of the branches of natural philosophy, the previous parts of this course have always shown us the positive spirit, so unjustly accused of being a disturbing influence, as rather confirming in its outline of each science the precious indications of common sense, of which any real science can only be a special and systematic prolongation, and which only a sterile metaphysics can disdain. Far from restraining the influence which human reason has always attributed to history in political planning, the new social philosophy augments it to the utmost; it is now not mere counsels or lessons that politics will demand of history, in order to perfect or to rectify inspirations not derived from it; it is its own governance that politics will seek from now on exclusively in general historical trends.

X

Restrictions on the Historical Operation 94

Historical appreciation has no other purpose than to show the reality and the fecundity of the theory of social development which we have already established,[95] through a wide-ranging and decisive application of it. Though such a demonstration would not leave any doubt as to the exactitude and the importance of the general law of evolution that I have discovered, nevertheless the extreme novelty of so difficult a subject, and the irrationality of the intellectual habits that still rule in such studies, would cause some apprehension that the best minds might not at present see the renovation that this great principle would bring about in social science, if its ability to constitute a true philosophy of history were not irrefutably confirmed by a rough sketch of the human past considered as a whole, and only in its principal phases. The usefulness of this novel attempt would not be impaired by its necessary imperfection at this stage, for it would both convey the experiential reality of our sociological conception, and demonstrate the mode of its gradual application; so that competent brains, suitably prepared, could proceed to extend the theory to new analyses of human development, viewed under more and more specialised aspects, in conformity with the logical conditions of social dynamics.[96] This course being devoted to the general system of political philosophy I will merely draw the attention of my readers to the principal conditions that must limit a first attempt at historical appreciation.

The most important of the restrictions appertaining to the historical method, a restriction that implicitly includes all the others, is the confining of scientific analysis to one social series only, that is to say to the development of the most advanced peoples, and the scrupulous avoidance of every digression to other centres of civilisation, whose evolution has so far been, for some cause or other, arrested at a more imperfect stage, unless the examination of these accessory series can throw a useful light on the principal subject. Historical exploration must therefore be limited to the élite or vanguard of humanity, comprising the greater part of the white race or the European nations, and even in the interests of accuracy, especially in modern times, it must be confined to the peoples of Western Europe. In any epoch study will mainly concern the political ancestors of this privileged population, whatever be their country. In a word only those social phenomena which have obviously exercised a real influence, even if indirect or distant, on the successive phases leading to the present state of the most advanced nations should be included in the historical material that contributes to the philosophic co-ordination of the human past. One cannot hope to grasp the true progress of human society except by the exclusive consideration of the most complete and distinctive evolution, to the elucidation of which all collateral observations relating to less complete and less notable progressions must be subordinated. Whatever interest attach to the latter, appreciation of them must be systematically adjourned until the principal laws of social movement have been ascertained in the case most favourable to their full manifestation, when it will become possible and even useful to proceed to an explanation of the modifications these laws have undergone among populations that for various reasons have lagged behind the main type of development. Till then, the puerile and inept display of sterile, ill-directed erudition at present tending to hamper the study of social evolution by the intermixture of the history of populations such as those of India and China etc., which have never exercised any real influence on our past, must be stigmatised as a source of inextricable confusion, as far as the discovery of the laws of human sociability is concerned, for the fundamental course and its modifications are thus being considered simultaneously, and the problem becomes insoluble. In this connection it seems to me that the great Bossuet,[36a] although guided only by the literary principle of unity of composition, instinctively divined the conditions imposed by the nature of this subject, when he confined his historical appreciation to the examination of one homogeneous and continuous series only, which he justly qualified, nevertheless, as universal; a sage limitation which strange to say has been blamed by many antiphilosophic persons, and to which we are brought back today by the analysis of the intellectual procedure proper to these studies.

Such a procedure must appear the more indispensable in that it will be seen to play a necessary part in the wise regulation of an important order of political relationships, those that concern the influence of the advanced nations on the development of the inferior civilisations. Metaphysical politics and even theological politics, because of the absolute nature of their principal conceptions, are led to pursue blindly the uniform and immediate realisation of their unchanging types, in spite of the diversity of conditions: which amounts to a kind of systematic adoption of that natural empiricism that inclines all civilised men to transfer their ideas, customs and institutions, indiscriminately and often very indiscreetly. It would be superfluous to point out an obvious danger: that such a tendency will excite and maintain the gravest political unrest. The more one meditates on this subject, the more one feels that practice, not less than theory, demands exclusive or at least principal consideration of the most advanced social evolution first of all, and the neglect of less complete types of progress. It is only when we have determined what belongs to the élite of humanity that we can regulate our intervention in the development of more or less backward peoples, by reason of the necessary universality of the fundamental evolution, with due appreciation of the characteristic circumstances of each case. Renewing in this way the spirit of international relations, positive politics will tend to substitute for action which has too often been disturbing or even oppressive, wise and benevolent protection, and the mutual advantage of this cannot be doubted; it would be almost always favourably received, as proposing only those modifications that are in real harmony with the particular state of the peoples concerned, and varying judiciously the realisation of the modifications according to what is suitable in each case. We will not further insist on these views,[97] but draw attention to the fact that this important transformation of policy could not possibly come about if all the various political evolutions were considered as being on a level, in spite of their necessary inequality: which confirms the scientific directive that sociological analysis should be systematically concentrated on the historical appreciation of the most complete development.

This limitation, so clearly imposed by the nature of the subject, fits in very well with the necessity for speed in a historical survey. It is enough to explain here that, taken as a whole, the past of the most advanced peoples consists essentially in the gradual development of a triple dualism,* constituting the fundamental evolution of humanity. By its nature this great law already offers the first co-ordination of the human past in its most general aspect and considered in its most distinct phases. I must leave to my successors the particularising of this primordial conception through the methodical interconnection of ever-decreasing intervals.

* (Translator's note) Of the theological, metaphysical and positive stages, presenting respectively the dualisms of people and priests, church and state, industry and science. cf. Cinquante-unième leçon in the *Cours de philosophie positive*. Harriet Martineau, *The Positive Philosophy of Auguste Comte II*, London, 1893, p. 148.

The final stage, doubtless never to be reached, would consist in establishing the line of every kind of progress from one generation to the next, since sociological chronology cannot demand the consideration of any smaller unit of time, for then political development would be almost always imperceptible.

If my sociological concept really succeeds, by the study of the most complete social series, in instituting a real scientific link between the historical facts with which all educated men are familiar today, by that alone, I venture to affirm, it will have attained the most difficult and important objective of this subject, both for theory and for practice. It will have established at the same time its capacity to furnish, by further elaboration, all the more specialised and exact explanations that progressively become necessary. In each of the previous chapters we have had occasion to observe that in general the commonest phenomena are always those that it is most essential to consider in true science. Now this maxim, whose truth strikes one so forcibly in astronomy, in physics, in chemistry and in biology, must apply still more to sociological studies, as being even better suited to the greater complexity and speciality of their phenomena. In the search for the true laws of sociability, the exceptional events and minute details that the anecdote-monger seeks out with insatiable curiosity must nearly always be ignored as essentially insignificant: science must attach itself to the most vulgar phenomena, which the participants see around them, constituting the principal material of their habitual social life. True, for that very reason such phenomena are more difficult to observe in such a way as to make of them the basis of sound scientific speculation. The prejudices and habits that still prevail almost universally in political philosophy, even in the best minds, are but one more proof of prolonged infantilism in this last department of natural philosophy: they recall the time, still not far distant, when in physics only the extraordinary effects of thunder, of volcanoes, etc., were judged worthy of attention, and in biology, monstrosities. There can be no doubt that the total reformation of these intellectual habits is much more necessary in social science than it has even been in any of the other basic sciences.

Generalising these considerations on the limitation of historical analysis, we can give to this important requirement of *restriction* the greatest degree possible of philosophic consistency, if we recognise that far from being peculiar to sociology, it is but a new application of an essential principle of positive philosophy, which is no longer disputed in any other order of phenomena, and which I carefully formulated at the beginning of these lectures (see the second lecture). One can see that this limitation simply means extending to the study of social phenomena the distinction that I established for all subjects between abstract and concrete science, a distinction generally expressed today, for want of more suitable terms, by contrasting the domain of physical science with that of natural history, the first alone constituting the principal field of positive philosophy, and being necessarily considered as the fundamental basis of the entire system of human speculation. It is a division, that certainly cannot be less necessary as the order of phenomena becomes more specialised and more complex, and that determines quite clearly and precisely the true function of historical observation in the study of social dynamics. It is true that abstract determination of the laws of individual life necessarily rests, as Bacon justly remarked, on facts borrowed from the real history of different living beings. But all good scientists are none the less used to separating physiological or anatomical conceptions from their eventual application to the concrete study of the mode of existence peculiar to each organism. Similar motives must prevent us from confusing abstract research into the fundamental laws of sociability with the concrete history of the various human societies, of which indeed a satisfactory explanation can only result from very advanced knowledge of all these laws. Thus however indispensable the part of history in nourishing and guiding the speculations of sociology, that part must remain abstract. It can only be a history without names of men, even without names of peoples, except that one must avoid the puerile affectation of abstaining from the use of names that may illuminate the exposition of a subject, or even facilitate and consolidate thought, especially in these initial stages of sociological science. The motives of this important logical distinction are still more powerful in the study of the collective life of humanity than in individual biology. As early as the second lecture, underlining this great precept of positive philosophy, I showed that each branch of natural history, besides requiring previous knowledge of a corresponding set of fundamental laws, presupposes also the collective application of the laws relating to the different orders of phenomena. This solidarity is seen still more clearly in the present case. For instance, it would be impossible to conceive of the history of humanity apart from the history of the terrestrial globe, which is the theatre of humanity's progressive activity, and whose successive states must have exercised a tremendous influence on the course of human events, from the time when the physical and chemical conditions of our planet first permitted the continuous existence of man. Conversely it is not less certain that any true history of the earth will demand, to a certain degree, the consideration of the history of humanity, because of the powerful impact, constantly reinforced, that the development of our activity must have exercised during all the ages of social life on the general state of the earth's surface. The more this great subject is gone into, the more it will be felt that natural history, which is essentially synthetic, cannot become fully rational so long as all the orders of elementary phenomena are not considered at the same time; while on the contrary natural philosophy must preserve a strictly analytic character, without which there would be no hope of arriving at the fundamental laws belonging to each of the general categories. Such an opposition of views and methods between the two great sections of the total system of human speculations, can leave no doubt as to the importance of preserving and emphasising this scientific dichotomy, which alone can ensure that the study of nature emerge from its confused primitive state, especially as regards the more complex type of phenomena. Thus a rational history of the different entities, both individual and collective, cannot even begin to be possible before the entire system of the fundamental sciences has been previously completed by the addition of sociology, as I have so often explained. Until then, all the historical information that will continue to be collected on any of the orders of phenomena must be set aside as future material for the true history, when the time is ripe; its immediate function in the development of true science, is to furnish the branches of natural philosophy with facts destined to illustrate or confirm the abstract general laws that philosophy seeks to establish. To this necessary and observed subordination social phenomena can be no exception; here indeed it is still more indispensable. If all naturalists agree today that the true history of the earth cannot yet be fully established, not only for want of sufficient data, but also because the various natural laws on which it depends are so far too little known, how much more fantastic must any attempt appear to set forth the infinitely more complex history of human societies! It is therefore evident that sociology can only borrow from the shapeless heap of facts improperly called *history* such information as exemplifies in accordance with the biological theory of man the fundamental laws of sociability: and this demands almost always that every item of such data undergo a certain preparation, often of some difficulty, in order to pass from the concrete to the abstract state, by being stripped of the purely individual and adventitious circumstances of climate, locality, etc., without its essential and general part being altered; and although this preliminary filtering is only an imitation of what astronomers, physicists, chemists and biologists now ordinarily practise with their respective phenomena, the greater complexity of social phenomena must render it more difficult, even when the positivity of these studies is finally recognised. As for the effect which the institution of social dynamics will have on the development of history, it will consist above all in the sequence of signposts that it will set up in the human past and that will serve to concentrate and guide further observation; these signposts will find themselves at ever shorter distances as we approach modern times, in view of the acceleration of social movement.

The historical operation[98] which constitutes dynamic sociology having necessarily by its nature and in conformity with its function an abstract character, is thus happily freed from a host of incidental and preliminary difficulties, which might otherwise have hindered it, and which the extreme imperfection of our knowledge would have prevented us from overcoming, even if we had put aside all the insoluble or fanciful questions on social origins that are still entertained by the majority of contemporary philosophers because of the prolonged infantilism of this study. Thus, for example, if we had to draw up a concrete history of humanity now, we should have a great deal of difficulty in combining sociological conceptions with geological considerations; however indispensable for our history this combination might be, it could not be made with success, because of the too imperfect state, not only of sociology, which is evident, but also, at bottom, of geology itself, although it is apparently well advanced. It would be the same with the various more or less adventitious influences of climate, race, etc. which would necessarily present themselves in the concrete study of human development, and which, without doubt, could not possibly be estimated at present in a truly rational fashion, since they will be measurable only after the sociological laws have been sufficiently worked out. The fundamental distinction made between the two points of view, abstract and concrete, here as elsewhere, does away with all these insurmountable difficulties; this serves to show the extreme importance of this philosophic dichotomy, which I recommend to your attention because, although today it is never contested in principle by intelligent men, it is not sufficiently appreciated, even by the most eminent. We must then learn to reserve for a more advanced scientific epoch a great number of questions incidental to concrete sociology, the immediate consideration of which would hinder the development of abstract sociology, however profound the interest aroused by such research. The human spirit, now habituated to such rational adjournments even for the simplest of phenomena, will not fail to show the same wisdom with regard to the most complex phenomena that our intelligence can ever be called upon to face.

The better to illustrate this great logical precept, without which I can state that social dynamics would be impossible, it will be enough to take one single important example of those interesting questions which today we must be ready to adjourn, because of their concrete nature. For this I choose, in view of its great importance, the explanation of the agent and the theatre of the complete social evolution that must form the almost exclusive subject of our historical operation from the motives noted above. Why does the white race possess in so marked a manner the privilege of the chief social development, and why has Europe been the theatre of that development? This two-fold subject for meditation must have more than once stimulated the intelligent curiosity of philosophers, and even of statesmen. But whatever be the interest and importance of such research, one must have the wisdom to set it aside until the fundamental laws of social development have been worked out in the abstract, for without these this question would always be premature, in spite of ingenious attempts that could only produce partial and isolated and therefore unsatisfactory insights. No doubt, on the question of agent, one can see in the characteristic bodily organisation of the white race, and above all in its brain, some germs of its superiority; although naturalists are today very far from agreement on this point. In the same way, on the question of place, one can see a little more clearly various physical, chemical and even biological conditions which must certainly have been influential up to a point in producing the peculiar capacity of European countries to serve as the theatre of the preponderant evolution of humanity.* Such is the vagueness of theologico-metaphysical philosophy, it

* Such are, for example, for the physical aspect, besides the situation, thermologically so advantageous, of the temperate zone, the existence of the admirable basin of the Mediterranean, around which the most rapid social development was bound to take place, as soon as the nautical art was sufficiently advanced to permit of using so valuable a means of communication, which offers to the assembled nations on its banks at once the contiguity that would facilitate continuous relationships, and the diversity that makes these nations important sources of mutual stimulation. Similarly, from the chemical point of view, the abundance of iron and coal that distinguishes these privileged countries must certainly have contributed to the acceleration of human evolution in them. Finally, as to the biological aspect, whether phytological or zoological, it is clear that in a milieu which has been specially favourable as this one has, on the one hand to the principal alimentary crops, and on the other to the development of the most valuable domestic animals, civilisation must have been particularly encouraged. But whatever be the importance attached to these aspects, they are very far from furnishing a truly positive explanation of the phenomenon in question: and when the formation of social dynamics

was bound to lead to these explanations being often accepted as satisfactory solutions to a problem that this philosophy was in actual fact little inclined to ponder at all. But even a mediocre intelligence, if sufficiently trained by the habit of positive speculation on the other natural phenomena would only need to juxtapose any real data acquired on this subject and the difficulty—properly enunciated—they are meant to resolve, to realise the inadequacy of such data. This inadequacy results not only from the information being too scanty and incomplete; it must be attributed above all to a more essential and potent cause, to the absence of any sound socialogical theory capable of measuring the true scientific import of each of the above-mentioned insights and even of directing its further elaboration; without such light on the subject one would not even know if one had brought together all the elements necessary to a real decision. Thus it is impossible to deny the logical necessity of postponing this great question of concrete sociology until the fundamental laws of sociability have been abstracted, at least in their general outline; and I have no doubt that the lesson of this particular case will induce an understanding in the reader of the need for philosophic reserve on each of similar questions that may arise through the association of ideas. Because of the extreme novelty and the great difficulty of the science which I am endeavouring to create, I may not myself be strictly faithful to this important precept of positive logic: but at least I shall have sufficiently warned my hearers who will thus be able to correct themselves the deviations into which I may be enticed.

These preliminary considerations make us aware of the spirit that must preside over the use of historical observation, and it only remains for me, before proceeding to a summary description of social development, to decide on the definition of the successive phases that are to be examined. My fundamental law of evolution no doubt determines automatically, to the exclusion of arbitrary choice, the principal attributes and the general co-ordination of these phases, by attaching them to the corresponding theological, metaphysical or positive state of human conceptions. Nevertheless there still remains the minor difficulty, which I hasten to remove, occasioned by the uneven progress of the different departments of thought. Unable to advance at the same rate, as we saw by the hierarchical law established at the beginning of these lectures, they frequently display the metaphysical state, for instance, of one intellectual category

---

has made possible the attempt at such an explanation, evidently each one of the preceding factors will need to be subjected to a scrupulous scientific revision, based on the whole of natural philosophy.

coexisting with the theological state of a later, less general and more retarded one, or with the positive state of an earlier, less complex and more advanced one, in spite of the human spirit's constant tendency to unity of method and homogeneity of doctrine. This apparent confusion must produce at first among those who have not understood its source a regrettable hesitation over the philosophic character of the epochs. In order to prevent this, or to remove it, all we have to do is to discern by what intellectual category we can judge the speculative stage of an epoch. And every motive combines to indicate that it is the most specialised and complicated order of ideas, i.e. moral and social ideas, that furnishes the basis of this decision; not only in virtue of their intrinsic importance, which is necessarily very great in the mental system of almost all men, but also by reason of their position at the extremity of the encyclopaedic hierarchy that we established at the beginning of these lectures, which makes them particularly important for philosophers. For these two reasons the intellectual character of each epoch must be constantly dominated by the character of this type of human speculation. It is only when a new mental regime has been extended to this ultimate category that we can regard the corresponding evolution as fully effected, so as to leave neither fear nor hope of a return to a previous state: the more rapid advance of the more general and less complicated ideas only serves to indicate for each phase the germs of the following one, without the proper character of the phase being affected; such accessory considerations could not be used except to subdivide epochs, to an extent that it would be premature to decide now. Thus we must regard the theological epoch as still subsisting as long as the moral and political ideas have preserved an essentially theological character, though the other intellectual categories may have reached the metaphysical stage, and the positive state have commenced for the simplest of these categories; similarly the metaphysical epoch must be prolonged until positivity appears in the overruling order of human conceptions. If we proceed thus, we shall perceive the essential aspect of each epoch quite clearly, as well as the preparation in it of the following epoch.

Now that these preliminary explanations are complete, it is open to the positive philosopher to commence his study of social development, following my law of evolution; he need not however go back as far as the preliminary age whose outlines are furnished by biology to sociology, and can be taken as complete today, so as not to slow down, contrary to the aim of this course, the rapid movement of the historical operation,[99] reserving for the special treatise on positive politics that I have already announced an important philosophic analysis that has never before been properly carried out. In general the positive philosopher should concern himself on the one hand with the appreciation of the character proper to each successive phase, and on the other with determining the filiation of the phase with the preceding one, as also with its inevitable tendency to prepare the following one, so as gradually to establish the positive interconnection of which I have made out the principle.

XI

Summary Appreciation of the Final Effect of Positive Philosophy [100]

None of the preceding revolutions of humanity, even the greatest one of all, the transition from the polytheistic society of antiquity to the monotheistic one of the Middle Ages, has been able to modify the whole of human existence, both individual and social, as profoundly as will the necessary advent in the near future of a fully positive society which, as we have recognised, is the sole issue possible to the immense crisis that has agitated the élite peoples of the earth for the last half century. This natural outcome of the various previous movements has now been so well prepared that its accomplishment depends only on the direct and systematic ascendancy of the corresponding philosophy.[101] It remains for us to indicate what will be the normal effect of the new philosophic regime when its universal ascendancy has been secured. We must consider this effect successively in each of the essential modes of human existence, first of all mental, then social. With regard to the latter we shall have to examine separately the purely moral order and then the political order. As for the mental existence, it also has two points of view, the scientific and the aesthetic. But as this latter must reflect the totality of human aspects, social and intellectual, it will be better to put our reference to it at the end of our analysis. It is therefore in relation to these four classes of ideas, first scientific, then moral, after that political and finally aesthetic that we must, in our last chapter, complete the description of the great philosophic regeneration which has been the object of these lectures.

The principal intellectual feature of the positive state will certainly be its capacity to determine and to maintain a complete mental coherence such as has never before existed even in the best ordered and most advanced minds. No doubt the polytheistic regime, which forms the most important phase of our theological stage, possessed a kind of speculative unity for a lengthy period, through the uniformly religious nature of all the great human conceptions, at least before the metaphysical solvent had spread. But although since then our intelligence has not been able to recover an equivalent harmony, this primitive consistency, apart from its relative instability, was far from being as complete as that which will necessarily result from the universal ascendancy of the positive spirit; for in the most benighted epochs the involuntary upsurge of the more particular and practical notions must always have modified the theological purity of general speculation in each and every department of life, while the new regime is destined to imprint on all our conceptions without distinction, from the most elementary to the most transcendent, a completely positive character, without the least admixture of any heterogeneous philosophy. There is no need to point out how superior is this ultimate harmony to the precarious and incomplete equilibrium that we have seen dragging out its existence for several centuries under the provisional rule of scholastic metaphysics, after the ascendancy of the monotheistic system, and before positive philosophy began to manifest itself distinctly. The profoundly self-contradictory situation peculiar to the present transition period, in which the best minds are subjected to three incompatible regimes, can still less convey the idea of this approaching unity, at once scientific and logical. We form a just conception of it only if we see in it the total and definitive extension of the fundamental good sense that has gradually taken possession of various parts of the speculative domain, after being long confined to partial and practical operations, so as to bring about at last an entire renewal of human reason, or rather the definitive ascendancy of reason over imagination.[102] When that happens our intelligence will have established even in the most sublime subjects the rule of that universal wisdom with which we are familiar through the demands of active life in the simpler subjects, and will give up once for all the search for essential causes and the inner nature of phenomena, devoting itself exclusively to the study of the effective laws of these phenomena, with the fixed intention of ameliorating as much as possible our real existence, public or private. Once the purely relative nature of all our knowledge comes to be recognised, our theories, under the natural dominance of the social point of view, will aim solely, with regard to a reality that can never be absolutely revealed, at approximations as satisfying as the corresponding stage of the great human evolution in each epoch permits. This logical attitude will be in complete scientific harmony with the basic feeling of a natural order which is independent of ourselves, independent even of the phenomena of ourselves, individual or collective, and which can only undergo minor modifications through our intervention, these minor modifications being infinitely precious as the principal basis of our effective power. We cannot as yet understand how our intelligence could come to be actually dominated by this feeling, either because the intrusive thought of continual or at least latent disorder, of which we are reminded by a vestigial theological belief, still inhibits even in the best minds the conviction that tends to produce the daily regularity of external life; or because the invariability of natural law is not yet sufficiently recognised as touching those most complex events with which public attention is justly preoccupied. The future power of this great idea, at once transcendent and popular, can be perceived at present only by minds sufficiently advanced to be near that normal position which every sensible man already regards as inevitable.

Finally there is a third elementary attribute, at once scientific and logical, equally peculiar to the true positive spirit, an attribute that must greatly accelerate the progress of sound speculation: the fundamental liberty which realistic theories necessarily give to our intelligence, and which in every department of life could be much more extensive than absolute theories have hitherto allowed us to suspect. For these various reasons our transitional situation is still so little in conformity with the nearby goal, that we cannot today measure the importance and rate of the progress that will be made towards it: in each case we can only vaguely estimate this progress according to what has already been realised during three centuries under an extremely imperfect and in some cases radically aberrant mental regime that continues to cause the waste of most intellectual effort. As all sciences have scarcely emerged from infancy, it is impossible for a widely systematic culture, in which even the slightest forces will be directly applied to the common thinking, not to determine a development vastly superior to that sanctioned by a dispersed empiricism, powerless to free itself sufficiently from metaphysical and even theological tutelage, of which the present state of these sciences offers so many significant traces. Let us consider the perfect mental harmony belonging to the positive state, first as regards abstract speculation, then with reference to concrete studies and finally to practical activities.

First as regards abstract speculation, which alone up till now it is possible to judge, every part of this course has emphasised that each department of knowledge must improve, as soon as rational advance replaces the preparatory stage. The ultimate regime will be principally distinguished by the solidarity of the different branches of abstract philosophy. It is enough to point out here that this interrelation will have a twofold influence, first in guaranteeing the independence due to each science, and then in consolidating the related ideas. When the normal ascendancy of the sociological spirit has replaced the scientific hegemony provisionally entrusted to the mathematical spirit, from now on confined to its own domain, the predominance of a science dependent on all the other sciences, and yet never to be absorbed by any of them, will certainly ensure the free development of each particular science, according to its own proper genius, and without irrational interference, while not hindering its contribution to the universal harmony, which the legitimate originality of each element will on the contrary render more essential and more stable. Instead of seeking blindly for a sterile scientific unity that would be as oppressive as unreal, forcibly reducing all phenomena to one single order of laws, the human spirit will come to regard the different classes of events as having their own special laws, convergent, it is true and even in some respects analogous laws. The most satisfying harmony will spontaneously develop between these classes of events, first from their being continuously subject to one fundamental method, then from their joint tendency towards the one goal, and finally from their simultaneous subordination to the same general evolution. While this definitive regime must certainly greatly augment the independence and dignity of all the sciences, it is the study of living bodies that will derive most advantage from it, as being the one that up till now has been the most exposed to disastrous encroachments, against which it does not seem to be able to find effective guarantees except under the still more dangerous, and yet very inadequate protection of theologico-metaphysical concepts. The deplorable conflict that results in biology from this contest alone keeps alive the ancient philosophic antagonism between materialism and spiritualism. For these two opposite tendencies, equally aberrant, destined by their intimate correlation to disappear simultaneously under the impact of the positive spirit, represent respectively the natural inclination of the lower sciences to absorb the higher ones, and the instinct of the latter to maintain their dignity through the obscurities of ancient philosophy: a twofold error that is no longer important except in biological studies, where it will not be able to resist the capacity of the final philosophy for regulating the constitution of each science so as to avoid both oppression and anarchy. If one considers in the second place the internal co-ordination of each science, the same philosophic discipline will guarantee through its universality the consolidation of the various concepts against the dissolution with which they are threatened today in every direction through the disorderly irruption of specialist impulses. Unmistakable symptoms even in the most advanced sciences demand that ambitious mediocrity be restrained in its tendency to obtain facile successes by the anarchic demolition of the doctrines considered to be the best established, but which cannot be confirmed except by a common adherence to the general system of true abstract philosophy. Just as the need to reconcile spiritualism and materialism, so the new need now everywhere appreciated, of holding specialism within bounds, should make itself felt especially in biological studies, which are more than usually exposed to destructive controversy by reason of their great complexity and recent formation, but which an intimate connection with the dominant science will naturally render more accessible to its salutary protection. To take the most decisive example, the deplorable scientific hesitation in so many enlightened minds on the subject of that great conception: the animal hierarchy, without which any real biological philosophy would be impossible, will be gone forever, when the ultimate philosophy has made plain the connection of this idea either with the entire speculative system or with the general principle of social classification. Even in cases where established notions could undergo unmistakable rectifications, a sage philosophic discipline would always maintain a just balance between the occasional contrary exigencies of connexity and exactitude: while the dispersive regime sacrifices blindly the first to the second, the second being often more specious than real.

The progressive elaboration of positive doctrine undertaken in these lectures, has justly given first place to the formation of abstract science, whose priority was so well perceived by Bacon. Yet it is clear that the construction of concrete science will constitute one of the principal functions of the new philosophic spirit, for without its ascendancy it would be impossible for a science demanding the continuous combination of various scientific points of view to develop. Concrete science must in every respect, as is indicated by its usual name of 'natural history', be historical, in so far as it involves the appreciation of the successive stages of existence proper to real beings. Besides the brilliant light that it will cast on the elementary laws of different modes of activity, and the valuable practical indications that it is bound to give, I must point out an important datum, especially with regard to the more complex and higher grade phenomena, which cannot be obtained except from it, and whose philosophic effect must be regarded as indispensable to the new intellectual regime, for the entire elimination of the absolute would not be assured without it. I refer to the determination of the duration assigned by the whole economy of the real to each of the principal natural existences, among others to the ascending evolution of humanity. Premature at present, in concrete science this would become directly accessible. That great evolution which has scarcely begun to emerge from a lengthy preparatory development is bound to remain still for many centuries in a progressive state, beyond which it would be as uncalled for as irrational to speculate at present. But it is very important for the further development of the true philosophic genius to recognise on principle, as clearly as possible, that the collective organism is subject as much as the individual organism, to decline, even independently of alterations in the environment. Vainly do people argue, to avert the fatal analogy, that there is a radical difference between the two cases arising from the continual rejuvenation supposed to be proper to the former. But clearly the latter is at bottom not less disposed to rejuvenation through the constant introduction of new elements, which ceases only with life, and yet does not prevent death, when a growing decomposition triumphs at last over a decreasing recomposition. Except for the inequality of duration, related to the comparative extent of the two organisms, and to their respective rate of development, there is nothing at all to prevent the collective life of humanity from suffering a similar destiny. This philosophic prospect, while dissipating all metaphysical illusions about infinite progress, should not discourage energetic attempts at judicious improvement, any more than for sensible men their certainty of inevitable destruction, even when that destruction is imminent. Sound philosophy, it seems to me, will miss very little the assistance of those who are not going to have the courage to co-operate in the long ascent of humanity without the artificial stimulus of chimerical hopes whose influence tends to prolong in other forms the dark dominion of the old absolute philosophy. Of course it would be idle to attempt now to forecast what will be the final character assumed in a very distant future by the true philosophic spirit, disposed as it is to recognise without vain despair an inevitable destiny, when the age of decline draws near, and it has to assuage a natural bitterness by sustaining the dignity of man. But it is not for those who have scarcely issued from childhood to be preparing their old age: this so-called wisdom is even less suitable to collective than to individual life.

If we consider the normal influence of the new intellectual regime on the working out of practical knowledge, it creates the most intimate and permanent harmony between the active and the speculative point of view. They are subordinated to the same philosophic spirit, the radical opposition which the old philosophy had established between them ceasing entirely. Practical advancement on the one hand, hitherto more or less suppressed by superstitious scruples or rejected through vain hopes, will necessarily be stimulated by the universal ascendancy of rational positivity, which will subject all ordinary operations to an illuminating systematic appreciation. Conversely technical expansion will create universal appreciation of the scientific regime as superior to the previous vain system of human speculations. Action and prediction being now members of one another in their common subordination to the principle of natural laws, their connexity can but contribute to popularise and consolidate the new philosophy, and everyone will recognise that the same general advance is being realised in all subjects accessible to our intelligence. These influences will be seen in the development of the two most difficult and most important arts: medicine and politics. They are still in their swaddling clothes, as befits the infantile condition of their theories, but will be promptly rationalised under the powerful impact of the true philosophic unity, once concrete studies have been properly instituted. As the most complex phenomena are also the most modifiable, it is chiefly in relation to them that the question of the true relation between speculation and action must be studied. So will emerge the mutual solidarity that unites practical activity and the intellectual regime most suitable to human nature as it is, once they have been completely freed from those alien forces that were indispensable to their initial development but that now hinder their twin progress and definite reconciliation.

Such, in brief summary, are the qualities that will be seen to be those of the positive spirit when, as a result of its final extension it has attained to its full universality, at present disguised by an initial dispersions that has been disastrously prolonged. Equally rapidly, we will now consider the capacity of positive philosophy to consolidate and perfect human morality, a capacity that has been still more denied than its other qualities, and is still more authentic.

We have already had occasion to observe[103] the fatal cleavage which has developed in the course of the great modern transition between intellectual and moral needs, and thanks to which it is taken for granted that the most suitable regime for the one will not be able to satisfy the other. To do away with this fatal prejudice which tends to neutralise regenerative activity, we need only point out that the opposition in question is the result, distressing but temporary, of an evolution in the course of which intellectual renewal was only possible in the higher studies, and excluded, as being too complicated, moral questions. These appeared therefore to adhere indefinitely to ancient philosophy, whose oppressive ascendancy the first stage of evolution was destined to destroy, before replacing it by a more complete and lasting system. The extension of rational positivity to the ultimate spheres of speculation puts an immediate end to this disastrous opposition, by conferring on the social point of view normal predominance, moral and political as well as logical and scientific.[104] Under the new philosophic regime the positive spirit will rapidly develop its native aptitude for the treatment of such questions, in reference to which theological and metaphysical concepts can only be a source of increasing danger, for they cast on the most important doctrines the discredit that inevitably attaches to an outworn philosophy, and one that is viewed by modern reason with an increasing antipathy, scarcely tempered by the absence of an alternative system.

Since the metaphysical intervention broke theological unity, while vainly endeavouring to replace it, its deep-seated impotence has been temporarily disguised by the great critical effort, in the absence of real moral principles, to arouse a general movement for some kind of repression of natural egoism. But as the negating operation is today, in all its essential aspects, as fully accomplished as it can be before renewal supervenes, and as revolutionary passions have subsided for want of an adequate goal, the fragility of the metaphysical foundations, and their inability to resist the slightest agitation, becomes ever more evident. The profound convictions, which theology has allowed to be destroyed, and which metaphysics has not been able to revive, can no longer be established in morals or in anything else except through the predominance of the positive spirit properly applied to them in the final working out of social theories. There is no need to insist on the high morality proper to the scientific ascendancy of the social point of view, and to the logical supremacy of holist concepts, both of which will characterise the ultimate fully positive philosophy. In the universal fluctuation that accompanies the present anarchy, where for want of satisfying principles the most indispensable notions may be openly contested, nothing can give a just idea of the energy and tenacity that moral rules are bound to acquire, in every domain, when they rest on the appreciation of the real influence, direct and indirect, particular and general, constantly received by human existence, public or private, from our acts and our tendencies, which must be judged by the laws of our nature individual and social. This positive proposition will leave no loophole for those facile subterfuges that have enabled many sincere believers to elude, every day, in their own eyes, and in the eyes of others, the strictness of moral prescriptions, ever since religious doctrines lost their main social sanction through the decadence of a corresponding power. The inborn feeling for order will now acquire in every domain through the convergence of the whole speculative process an intensity that will enable it to persist throughout the utmost disorder. While the perfect intellectual unity that characterises the positive state will bring about active moral convictions in each and every cultivated mind, it will create no less inevitably powerful public prejudices by developing a plenitude of assent that has never before existed to the same degree, and whose irresistible and constant ascendancy will make up for any insufficiency of private effort, should culture be too imperfect or impulse too strong. The moral effect of the final philosophy presupposes not only the direct influence of the doctrines, which, whatever be their speculative power, would rarely be able to control vicious impulses in view of the weakness of the intellectual impetus relatively to our whole state of being. We have fully recognised that under the most favourable regime moral results will demand, besides doctrine, the action of a suitable system of universal education, and after that wise and continuous discipline, both public and private emanating from the same moral power as guides the common initiation. Too often today these factors are forgotten in superficial and premature, often unjust and sometimes malevolent comparisons of positive morality, of which we scarcely have a mental outline, without institutions of any kind, with religious morality, which has been completely developed by the efforts of centuries and assisted by all the social apparatus needed for putting it into practice.

Since, then, we can only judge of the influence of positive philosophy from its doctrines, without any corresponding institutions, in order to make this judgement it is necessary to distinguish in these doctrines the three grades proper to universal morality,[105] namely the personal, the domestic and the social.

As for the first, positive morality, properly organised, will produce far better moral results than religious morality, even in the monotheistic stage, has ever been able to obtain in spite of the powerful means at its disposal. Besides the fact that individual appreciation of systems of conduct is in the positive state easier and more direct, personal morality will be seen in its true guise, not as related to private utility, but as the basis of all moral development, and for that reason removed from the arbitrament of personal prudence in order to be incorporated in public prescription. The ancients were not able to secure this result, although they felt its importance, and Catholicism itself has not completely attained it

—an inevitable consequence of the predominance it always accorded to an imaginary goal. Exaggerating the momentary dangers of renouncing all hope, we have ignored the permanent advantages that must result, under wise philosophic direction, from concentrating human effort on real life, individual and collective, whose total economy man would thus be impelled to improve as much as possible by all the proper means, among which moral rules occupy the first rank, as they are destined to promote that universal co-operation in which is our chief strength. If this restriction to the present life tends to prevent overmuch foresight by making us appreciate the value of the present, such an influence can easily be regulated, and will be of use in advancing the common harmony by preventing excessive hoarding. A sound estimate of our own nature, in which vicious or excessive inclinations predominate, will secure widespread acceptance of the obligation to exercise a wise discipline over our inclinations, stimulating or restraining them as the need demands. Finally the general idea, at once scientific and moral, of the true situation of man, as natural head of the real order of things, will always underline the necessity of ceaselessly developing by their judicious exercise, the noble attributes, not less of feeling than of intellect, which place us at the summit of the living hierarchy. The just pride that the consciousness of this pre-eminence must excite, especially as it succeeds age-long acceptance of man's inferiority to the angels, will not lead to any apathy, since always the type before our mind's eye will be one of real perfection, to which we shall be constantly aware that we never attain, though persevering efforts may bring us nearer to it. Hence a noble audacity in developing the greatness of man in every direction, secure from oppressive terrors and knowing no limit but that imposed by the collective force of the real. This real, however, we must seek to modify to our advantage as much as possible, through an exact and continuous estimation of it.

As for domestic morality, comparison will soon demonstrate the vast superiority of positive philosophy,[106] alone capable of restraining the dangerous aberrations caused by metaphysics, aberrations that theology has not been able to contain. Perhaps it was necessary for the present anarchy to be carried as far as the existing disorders of domestic life, to bring home to people the necessity of putting all our moral notions on a new intellectual basis, fit to resist corrosive discussion, and even to do away with such discussion entirely by presenting the immutable reality of that subordination which constitutes the basic order of human societies. It is indeed in relation to domestic union, where sociological analysis almost merges with biological, that the profound naturalness of social relationships will most easily be felt, since they are part of the way of life peculiar to the upper strata of the animal hierarchy, of which man is simply the most complete development. A judicious application of the principle of classification, first abstract and then concrete, proper to positive philosophy, will strengthen the subordination principle, by linking it to the whole of the speculative scheme. Finally, a more thorough study of human evolution under this all-important domestic aspect will demonstrate clearly that the natural diversities on which its system rests develop through the common progress, so that each element tends more and more towards the existence most in conformity with its true nature and most suitable to the general harmony. While the positive spirit will systematically consolidate the great moral notions that relate to this first stage of association, it will underline the growing preponderance of domestic life for the immense majority of humanity, as modern sociability approaches its normal state. That natural sequence which, except for a few rare anomalies, makes of domestic existence the necessary preamble to social existence, will thus be guaranteed against any sophistical alteration.

If in the third place positive philosophy is judged in relation to social morality, here also, and still more than in the other two cases it will display its high powers. Neither metaphysical philosophy, which ratifies egoism, nor theological philosophy, which subordinates real life to an imaginary destination, has ever directly brought out the social point of view, as of its very nature the new philosophy will be able to do, for it takes it as the basis of its definitive systematisation. Domestic and personal morality give so little scope to the benevolent and disinterested affections that they have often led to a dogmatic denial of their existence, in accordance with vain scholastic subtleties in the domestic sphere, and in the personal under the regime of continual preoccupation with personal salvation. As no sentiment of any kind can be fully developed unless it is specially and constantly exercised, especially if it is not naturally very strong, one must regard the moral sense, of which the social stage is the complete manifestation, as being up till now but the stunted growth of an indirect and artificial cultivation, which was however a necessary preliminary. When a true education has familiarised modern minds with the notions of solidarity and perpetuity that the positive contemplation of social evolution suggests in so many cases, then will be felt the essential moral superiority of a philosophy that binds each one of us to the whole existence of humanity, seen against a background of all times and places: religion on the contrary could only recognise individuals brought together for a time, absorbed in the thought of their own personal destination, and whose final reunion, vaguely assigned to heaven, offered the human imagination a sterile typology in the absence of any realistic goal. The restriction of our hopes to real life, individual or collective, under a wise philosophic direction, may well furnish new means of linking private advancement to universal progress, of which the idea will gradually predominate and constitute the sole means of satisfying the need for eternity that is inherent in our nature. For example, the scrupulous respect for human life, which has always developed in proportion to our sociality, can only increase with the complete extinction of a vain hope that disposes people to underrate, quite openly, every present existence, as purely incidental to the final goal. In spite of the declamation of the various religious schools, positive philosophy, extended to the social phenomena of its principal sphere, shows itself to be more capable than any other of seconding the natural expansion of human sociability. The true philosophic spirit being at bottom nothing but fully systematised good sense, it can be said that at least in its natural form it has maintained the general harmony for three centuries against the dogmatic assaults inspired or tolerated by ancient philosophy, whose theologico-metaphysical divagations would have upset the entire system of modernity, if the instinctive resistance of the vulgar mind had not restrained its disastrous social application. The effects of the theologico-metaphysical philosophy are but too apparent, and are the consequence of the insufficient practical opposition that only acts against very notorious disorders, and cannot stop their ever imminent renewal by arresting the mental anarchy from which they proceed.

Triply endowed in the personal, domestic and social spheres, positive morality will tend to present each man's happiness as dependent on the extension of benevolent acts and sympathetic emotions to our species as a whole, and even, by a necessary gradation, to all those sentient beings that are our subordinates, proportionally to their animal dignity and their social utility. Its continuous effectiveness will be the more assured in that it will always be able to adapt itself spontaneously, opportunely, yet without inconsistency to the various demands of each special case, whether individual or social, in accordance with the relative nature of the new philosophy; while the necessary immobility of religious morality was bound to deprive it of all its strength, even in the time of its ascendancy, in situations that had not been foreseen, as they had developed after it was first constituted. The future will see the full development of these eminent moral attributes belonging to positive philosophy, but before this happens it is for true philosophers, those natural forerunners, to establish them in the eyes of all by the superiority of their conduct, personal, domestic and social, contrary to the pernicious metaphysical maxim that all public judgement of private life is religiously excluded. In this way example will prove the possibility of developing for solely human reasons a feeling for universal morality keen enough to produce a real feeling of repugnance at any violation of it, as also an irresistible inclination to serve it.

Now that we have defined the mental and moral influence that positive philosophy is destined to have, we must proceed to an estimate of its political influence—which will always be its principal objective. But as there has been implicit consideration of this subject throughout our eighth, ninth and tenth chapters,[107] in which the past has been constantly viewed in relation to the future, what remains is to indicate the fundamental division between the spiritual or theoretical organism and the temporal or practical one.

The premature attempt of Catholicism in the Middle Ages, in spite of its merit and its efficiency, could only indicate the aim of modern civilisation on this point, by leaving an indelible though imperfect impression, but no suggestion for a political solution that was to depend on an entirely different philosophy and relate to an entirely different sociability. Like all the great social notions placed hitherto under the inefficient protection of monotheism, this conception has necessarily been more and more discredited during the five centuries of transition spiritual and temporal, because of its connection with reactionary doctrines that had become profoundly oppressive. And in its place we have the pedantocratic utopia transmitted by modern metaphysics in increasing ascendancy, with its profoundly perturbing effect clear for all to see. All that now exists on this subject is a feeling, vague and uncertain, but spontaneous and indestructible, of the political necessities inherent in the nature of modern civilisation, which assigns in every department distinct participations to the material and the intellectual power, whose separation and co-ordination, till now confused, are reserved for the future. Their temporary equilibrium in the Middle Ages resulted from a purely empirical antagonism caused by the development of the monotheistic system under a former type of sociability that a monotheistic system could only modify, although its instinct was to dominate it as, at the end of this great historical phase, its directly theocratic tendency showed—a tendency happily blocked by the temporal powers. Great as was the gain of human evolution from this first consecration of morality's independence of politics, the future will certainly take up the modern constitution right from the initial operation that determines its general spirit; for the Catholic system could conceive it and guide it only in an inadequate and even deleterious manner, because of the ineptitude of its philosophy. For it was not from a sane and systematic appreciation, at once intellectual and social—at that time impossible—that Catholicism roughed out a separation between the universal rules of human conduct, public and private, and their flexible application to cases. Such a division could be instituted at that time only in accordance with the mystical opposition between celestial and terrestrial interests, as the customary nomenclature reminds us. If the instinctive appreciation by the vulgar of the new social situation and the inevitable preponderance of practical impulse had not automatically guided so imperfect a logical tool towards its political destination, modern societies would have been converted into sterile Thebaids, in which vain preoccupation with personal salvation would have absorbed every realistic consideration. So when the terrestrial point of view had finally prevailed over the celestial, morality's independence of politics, though so much in harmony with the nature of modern civilisation,[108] found itself theoretically compromised because at bottom it had no rational foundation capable of resisting revolutionary divagation. The positive future, having to resume from the bottom upwards this divisive operation, of which the past can furnish no real type, will rectify it in accordance with a just appreciation of the entire course of human evolution. The Christian principle turned morality's independence into a vicious isolation, as fatal as it was irrational. As positive philosophy everywhere establishes the preponderance, at once logical and scientific, of the social point of view, it will certainly not be able to deny it with regard to morality, where all see its principal application, and where, even in a purely individual case, everything must be constantly related not to the man, but to humanity. Obviously we can extend to moral laws the rule that intellectual laws are of their nature and without exception much more perceptible in the collective than in the individual organism. The type of human progress is necessarily identical in the individual and in the species, but its character will emerge more clearly from an examination of social rather than of personal evolution. It is therefore certain that morality properly so called will always in a sense have its point of departure in politics. The necessary division between the two will come about through an internal decomposition of the amalgam of theoretical and practical views, a decomposition indispensable to their common destination. Apropos of this subject, we are now in a position to sum up for positive philosophy the ultimate conditions of its principal political function, which are that it must conciliate the opposite attributes of human wisdom as manifested in antiquity and in the Middle Ages. For even though the monotheistic regime had the merit of proclaiming at last, though without much success, the legitimate independence of morality, or rather its superior dignity, in the antique subordination of morality to politics there existed without a doubt an eminently social tendency, although the polytheistic regime made of it a pernicious confusion, impossible to avoid at the time; even indispensable for military purposes. Antiquity alone has been able up till now to offer a complete political system, possessing homogeneity, and capable of preserving its identity over a long period of time: what we have had since then has been an endless series of transitions, first of all in the Middle Ages, and then in modern times. Now the polytheistic organism presented two distinct modes, though intimately combined: the one conservative and stationary, under the theocratic ascendancy, the other active and progressive, under the military impulsion. The great political task, prematurely attempted in the Middle Ages, and which the future alone will be able to accomplish, is that of reconciling in one milieu, and with quite different aims and principles the distinct properties of these two regimes, the one conferring social preponderance on theoretical power and the other on practical power. This conciliation will directly depend on the systematic distinction between the just exigencies of education and action respectively. But while instituting such a division, without which modern politics cannot take a single important step, it is extremely important[109] to consign the day-to-day direction of operations to practicality, theoretic authority remaining purely consultative, under pain of pedantocratic disturbances. The definitive elimination of religious influences must now happily prevent the oppression caused by ambitious speculations, but their irrational pretensions can still excite grave disorders producing reaction and even fear. Hence the denial to theoretic exigency of every legitimate political satisfaction, for from such satisfaction that indispensable thing, practical conservatism, dreads, by a kind of blind instinct, that a subversive movement might arise that it would no longer be able to control. In spite of the great difficulties both mental and social that the proper weighting of theory and practice respectively—that necessary basis of the positive organism—is bound to present, there is a prefiguration of it in the day-to-day relation of science and art. It is only a matter of giving this definitive shape by extending it to the most important and difficult operations under the inspiration of a sound philosophy which is always attentive to the totality of human relations. The inevitable imperfection of the science-art typology does not prevent it from furnishing valuable directives on the correspondence between theory and practice, in politics as elsewhere, thus confirming the characteristic tendency of the positive spirit to attach every systematic judgement to an instinctive manifestation. The positive spirit recognises simultaneously both the necessary independence of theory, without which its development, and in consequence that of practice itself, would be greatly hampered, and the radical inability of theory to direct real operations, in which practical wisdom alone must preside over the controlled use of speculative insights. If the long experience of modern skills has established through a multitude of daily tests the science-art situation in simple cases, perfectly analogous motives must *a fortiori* make its need felt in complex cases. In systematising the universal supremacy of good sense, positive philosophy will tend to dissipate the political illusions of speculative ambition, offshoots of the mystical and absolute nature of primitive theories, instilling a profound disdain for the practical instinct; while from now on mutual appreciation of their identity of origin, conformity of procedure and common goal will bind together the two equally indispensable modes of human wisdom, whose progress depends on their convergence. The political art, which calls for the spontaneous co-operation of all individual effort, is calculated to inspire the greatest respect for practical wisdom, for in this art it has generally shown itself very superior to theoretical wisdom, under the compulsion it is true of a general situation that is much more irresistible and more clearly defined than vain metaphysical doctrines suppose. We should recognise as a universal principle that the more eminent the art, the more it is important both that theory should be separated from practice, and that practice should always keep the direction of each operation. The more the positive study of politics, especially modern politics, even contemporary politics, is pursued in depth, the more it will be felt that measures directly inspired by a situation are as a rule superior, not only as far as the present is concerned but also the future, to the inspirations of ill-established theory. Although the gap is bound to narrow under a better system of social theorising, the common interest will always require a day-to-day preponderance of the practical or material power, provided it has due respect for the independence of theoretical or intellectual power, and recognises the necessity of including abstract considerations among the regular elements of every concrete decision. This certainly no true statesman would dare to dispute, once theoreticians, on their side, have given proof of the scientific character and the political attitude that befit their social function. As the whole of this course is directed to the constitution of a new spiritual power, in terminating it I was bound, in anticipation of the future, to indicate measures for preventing the encroachment of moral government on political government. Without such measures it would be impossible to remove the prejudices that today oppose themselves to the advent of this power, which I have shown to be the first condition of final regeneration.

Regarding the initial preparation of its advent,[110] I must insist on the necessity of restricting it at first to the populations of Western Europe,[111] the better to guarantee its distinctness and originality against the vague, confused tendencies of contemporary speculation. But with regard to the ultimate stage, we must envisage the extension of the positive organism first to the whole of the white race, and then to the whole of the human species when it has been properly prepared for it. However, the natural aptitude of positive philosophy for creating a spiritual association much vaster than was ever compatible with previous philosophy is already so obvious that there is no need to stress it. That quality of the positive spirit which brings about a mental harmony hitherto impossible in the individual, will also create collectively an intellectual and moral communion more complete, more extensive and more stable than any religious communion. In spite of the veneration accorded from sheer habit to the outworn pretensions of theological philosophy, it is under the inspiration of that philosophy that the European West has broken up during the last five centuries into independent nationalities. Their basic solidarity, rooted in a common evolution, cannot be systematised except through total renewal. As the European case is better fitted than the national case to arouse appreciation of a truly spiritual constitution, such a constitution is destined to acquire new consistency and efficacity with every positive organism added to it, and will thus have become more and more moral and less and less political, without practical power ever losing its active predominance. Through an inevitable reaction this progression will be not less favourable to just liberty than to indispensable order; for as intellectual and moral association extends and consolidates itself, that concentration of temporal power without which a break-up would be imminent will diminish of its own accord for lack of urgency, so as to allow each political element to expand according to its nature. Today such a process would lead to disastrous anarchy, with dangers much graver than the various disadvantages suffered at present from excessive centralisation.

As for the conflicts that the inevitable discords of human passions will naturally bring about, in spite of the wisest measures, in the positive system, as in any previous one, they will be neither as stormy nor as obstinate. They will be most intense at the initial installation of the new regime, much more intense than during its normal development. Indeed the disastrous outbreaks of the great internal struggle that is inseparable from our mental and moral anarchy belong to the near future, and their grave material consequences are already beginning to threaten us, first in the relations between industrialists and workers, and then in the attitude to one another of town and country. The only things that are systematised today are those that are destined to disappear; and everything that is not yet systematised, that is, that has life, must engender unavoidable collisions that cannot be sufficiently foreseen or contained during the slow development of a different systematisation, rejected by the spontaneous combination of the most contrary tendencies; although the advent of this as yet unsystematised life would be quite natural. In this stormy situation positive philosophy will find the first test of its political efficiency, and a spur to its necessary social ascendancy, the only satisfactory solution left to the legitimate desires of order and progress which this philosophy alone can reconcile. When its painful introduction has been accomplished, the continual difficulties proper to the normal action of the new regime will have far less intensity, and will be resolved as before. It is unnecessary here to dwell on them.

Nor is it necessary to insist on the close solidarity between philosophic tendencies and popular movements. This powerful affinity, which determined the political advent of the positive system, will naturally become its most solid support. The same philosophy that has brought about the recognition of the supremacy of common reason, will also secure the social preponderance of true popular needs without any danger of anarchy, by bringing about the universal ascendancy of morality, which will dominate both scientific inspirations and political decisions.

The storms, due above all to an extremely unequal development of practical exigencies and theoretic satisfactions, will be violent, but they will pass, and positive philosophy politically applied will lead humanity to the social system most suited to its nature one that will greatly surpass in homogeneity, extension and stability everything that the past could ever offer.

While opinions, manners and institutions ultimately suited to modern sociability are being gradually worked out under the impact of decisive events, positive philosophy will display a fourth aptitude, complementary to the other three, and less suspected today than any of them: it will develop the aesthetic constitution that corresponds to our civilisation, and that has been so vainly sought for five centuries. One would have a very inadequate idea of this new quality of the positive spirit if one reduced it to a systematised general philosophy of the fine arts.[112] Whatever the importance of such a philosophic enterprise, which up till now has been impossible and even today would be premature, since the best 'poetics' are certainly not capable of bringing true poets into existence there would certainly be no justification for considering here the aesthetic action of the ultimate philosophy if it were not to have an entirely different character, a higher and more effective character, at once mental and social.

Aesthetic life[113] has a felicitous influence on our existence as a whole, both individually and collectively. Midway between the speculative tendency and the active impulse, it must always charm and improve, elevating the vulgar, humanising the great. Under this aspect which will become more and more evident as the new philosophy develops, the fine arts have much to gain from the advent of the positive regime, which will give them a dignified place in the social system, outside of which up till now they have always remained. The preponderance of a human point of view,[114] and the corresponding ascendancy of a community spirit must in the nature of things be favourable to the development of aesthetic inclinations, whether moderately, which is enough for the creation of taste, or with that extra intensity that signifies a vocation. And history both of the ancients and the moderns shows that there is a social condition indispensable to the full development of the aesthetic sense: a sociability that is markedly progressive, and at the same time markedly stable. For these various reasons, which can only be strengthened with time, all intelligent people will soon perceive, in spite of prejudices that have no force except as regards the preliminary spadework of the system, the great aesthetic resources that our future will hold.

The mental and social conditions necessary to the flourishing of the fine arts have not up till now converged except under the polytheistic regime of antiquity. This flourishing condition was connected with a constant, vigorous public life, characterised by the energetic development of military life. Idealisation of the military life is now entirely at an end. But this is not the case of the hard-working and pacific activity of modern civilisation, whose outlines up till now have been barely visible, and could not be aesthetically evaluated, for want of a philosophic direction and a political consistency suitable to its nature. Modern art, therefore, as well as science and industry, far from growing old, is really not sufficiently formed. It has not been able to free itself from the antique type. In spite of its obvious inopportuneness this type has not lost in the artistic field the provisional preponderance that the prolongation of the transition to positivism was bound to assure it. The admirable productions of the last five centuries have certainly asserted, without a doubt in the most emphatic manner, and against vain prejudices, the unchanging persistence of aesthetic faculties of humanity, and even their continued growth, in spite of the most unfavourable of environments. Nevertheless collectively they can only be regarded, in comparison with what the future has in store, as a preparation, whose most original and popular portion has generally been kept down to private life, for want of a suitable pabulum in public life. As the true intellectual, moral and political character of modern life develops in the near future, one can be certain that it will soon find its continuous idealisation. The sense of the true and the good would not find expression in modern life without the sense of the beautiful, which is nothing but the instinct of rapidly appreciated perfection everywhere erupting. So this last general effect of positive philosophy is closely linked to each of the three that have just been examined. Besides, the systematic regeneration of all human conceptions will certainly furnish new philosophic means of aesthetic development, thus assured of a lofty aim and continuous stimulation. The better to appreciate this judgement, we will first of all frankly admit that theological philosophy, applying universally the human type—and this is its real and essential activity—must long prove favourable to the impulses of the imagination. But this initial aptitude was certainly limited to the polytheistic state: the monotheistic decline so effectually brought it to an end that it could only maintain itself by the strange expedient of prolonging specially in the midst of the most fervent Christianity, the contradictory ascendancy of the longest religious epoch. One may therefore regard the conception of divinity or rather of the gods as having been for a long time still more impotent in its aesthetic aspect than it has become in its intellectual and even in its social aspect. As for the vain entity of nature, by which metaphysics endeavoured to replace primitive belief, its organic sterility is as evident in poetry as it is in philosophy and politics. It is not surprising that the dim feeling of a want and a gap has often led people to regard the mental springs of art as dried up in those who, not finding in themselves a deep enough conviction of the spontaneity of aesthetic life, exaggerate the importance of the intellectual impulses in it —impulses of which indeed they have a quite inadequate appreciation. For want of perceiving the positive side of modern evolution as clearly as the negative side, which alone has been understood up till now, superficial observation, on this subject as on others, engenders too frequently a kind of philosophic despair among those advanced enough to feel the absolute impossibility of a true restoration of the past. But sound historical theory has always shown us on the contrary, even on this particular point, the advance of construction correlatively with demolition. The principal philosophic result of this progression is the convergence of all modern concepts in the great notion of humanity, whose final preponderance in every department of life will replace the ancient theologico-metaphysical co-ordination. Now this new mental unity, necessarily more complete and more lasting than any other, will certainly be associated with a tremendous and quite spontaneous aesthetic aptitude, once it has prevailed, an aptitude that will soon prove superior to anything of the kind that theological philosophy has ever been able to offer, even in its polytheistic splendour. For if art which everywhere sees and seeks man, has for that reason long had to sympathise with the primitive philosophy that offered a fictitious idea of him, it will adapt itself much better to a fundamental doctrine substituting for that fanciful and indirect representation the real and immediate notion of human preponderance in all the subjects of our habitual speculations, from now on to be circumscribed by the order of reality, unknown to primitive man. Certainly, for those capable of appreciating it, there is an inexhaustible source of poetic grandeur in the positive conception of man as the supreme head of the system of nature which he unceasingly modifies to his advantage, with a wise boldness completely liberated from any vain scruple or oppressive terror, and recognising no other limits than those of the positive laws revealed by his active intelligence: while up till now humanity remained, on the contrary, passively subject in every respect to an arbitrary external direction, on which all of its enterprises were always dependent. The action of man on nature, still very imperfect, has only been able to manifest itself to any extent with the moderns, as the final result of a painful social evolution, long after the aesthetic development corresponding to the primitive philosophy was essentially exhausted, so that it was not accompanied by any idealisation. Irrationally imitating the poetry of antiquity, modern art has continued to sing the marvellous wisdom of nature, even after science had ascertained the extreme imperfection of the vaunted order of nature, in all its important aspects. When

the theological or metaphysical hypnotism does not prevent true judgement, everyone feels today that human works, from the simplest
mechanical apparatus to the most sublime political constructions, are in
general very superior, both in aptitude and in simplicity, to the most perfect things offered by the system that man does not guide, and where
mass alone has been the principal source of admiration. Thus it is in sing-
ing of the wonders of man, his conquest of nature, the marvels of his
sociability, that true aesthetic genius will henceforth find, under the
active stimulus of the positive spirit, a fruitful source of new and powerful inspiration, enjoying a popularity without parallel because it will be
in full harmony both with the noble instinct of our mental superiority
and with the entire body of our rational convictions. The most eminent
poet of our century, the great Byron, who in his fashion has divined
better than anyone hitherto, the true nature of modern existence, mental
and moral, alone has attempted this audacious poetic regeneration, the
one way left open to contemporary art. No doubt sound philosophy was
not then sufficiently advanced to allow his genius to appreciate adequately in our situation anything beyond the purely negative aspect. This, it
is true, he admirably idealised. But the profound merit of his immortal
compositions, and their immense immediate success among the élite of
all nations, in spite of vain national antipathies, have already rendered
undeniable both the aesthetic power proper to the new sociability, and
the universal tendency to the renewal in question. All true philosophic
spirits can therefore now understand that the necessary advent of universal reorganisation will of itself provide at the same time inexhaustible
food for modern art, in the spectacle of human marvels and in a lofty
social destiny, that of making the ultimate social system adequately
appreciated. Although dogmatic philosophy must always preside over
the creation of the different types, intellectual or moral that the new spiritual organisation will require, aesthetic participation will nevertheless
become indispensable both for their active propagation, and even for
their preparation, so that art will thus find in the positive future an
important political function, equivalent to that which the polytheistic
past had conferred on it, and which since has been effaced under the
sombre monotheistic domination. We must here set aside all indication
of the new means of aesthetic execution, as not near enough in time for a
present appreciation of these means to be useful. But even if we avoid on
this issue premature and misplaced discussion, it is necessary to declare
here and now that the obligation imposed on modern art, as on science
and industry, of subordinating all its conceptions to real laws, will in no

way tend to deprive it of the precious resource of fictitious characters, and will compel it only to impose a new direction on that resource, in conformity with the direction that this powerful logical artifice will receive also under the two other universal aspects. There is a useful scientific and even logical employment that sane biological philosophy can now extract from the suitable introduction of imaginary organisms in full harmony with vital notions:[115] when the positive spirit has sufficiently prevailed, I do not doubt that such a procedure, essentially analogous to that at present adopted by geometrists in many important cases, can really facilitate in biology the development of judiciously systematic conceptions. Now it is clear that the aim and conditions of art must permit in it an application much more extensive of similar means. Their merely theoretic use might easily lead to abuses, and everyone feels that their aesthetic use should relate principally to the human organism, which is supposed to be modified either for good or for ill, more especially for good, so as to augment the effects of art, without violating the fundamental laws of reality.

In this rapid appreciation of the aesthetic action proper to positive philosophy, I have had to confine myself to the first of all the fine arts, the one which by its superior plenitude and generality has always dominated the development of the fine arts. But obviously the regeneration of modern art cannot be limited to poetry alone, and will extend itself from poetry to the four other fundamental means of ideal expression, in the order indicated by their natural hierarchy. The positive spirit, which as long as it remained in the initial mathematical phase seemed to deserve the reproach of antiaestheticism—still repeated in routine commentary —will become, conformably to sociological systematisation, the principal basis of an aesthetic organisation, not less indispensable than the mental and social renovation from which it is inseparable.

Thus the triple positive movement, ever dominated by one and the same fundamental principle, will lead humanity to the universal regime most in conformity with its nature, one in which its characteristic attributes will find their most perfect consolidation, their most complete harmony, and freest common development. Immediate destination of the movement will be the European occident, and the five essential elements of that noble élite of our species will each participate in the terms of its own proper genius, collaboration intimating future actual combination. Under the salutary predominance, both philosophic and political which is assured to the French spirit by the general tendencies of the modern transition, the English spirit will assert its predilection for reality and utility, the German spirit will apply its native aptitude for systematic generalisation, the Italian spirit will permeate the whole with its admirable aesthetic spontaneity, and finally the Spanish spirit will introduce its feeling both for personal dignity and universal fraternity.

CONTENTS OF THE SIX VOLUMES

OF THE *COURS*

From *Cours de Philosophie Positive*, Vol. VI, Paris, 1842
(Bachelier, Imprimeur–Libraire)

General Preliminaries and Mathematical Philosophy
(The whole of this first volume was written in the first six months of
1830.)* Note (1) by Comte: From the motive indicated at the end of the
Preface, I thought I must note here exactly the time and duration of each
of the successive parts of this long composition, whose vicissitudes will
thus be more easily understood.

1st lecture.   Exposition of the aim of the course, or general considerations on the nature and destiny of positive philosophy
2nd lecture.   Exposition of the plan of the course, or general considerations on the fundamental hierarchy of the positive sciences
3rd lecture.   Philosophic considerations on the whole of mathematical science
4th lecture.   General view of mathematical analysis
5th lecture.   General considerations on the calculus of direct functions
6th lecture.   Comparative exposition of the general points of view from which the calculus of inverse functions may be envisaged
7th lecture.   General table of calculus of inverse functions
8th lecture.   General considerations on the calculus of variations
9th lecture.   General considerations on the calculus of finite differences
10th lecture.   General view of geometry
11th lecture.   General considerations on *special* or *preliminary* geometry
12th lecture.   Fundamental concept of *general* or *analytic* geometry

---

* Except Lecture I which as we have seen ('History of the *Cours*') was ready towards the beginning of 1829.

36th lecture.   General considerations on chemistry properly so-called or *inorganic* chemistry

37th lecture.   Philosophic examination of the chemical doctrine of definite proportions

38th lecture.   Philosophic examination of electro-chemical theory

39th lecture.   General considerations on the chemistry called *organic*

40th lecture.   (Written from 1–30 January 1836.) Philosophic considerations on biological science as a whole

41st lecture.   (Written from 1–6 August 1836.) General considerations on anatomical philosophy

42nd lecture.   (Written from 9–15 August 1836.) General considerations on biostatic philosophy

43rd lecture.   (Written from 20 November to 15 December 1837.) Philosophic considerations on the general study of vegetative or *organic* life

44th lecture.   (Written from 17–22 December 1837.) Philosophic considerations on the general study of *animal* life properly so-called

45th lecture.   (Written from 24–31 December 1837.) General considerations on the positive study of the intellectual and moral, or cerebral functions

VOLUME IV *containing* The Dogmatic Part of Social Philosophy

(The whole of this fourth volume was written, with few interruptions from 1 March to 1 July 1839.
Publisher's Note.)
Author's note.

46th lecture.   Preliminary political considerations on the necessity and the opportuneness of *social physics*, based on a thorough analysis of the present state of politics

47th lecture.   Brief appreciation of the principal philosophic attempts undertaken so far to found social science

48th lecture.   Fundamental characteristics of the positive method in the rational study of social phenomena

49th lecture.   Necessary relations of social physics to the other fundamental branches of positive philosophy

50th lecture.   Preliminary considerations in social statics, or general theory on the spontaneous order of human societies

51st lecture.   Fundamental laws of social dynamics, or general theory of the natural progress of humanity

VOLUME V *containing* The Historical Part of Social Philosophy, in everything that concerns the Theological State and the Metaphysical State

52nd lecture. (Written from 21 April to 2 May 1840.) Preliminary limitation of the historical account—General considerations on the first theological state of humanity: the age of fetishism. Quick sketch of the theological and military regime

53rd lecture. (Written from 7–30 May 1840.) General appreciation of the principal theological state of humanity: the age of polytheism. Gradual development of the theological and military regime

54th lecture. (Written from 15 June to 2 July 1840.) General appreciation of the last theological state of humanity: the age of monotheism. Radical modification of the theological and military regime

55th lecture. (Written from 10 January to 26 February 1841.) General appreciation of the metaphysical nature of modern societies: critical epoch, or age of revolutionary transition. Growing disorganisation, at first spontaneous and then systematic, of the entire theological and military regime

VOLUME VI *containing* Completion of the Historical Part of Social Philosophy, and General Conclusions

Personal preface (Written from 17–19 July 1842.)

56th lecture. (Written from 20 May to 17 June 1841.) General appreciation of the fundamental development of the different elements proper to the positive state of humanity: the age of specialism, or the provisional stage, characterised by the universal preponderance of the spirit of detail over the spirit of the whole. Progressive convergence of the principal spontaneous developments of modern society towards the final organisation of a rational and pacific regime

57th lecture. (The historical part of this lecture was written from 25 June to 14 July 1841, and the dogmatic part from 23 December 1841 to 15 January 1842.) General appreciation of the already accomplished portion of the French or European revolution

—Rational determination of the final tendency of modern societies, in accordance with the human past as a whole: a fully positive state, or age of generality, characterised by a new normal preponderance of the spirit of the whole over the spirit of detail

58th lecture. (Written from 17 May to 16 June 1842.) Final appreciation of the positive method as a whole

59th lecture. (Written from 23–28 June 1842.) Philosophic appreciation of the results viewed as a whole, conducive to a preliminary constitution of positive doctrine

60th and last lecture. (Written from 9–13 July 1842.) General appreciation of the definitive influence proper to positive philosophy

PLAN OF THE *COURS*

Cours de Philosophie Positive

Préliminaires généreux		1. Exposition de tout ce cours
2 séances		2. Exposition du plan
mathematiques		Vue générale 1 séance
16 séances		Calcul 6 séances
		Géométrie 5 séances
		Mécanique rationnelle 4 séances

Science des corps bruts
Astronomie	9 séances	Géométrique	5 séances
		Mécanique	4 séances
Physique	9 séances		
Chimie	6 séances		

Physiologie	12 séances	Végetale	3 séances
		Animale	5 séances
		Intellectuelle et affective 4 séances

Physique sociale	15 séances	Introduction	2 séances
		Méthode	3 séances
		Science	10 séances

Résumé général et Conclusion 3 séances
1. Résumé de la méthode positive
2. Résumé de la doctrine
3. De l'Avenir de la philosophie positive.

The note adds:
This course of lectures was begun Sunday, 4 January 1829, before an audience where were present M. Fourier, secrétaire perpétuel de l'Académie des Sciences; MM. de Blainville, Poinsot, Navier, membres de la même Académie; MM. les professeurs Broussais, Esquirol, Binet, etc. The same course will be given again, from December on, at the Athénée royal, with this difference that the usages of that establishment necessitate a certain reduction in developments of certain themes, which however will be found complete in the publication which the professor proposes to make of his lectures, as they have taken place this year.

(It was Comte himself who had sent his first lecture in January 1829 to the *Revue Encyclopédique* which published it only in November.)

BIBLIOGRAPHICAL NOTES

The edition of the *Cours de Philosophie Positive* is that published in Paris by Bachelier, 1830–42. Volume I bears the date 1830, but as the contract for publication was only signed with Bachelier in 1833,[1] it is a reprint of the volume published by Rouen Frères in Brussels[2] in July 1830, during the revolutionary troubles.

Volume II was published in 1835, Volume III in 1838, Volume IV in 1839, Volume V in 1841, and Volume VI in 1842.

In the list of chapters or lectures which precedes the notes of this selection, and which is to be found at the end of Volume VI of the Bachelier edition, Comte gives particulars of dates of composition.

1. Henri Gouhier, *Vie d'Auguste Comte*, Paris, 1965, p. 149.
2. See photograph of title-page in *Auguste Comte et la théorie sociale du positivisme*, by Angèle Kremer-Marietti, Paris, 1970, facing page 64. This first volume is not listed in the *Bibliographie de la France* for 1830; what are listed are the different parts appearing singly throughout the year up to lecture 17 of Volume I: January, 1st lecture, 2nd lecture (two parts); March, 3rd and 4th lectures; 5th and 6th lectures; 7th, 8th and 9th lectures; 10th lecture. (4 parts). July, 11th and 12th lectures; 13th and 14th lectures; 15th lecture; 16th lecture (4 parts). September, 17th lecture (1 part). They were published in France by Rouen Frères, 13 Rue de l'Ecole de Medecine, 13. Rouen Frères is also the publisher of the Brussels Volume I, which also names Paris, before Brussels, yet could not have been published at that date in France or it would be in the *Bibliographie de la France*. All the other volumes as having appeared in France are listed there at their due dates.

History of the Cours de Philosophie Positive

The course was planned to be given 1 March 1826 to 1 March 1827 in

Comte's flat, 13 rue du Faubourg Montmartre. It was to consist of 72 lectures, given on Sundays and Wednesdays.

It opened on Sunday 2 April. The audience included Alexander von Humboldt, and de Blainville and Poinsot, members of the Académie des Sciences.

The first three lectures, as we have them in the printed *Cours*, on general survey, hierarchy of the sciences, mathematics, the third given on Sunday 9 April, passed off normally. But when the audience turned up on Wednesday 12 April they found the flat closed, and Comte's friends began receiving letters indicating that he was insane.

He recovered, and the whole course was given in his flat at 159 Rue Saint Jacques beginning 4 January 1829. He sent a copy of the first lecture to the *Revue Encyclopédique* after it was given, but it was not printed in that journal till November 1829. If we compare the version in the *Revue Encyclopédique* with the printed one in the *Cours* they tally absolutely except for insignificant and very infrequent substitution of a synonym: ouvrage—recueil, leçon—séance, and one short paragraph added in the *Cours*, on Descartes. Comte himself indicates in his author's Avertissement to Volume I that the lectures in it are as he gave them during 1829. But the Athénée that distinguished scientists' club where scientists gave unofficial courses of lectures, wanted the course, and he repeated it there beginning in December 1829. But, as he stated in his Avertissement, he had to curtail the lectures for the Athénée, in obedience to its usages, and so was particularly attached to the printing of the course as he had given it throughout 1829. The fascicules published in France in 1830 would also be the lectures as he gave them during 1829. This course also, like the 1826 beginning, had a most distinguished audience, who doubtless were responsible for its being repeated at the Athénée: Fourier, secrétaire perpetuel de l'Académie des Sciences; Blainville, Poinsot, Professors Broussais, Binet.

The plan of the whole course is given in a footnote by Comte to Lecture 1 as printed November 1829 in the *Revue Encyclopédique* (Volume 44), p. 274. It is for 72, not 60 lectures, but follows very closely the course as we have it in print, i.e. Comte had anticipated the whole scheme that he followed during twelve years of preparing his lectures for the press.

NOTES

1. See 1st lecture.

2. Claude-Louis Berthollet, 1748–1822, French chemist. Professor at the École Polytechnique and the École Normale. He claimed that chemical reactions depend upon the masses of reacting substances, and maintained against Joseph Louis Proust that the elements unite in all proportions. The latter had established the law of definite proportions, that two bodies to form the same compound always combine in the same proportion. The controversy lasted from 1801–08 and finished in Proust's favour.

3. Jean-Baptiste Joseph Fourier, 1768–1830. French mathematician and physicist. Professor of Analysis at the École Polytechnique. Made elaborate investigations in conduction of heat. With Cuvier joint secretary of the Academy of Sciences from 1822. His *Théorie analytique de la Chaleur* was published in 1812. In this work he developed what is known as the Fourier series, which had been developing since the first half of the eighteenth century, and which he used for the solution of boundary-value problems in partial differential equations.

4. Henri Marie Ducrotay de Blainville, 1777–1850, French comparative anatomist. In 1832 he succeeded Cuvier in the chair of comparative anatomy at the Museum of the Jardin des Plantes. He defended the idea of evolution from one animal creation of all forms of animal life. *De l'organisation des animaux ou principes d'anatomie comparée* was published in 1822.

5. Georges Léopold Chrétien Frédéric Dagobert Cuvier, 1769–1832, French zoologist and palaeontologist. In the *Leçons d'anatomie comparée* he developed a theory of the correlation of parts (1799). *Le regne animal distribué d'apres son organisation pour servir de base a l'histoire naturelle des animaux et d'introduction à l'anatomie comparée* (1816), applied a natural method of classification to animals on a principle of subordinated characteristics. Like Comte, he gave a course at the Athenaeum. First to say fossils were of extinct animals.

6. Allusion to Berthollet–Proust controversy. See note 2.

7. Joris-Jacob Berzélius, 1779–1848, Swedish Chemist, one of the founders of modern chemistry. By precise experiment he determined the composition of many elements, publishing his results in 1818, and sought to explain chemical reactions by electrochemistry. He developed Lavoisier's idea of chemical nomenclature and his system of a letter of the Latin alphabet for the name of the element with small numeral subscript to denote the number of atoms of each present is the present system.

8. Pierre Simon de Laplace, 1749–1827, French geometrist and astronomer, helped to organise the École Polytechnique; his *Traité de Mécanique céleste* (1700–1825) brought together as homogeneous doctrine the work of Newton, Halley, Clairaut, d'Alembert, and Euler on the consequences of the principle of gravitation. His *Essai philosophique sur les*

probabilités was published in 1814. He was also a great physicist (work on static properties of electricity etc.)

9. See lecture 2.

10. Jean le Rond d'Alembert, 1717–83, French mathematician and philosopher. Among his mathematical works are the Traité de dynamique (1743), and *Recherches sur le calcul intégral*. (1746 and 1748). He was the partner of Diderot in the free-thinking and materialistic *Encyclopédie* (1751) . . . and discusses in his *Discours preliminaire de l'Encyclopedie* (1754) the ladder of knowledge put forth by Diderot in the *Prospectus* for the Encyclopedie which the latter published before the first volume appeared. In his *Discours* he points out how it differs from Bacon's.

11. Marie-Jean-Antoine-Nicolas de Caritat, Marquess of Condorcet, 1743–94, French philosopher, mathematician and politician. Member of the Academy of Sciences from 1769. Guillotined as a Girondist. While in hiding in 1794, wrote his *Esquisse d'un tableau historique des progres de l'esprit humain*.

12. Apollonius of Perga, *ca.* 261 BC. . . . Greek geometer of the Alexandrian school. Four books of his *Treatise on Conic Sections* survive.

13. Gottfried Wilhelm Leibnitz, 1646–1716, German philosopher, continued the rationality of Descartes, but by combining the various systems of thought. Energy is the substance of nature, and the monads are its atoms. He believed in an evolution of the philosophia perennis. Rivalled Newton as the inventor of the differential and integral calculus (1846).

14. See 3rd lecture.

15. Of Joseph Louis Lagrange, see note 72.

16. See 19th lecture.

17. See note 3.

18. See 28th lecture.

19. Hans Christian Oersted, 1777–1851, Danish physicist and chemist. Showing the action of electric currents on a magnetic needle, he indentified electrical and magnetic forces and founded the science of electro-magnetism. The unit of magnetic field strength is called an oersted. He was in communication with the French scientists Cuvier, Berthollet and Biot.

20. Leonhard Euler, 1707–83, Swiss mathematician. He held the Chair of physics in the Academy of Sciences of St Petersburg, before being called to Berlin by Frederick II in 1744, where he became Director of the Mathematical class in the Academy of Berlin. He identified himself with the wave theory of light (*New Theory of light*, 1746) from which is derived the theory of the ether; magnetism consisted of vortexes in the omnipresent ether and light was in the ether the same thing as sound in the air. Ether was the bearer of all electro-magnetic phenomena. He was an Associate of the French Academy of Sciences from 1755. Chief mathematical works: *Introduction to the analysis of the infinitely little*, and *Institutes of Differential and Integral Calculus*.

21. Comte's cross-reference: 19th lesson (Chapter 4).

22. See 35th lecture.

23. Comte's cross-reference: Volume IV.

24. See note 2.

25. Torbern Olof Bergmann, 1734–84, Swedish chemist. He was Professor of Chemistry and metallurgy at the University of Upsala; the founder of analystic inorganic chemistry. He established laws of affinities of atoms, and a chemical classification of minerals.

NOTES

26. Comte's cross-reference: second part of Volume III, on biology, 40th–45th lectures. (Chapter VI).

27. The binary and ternary combinations of atoms and elements or molecules. A binary compound had two atoms; a ternary three atoms; a quaternary four atoms, according to the system of compound atoms and elements established by John Dalton (*New System of Chemical Philosophy* 1808) as against Berthollet's insistence on the interpenetration of atoms: atoms were *added* to one another to make new compounds. His system was confirmed and developed by the experiments of Stas, Dumas and Berzelius, and is the basis of modern chemistry.

28. Joseph Priestley, 1733–1804, English Chemist, philosopher and theologian. A member of the Royal Society who because of his enthusiasm for the French Revolution had to emigrate to America in 1794. Through masterly experiments he isolated gases; with the aid of a burning glass not a new gas from mercuric oxide; published in 1772 *Observations on the different kinds of air*. He met Lavoisier in Paris.

29. Antoine Laurent Lavoisier, 1743–94, French chemist. He discovered oxygen by experiment, using the same methods as Priestley. He applied chemistry to physiology, and invented a chemical nomenclature.

30. See 40th lecture.

31. George Ernest Stahl, 1660–1734, German doctor and chemist. Professor at the University of Halle. He believed in animism throughout nature. *Fundamenta chymiae*, 1723.

32. Hermann Boerhaave, 1668–1738, Dutch doctor. Professor of chemistry at the University of Leyden. A clinician. *Institutiones medicae*, 1708.

33. Albrecht von Haller, 1708–77, Swiss physiologist, Professor of anatomy at Berne university. He made discoveries on the generation and properties of tissues, and published *Elementa physiologiae corporis humani*, 1757. He did not practise the medical profession but pursued physiology independently of it.

34. 3rd–18th lectures on mathematics.

35. Gaspard Monge, 1746–1818, French mathematician. He founded the École Polytechnique, and when the École Normale opened taught descriptive geometry there, in the course of which he gave his fine lectures on the theory of surfaces.

36. Comte's cross-reference: 42nd lecture.

37. Comte's cross-reference to 3rd–18th lectures on mathematics, cf. especially 14th lecture, pp. 528–38, vol. I

38. Comte's cross-reference to 35th–39th lectures on chemistry. Cf. especially lecture 36. pp. 117–32.

38a. Bernard de Jussieu, 1699–1777, French botanist. He instituted a botanic garden at the Trianon for Louis XV, distributing the plants in 65 orders, subdivided into genera, based on the nature of the embryo.

38b. Carl Linnaeus, 1707–78, Swedish naturalist and doctor. Friend of Jussieu. Classification of plants based on stamens and pistils.

39. Comte's cross-reference 35th lecture, Vol. III, p. 69, chapter not part included in selection).

40. Comte's cross-reference: Vol. II, 19th–27th lectures.

41. Comte refers here to establishing this point p. 295 ff, Vol. III, 40th lecture, part not included in this chapter.

42. See note 4. Comte's cross-reference, 1st lecture (Chapter 1).

43. See 46th lecture.

44. The *Système de politique positive ou Traité de sociologie instituant la religion de l'humanité*, 1851–4, Paris. Republique occidentale. Ordre et progrès. Vivre pour autrui. Vol. I Discours preliminaire et introduction fondamentale. Vol. II Statistique sociale, ou Traité abstrait de l'ordre humain. Vol. III Dynamique sociale, ou Traité général du progrès humain. Vol. IV. Tableau synthetique de l'avenir humain.—Appendice general du systeme de politique positive, contenant tous les opuscules primitifs de l'auteur sur la philosophie sociale.

45. Comte's cross-reference, Volume IV of the Cours. See 46th–51st lectures.

46. Comte's cross-reference: Volumes I, II and III, for which see 1st–45th lectures.

47. Comte's cross-reference: 46th and 47th lectures.

48. Comte's cross-reference: 40th lecture.

49. Comte's cross-reference: Volumes I, II and III of the *Cours*.

50. Comte's cross-reference: 'This volume as a whole', but as he had believed that Volume IV would also comprise Volumes V and VI, as one subject, reference is to 46th to 60th lectures.

51. Comte's cross-reference: 52nd–57th lectures.

51a. The 'concert of Europe' against the French Revolution was launched in 1791, and renewed in a Treat of alliance between Russia, Austria, Prussia and England, from which France was excluded in 1815 (The 'Holy Alliance').

52. Félicité Robert de Lamennais, 1782–1854, French religious and political thinker. Under the Restoration (1815–30) he was anti-liberal: *Essai sur l'indifférence en matière de religion* (1823), *De la religion considerée dans ses rapports avec l'ordre politique et civil*, (1824), and *Les progrès de la Révolution et de la guerre contre l'Eglise*. After the July Revolution 1830, he founded the paper *L'Avenir*, with Henri Lacordaire and Charles de Montalembert, in which he advocated an alliance between the Church and democracy. It was suspended in 1831, on being condemned by the Pope, and in 1834 Lamennais published the *Paroles d'un croyant*, in which he in his turn condemned the Church. On being condemned himself in the encyclical *Singulari nos*, he left the Church and pursued his course as revolutionary thinker.

53. Comte is referring to the reactionary party which had power under the Restoration 1815–30.

54. The July revolution, caused by Charles X's ordinances against the Press; he took flight and the elder branch of the Bourbons was replaced by the younger Orleans branch, Louis Philippe, the 'citizen king' who was supposed to introduce a 'juste milieu' or golden mean between revolution and reaction.

55. Bound by an equal hatred of the 'juste milieu' the extreme left and the extreme right allied themselves under Louis Philippe (1830–48).

56. The right did aim at the restoration of the elder branch, with all that this implied, in spite of its alliance with the republicans.

57. Comte is referring to the substitution of the Orleans branch of the Bourbons for the elder or 'legitimate' branch, which would seem to have left intact the theory of monarchy, yet caused these tremendous upheavals in political strategy.

58. Joseph de Maistre, 1753–1821, French–Italian political thinker, born in Savoy, whence he fled before the French revolutionary armies. 1802–16 he was Ambassador of Savoy in St Petersburg. He was an extreme anti-revolutionary, advocating the rule of the Pope for Europe. (*Du Pape*, 1819). Nothing should prevail but the power of God, the Pope and the King.

58a. See note 96a.

59. The Gallican church from the time of Louis XIV had vindicated liberties for the Church in France against the rule of the Pope. The French episcopacy, in particular the great Bossuet, were Gallicans. De Maistre attacks their position in *De l'Eglise gallicane*, 1821.

60. See 48th lecture.

61. Comte's cross-reference: Volumes I, II and III of the *Cours*.

62. Comte's cross-reference: 'the beginning of this volume': i.e. 47th lecture, Vol. IV, p. 225; and a law expounded in the preceding volume (III). See Chapter 7 (40th lecture).

63. Comte's cross-reference to Chapter 8 (46th lecture).

64. Comte's cross-reference, idem.

65. An earlier version of the *Système de politique positive*, (see note 44), published in Saint-Simon's series *Catéchisme des industriels*, cahier 3, as *Système de politique positive*, tome 1er, 1e partie, Paris, 1824 (no more published).

66. Comte's cross-reference: 49th to 60th lectures.

67. Comte's cross-reference to Chapter VIII, 46th lecture. see note 44.

68. Comte's cross-reference: 50th lecture.

69. Comte's cross-reference: Volume II. (Chapter IV).

70. Here Comte notes that in lectures 49–60 social dynamics will dominate.

71. Comte's cross-reference: 52nd to 57th lectures.

72. Joseph Louis Lagrange, 1736–1813, French-Italian geometrist. Euler made him a member of the Berlin Academy. He applied isperimetrical problems to hydrodynamics and the calculus of variations grew out of this. He founded the Turin Academy of Sciences. His *Analytical Mechanics* was published in 1787. In 1797 he was a professor at the newly founded École Polytechnique in Paris, and published his *Theory of Analytical Functions*.

73. Marie François Xavier Bichat, 1771–1802, French anatomist; founder of general anatomy and of embryology. He was also a physiologist: *Treatise on membranes* (1800); *Physiological researches on life and death* (1800); *General anatomy* (1801).

74. Bernard le Bovier de Fontenelle, 1657–1757, French writer and philosopher. He launched the eighteenth-century religion of reason and science in his *Entretiens sur la pluralité des mondes* (1686), and *Historie des Oracles* (1687).

75. Comte's cross-reference, 16th lecture, Volume I, on statics.

76. Comte's cross-reference to historical treatment, 52nd–57th lectures.

77. Jean-Baptiste Pierre Antoine de Monet, chevalier de Lamarck, 1744–1829, French naturalist. A botanist and zoologist, he published his *Philosophie zoologique* in 1809, and *Histoire des animaux invertébrés* 1815–1822. He advocated spontaneous generation and evolution through the hereditary transmission of acquired characteristics.

78. Comte's cross-reference to historical treatment as in 76.

79. Comte's cross-reference to his remarks on climate, 47th lecture, Vol. IV, p. 248.

80. Julian the Apostate, ca. 331–363, Roman Emperor 361–363. On becoming Emperor he abjured Christianity and endeavoured to reintroduce paganism as the religion of the state.

80a. King of Spain, 1556–98, led the Catholic Counter-Reformation.

80b. Comte saw Napoleon as regressive and reactionary.

81. Adam Ferguson, 1723–1816, Scottish philosopher and historian, professor, first of Natural Philosophy, then of Pneumatic or Mental Philosophy in the University of Edinburgh. His *Essay on the History of Civil Society* (1767) was translated into all the main European languages. His *Principles of Moral and Political Law* was published in 1792. He

treats man as a social being. Victor Cousin in his *Cours d'histoire de la philosophie morale du* 18e siècle 1839–40, praised him.

82. *Prospectus des travaux scientifiques nécessaires pour réorganiser la société*.

83. Blaise Pascal, 1623–62, French mathematician, physicist and religious thinker. Humanity as one man continually progressing in knowledge is a concept put forward by him in his *Préface pour le Traité du Vide*. 'Tous les hommes ensemble font un continuel progrès à mesure que l'univers vieillit.'

84. For the second tool, Comte gives the cross-reference to the 49th lecture.

85. Comte's cross-reference: Volume II, Chapters IV and V in this selection.

86. Here Comte says that lectures 49–60 will show how he has acquitted himself of the difficult task of combining exploratory research with fundamental theory guiding it.

87. Comte's cross-reference: Volumes II and III (Chapters IV, V, VI and VII in this selection).

88. Comte's cross-reference to Volume III (see Chapter VI).

89. Francois Joseph Victor Broussais, 1772–1838, French doctor, professor at the Faculty of Medicine. He had a theory that pathological states were merely an exaggeration of the irritability that was normal in healthy tissues. He published a *History of phlegmasias and chronic inflammation*.

90. See note 81.

91. Here Comte refers to his historical lectures.

92. Here Comte refers to the 49th lecture.

93. Comte's cross-reference is to this chapter.

94. See 52nd lecture. The selection stops when the detailed account of human history begins, in this lecture, with fetishism. The detailed and chronological account continues to lecture 57, and is omitted in the selection. This paragraph has been curtailed in so far as it makes particular reference to the treatment in the omitted historical part. The sense has been summarised.

95. Comte's cross-reference: 51st lecture.

96. Comte's cross-reference to 48th lecture (Chapter IX).

96a. Jacques-Benigne Bossuet, 1627–1704, French theologian and perhaps the greatest of French prose writers in his sermons and funeral orations. Bishop of Meaux. His *Discours de l'Histoire universelle* is considered a masterpiece, and follows the lines indicated by Comte: it confines itself to tracing the European tradition from the Middle East, Greece, and Rome.

97. Comte's cross-reference: 57th lecture.

98. In this paragraph Comte summarises his historical treatment as something he is about to undertake. The substance has been translated as he gives it with the few grammatical alterations necessary.

99. See note 94.

100. See 60th lecture.

101. Here Comte refers to the second half of the 57th lecture, as showing that political effect will be the chief aim of the positive philosophy.

102. Comte's cross-reference: 58th and 59th lectures.

103. Idem.

104. Idem.

105. Comte's cross-reference: 50th lecture.

106. Idem.

107. Comte's cross-reference is to Volumes IV, V and VI.

108. Comte's cross-reference: 54th and 57th lectures.

109. Idem.

110. Comte's cross-reference: 57th lecture.

111. Comte here says that he has exactly defined Western Europe in lecture 56.

112. Comte's cross-reference: 58th lecture.

113. Here Comte refers particularly to the 53rd and 56th lectures in his historical sketch as treating of the aesthetic life.

114. Comte's cross-reference: 58th lecture.

115. Comte's cross-reference: 40th lecture (Chapter VII).

INDEX

Auguste Comte proclaimed himself the founder of sociology and, on the whole, this claim is accepted.

His most important work, on which his reputation rests, is the six-volume *Cours de Philosophie Positive* of which this present book is a selective abridgement. Comte was born in Montpellier in 1798 and produced the *Cours* when in his thirties. His later years were interrupted by more or less serious bouts of insanity and the young advocate of scientism ended as a mystic prophet and the self-proclaimed Grand Priest of the Religion of Humanity.

Comte, as this selection from the *Cours* illustrates, was above all a methodological visionary. He was an eminently successful terminological innovator and to him we owe not only 'sociology' and 'posivitism' but also 'biology' and 'altruism'. Professor Andreski, in his lucid introduction, assesses Comte's place under six headings, as scientist, as philosopher, as sociological theorist, as sociological historian, as reformer and as methodologist. But this selection from Comte's works will be most welcomed because it provides a modern English translation of the main body of Comte's thought.

Stanislav Andreski has been Professor of Sociology at the University of Reading since 1964. He is the author of numerous books and articles including the highly successful *Social Sciences as Sorcery* (1972).

Margaret Clarke, the translator of this selection, was born in Scotland and educated in Australia. She is the author of *The Archaic Principles in Education* (1962) and has written many journal articles.

ISBN: 06-490182-3